ACE IN RET

m you
due.
lested

DUE

DEMOCRATIC-REPUBLICAN
SOCIETIES, 1790–1800

———

Number 9 of the Columbia
Studies in American Culture

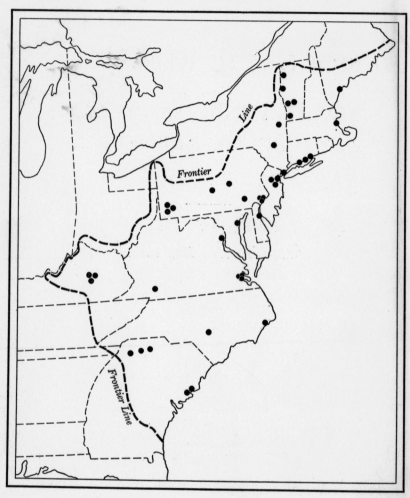

MAP SHOWING THE DISTRIBUTION OF THE SOCIETIES

Eugene Perry Link

DEMOCRATIC-REPUBLICAN

SOCIETIES, 1790-1800

COLUMBIA UNIVERSITY PRESS

Morningside Heights, New York : 1942

FOREWORD

IN VIEW OF the turmoil today associated with the words "democracy" and "democratic," original and thoughtful examinations of democracy in earlier periods of crisis are timely. It is clear that the meaning attached to the words "democracy" and "democratic" has changed with time and circumstance, yet beneath the changes there are elements of permanence. Dr. Link has, in the present monograph, indicated the meanings and values attached by different groups of Americans in the terms "democratic" and "democracy" in the last ten years of the eighteenth century—a period, like our own, of acute and world-wide crisis. The present study rests on a wealth of materials. Dr. Link, in addition to making use of printed records, such as newspapers, periodicals, brochures, and government publications, has upturned much unused manuscript material. To the pioneer studies of Hazen, Fäy, and Miller, he has added new knowledge; his work also suggests modifications of some of their conclusions.

While finding new evidence which supports the thesis that American democratic philosophy and practice in this period were closely related to similar patterns in France and, especially, in England, Dr. Link has also found evidence of ties between the upsurge of the democratic spirit in the 1790's and the indigenous tradition of the American Revolution. The reader will find new material on the ideas and interests of aristocratic as well as democratic leaders. Dr. Link has for the period of his study done interesting work in the extremely difficult field of popular thought and action, as distinguished from that of the leaders. He has also dealt with the controversial problem of the relative importance of the frontier and of cities in shaping characteristically American outlooks.

When studies of this subject are made for other decades, we shall be in a better position to understand and to evaluate the history of democracy in America. Meantime, investigators of the particular period in which Dr. Link has worked, and students of American democracy in general, will be indebted to him for his vigorous monograph.

MERLE CURTI

COLUMBIA UNIVERSITY
October, 1941

PREFACE

THE PERIOD following the adoption of the Constitution and the inauguration of George Washington to the presidency of the new republic, was, until the rise of modern critical scholarship, treated as though it were some mythical time when the administrators of government were demigods; nor are all recent scholars entirely free of this tendency. Many have written as though they believed that all the actions of the great Revolutionary hero and first president were infallible, and that any dissent from this belief is both untrue and unpatriotic. Consequently, the loud voice of dissidence that arose in the 1790's has too often been lightly dismissed as an aberration from fundamental American principles, the result in a large part of the subversive activities of French origin. According to this view, numbers of people and leaders went awry, and the period of their apostasy is of little importance to the main sequence of American development.

This study presents a different approach to the closing decade of the eighteenth century. It has been concerned not alone with the deeds of the influential, but also with the thought and action of those whom some have called the unimportant people. The frame of reference of the dissertation is the author's firm belief in the philosophy and methodology of democracy. To the writer, democracy has as its principal tenet that men, women and children can and should share increasingly in the decisions that affect their lives; and that the vast body of humble people are, in the long run, the best able to determine the direction of their affairs.

The results of a democratic approach to the study of post-Revolutionary America are here presented in the following pages. The author makes no claim that this approach is unique. The inimitable scholar, Charles A. Beard, in his own words, "has spent

his life discovering a few obvious things" in history. The work of
Vernon L. Parrington is of great significance. Among many mono-
graphs in this tradition, the recent study by Merrill Jensen, entitled
The Articles of Confederation, probes into the period immediately
preceding the one discussed here. Still others might well be mentioned.

The story about to be related in this monograph tells how farmers,
artisans, tradesmen, and sailors, among others, in the spirit of '76,
rolled up mass opposition to the anti-democratic tendencies of the
period. It gives setting for the fact that Thomas Jefferson "took a
walk" toward a new party alignment in 1793. And perhaps in a
day when democracy is again in greater danger of betrayal from
within, than attack from without, the record of a similar threat in
our early national history may be illuminating.

In travels to libraries and historical societies extending from
Maine to Georgia and as far west as Madison, Wisconsin, the investigator read the many well preserved manuscript collections of
"important" men in the post-Revolutionary period. But a democratic search, in the sense of finding materials from both sides, made
more stringent demands. One must uncover the opinions of the
"unimportant" people and gain a deeper understanding of the entire
period by knowing what the common man thought and did. The
difficulty of this task is at once apparent, for such gems as *The Kentucky Miscellany* with its tavern poetry, *The Feast of Merriment*
with its anti-aristocratic ribaldry, or *The Key of Libberty* with its
agrarian wisdom, are rare indeed. Yet, the search was not in vain.
Cordial librarians opened their collections in the quest for treasures,
and often joined the hunt for the archival erratics that would tell of
the "subterranean gentry," their convictions, their feelings and their
organizations. The fact that three collections of the manuscript
minutes and papers of the popular societies, never before used by
historians, are now brought forward indicates a part of the reward
of the long inquiry.

The author is indebted to so many who have been of the greatest
aid that it is quite impossible to give personal recognition to all.
The staffs of every state library, historical society and hall of record

from Georgia to Maine have given the kindest assistance. The university collections of manuscript and printed Americana at South Carolina, North Carolina, Duke, Virginia, William and Mary, Transylvania, Pittsburgh, Chicago, Wisconsin, Yale, Brown, Harvard, and Vermont were all made available by the gracious people in charge. The Boston Athenæum, the Peabody Institute, the Philadelphia and the Charleston Library Societies, the New York and the Boston Public Libraries were visited and their librarians are to be thanked. The longest periods of study were spent in research with the excellent newspaper collection in the American Antiquarian Society, and with the virtually inexhaustible sources to be found in the Rare Book Room and the Manuscript Division of the Library of Congress. To the staff members of these institutions the writer is deeply indebted.

Nor can one overlook extending a word of thanks to the numerous local historians, many of whom have valuable items of historic interest, and the Works Progress Administration employees, all of whom helped in so many ways.

To Miss Honor McCusker of the Boston Public Library, the author is especially grateful for her translation of and her efforts to decode the difficult French letters in "The Correspondence of the Republican Society of Charleston, South Carolina." To Dr. Henry Johnson for his direction in the early stages of this study through his inspiring course on "The Literature of American History"; to Dr. John M. Brewster, an editor of the posthumous works of George H. Mead, for his criticisms and suggestions for chapter five; to Dr. Harry Carman who has encouraged and helped in innumerable ways; to Dr. George S. Counts for suggesting the subject at hand and for guiding its development; to Dr. Imogene N. Cowles for her help with the style and with the proprieties of expression; to the Advanced School of Education for a grant which made possible a summer in the Library of Congress; and to Dr. Erling M. Hunt and Mr. Donald E. Stewart who read the manuscript and made important suggestions—to all these I express my appreciation.

But this study could never have been written had it not been for the indefatigable efforts and kindly patience of Dr. Merle Curti. If the author has failed to consider any sources or facts relative to the subject matter, it is entirely his error and not that of his sponsor. My wife, Beulah Meyer Link, deserves great credit for her generous and intelligent help, and for her good cheer at those moments when the road seemed endless.

EUGENE P. LINK

Columbia University
July, 1941

CONTENTS

DEMOCRATIC-REPUBLICAN
SOCIETIES, 1790–1800

Chapter One

THE APPEARANCE OF POPULAR
SOCIETIES

How did the Republicans of that day [*1790's*] *face and avert the first grand conspiracy to destroy the republic? By the establishment, wherever possible, of what were called Democratic Societies, in which the people met, discussed the designs of their enemies, contrived the means of defeating them, encouraged each other in the good fight for liberty, and directed and concentrated public opinion so as to make it most effectual. These societies were mighty engines in the politics of that gloomy period. They spoke the voice of the people and made it respected. The result was the complete overthrow of the Federal party.*

From the statement of purpose of the
JEFFERSON DEMOCRATIC ASSOCIATIONS, 1880

A DEMOCRACY might well be defined as a form of government in which popular associations have a free and recognized indispensable function. A popular association is any informal, unofficial group of citizens, convened without limitations of class, race, or creed, for the purpose of participating, through the expression of their sentiments, in the decisions of their government. The term "popular society" was used in the eighteenth century to designate the formal organization of the town meeting or the courthouse gathering of the citizenry. Through such associations a truly democratic government is an augmented "we group," in which government is not a taskmaster to be accepted in sullen silence or grumbletonian submission, but a social organization in which all citizens play an integral role. The popular society represents the attempt to bring the sense of "we" and "our" into the community and national life. The more democratic epochs of all history have been those periods when men spoke of their government as "ours" and their collective actions as "us." In direct contrast, in the less democratic epochs the circumscribing voice of individual or oligarchic desire has induced men to refer to their government as "it" or "they." The former epochs are so few they can be numbered on the fingers of one hand, and each is marked by this greater degree of informed and active participation of the body of citizens. The dichotomy between the people on the one hand and the government on the other no longer exists. Democracy and popular societies function together, the first encouraging the second, and the second, by constant reconstruction, preserving the first.

This reciprocal relationship existed in the tense and turbulent years during and following the American Revolution. Some who organized the movement for independence, and many others who fought for it, through semimilitary popular bodies such as the Committees of Safety and the militia, were defending the right to express their will in government, to gain greater social equality, and to extend and maintain the principle of liberty and justice for all. Of the many currents and cross currents that churned and tossed life in this eventful era, the democratizing stream was especially strong and significant. More than a few conservatives, who had loyally defended the freedom from Great Britain, felt that the tendencies toward egalitarianism must not get out of hand and move toward extremes. They believed that democracy—direct rule by the people—was premature and that it threatened chaos. The issue between those who wanted more democracy rather than less appeared, after the Revolution, in the state constitutional discussions, and the movement for framing the Articles of Confederation. The same issue was intensified in the ratification of the national Constitution and burst out in party vituperation in the 1790's.

Most of "the fathers" had the future welfare of the nascent nation as their chief concern. They were troubled about a variety of perplexing issues: The Indian problem on the frontier, foreign and domestic trade, stabilization of the currency, securing markets abroad, the raising of revenue, and, of course, the fundamental problem involved in working out a new governmental organization. It was natural that these "fathers" should not have been entirely agreed on the methods for solving these problems and advancing the welfare of the struggling young government. Conservatives doubted whether these complicated problems would yield to solution through an unhampered democratic process.

All were deeply concerned about their government and its policies. Dissension and resentment were inevitable. The clashes, acrimonious though they were, marked the construction of the framework of a great nation. Here and there an individual became so incensed by the ideas and actions of another that challenges to duels were not uncommon. Others, both Federalist and Republican, were so certain their panacea for the ills of the struggling government was right that they did not hesitate to use what seems today unethical means to gain their end. Broadsides and newspapers, pamphlets and "patriotic" speeches were the vehicles for their seething emotions. The processes of democracy were vigorously at work.

The broad and basic question was, should the infant nation follow the democratic tendency stirred up by the Revolution, or should it turn its feet into more familiar paths of governmental organization? Popular societies came forward to answer this question with a positive democratic affirmation. Moderate and radical democrats joined forces to stem a tide against their political ideals. Many thought Shays's farmers had just complaints. Many more looked with dissatisfaction upon the conservative trends in state and national constitution making, where the direct representation of the people was being compromised. Others disapproved of the hated excise system. This was especially true in those sections of the country where it was thought the popular voice was not heard in government—adumbrations of "taxation without representation." And still others, influenced by Rousseauian ideas, feared and distrusted apparent efforts to centralize the power of the state. Back to the ideals of July 4, 1776, was their cry.

This ubiquitous discontent, involving well-to-do merchants and farmers, poor settlers and craftsmen, sailors and militiamen, was the soil in which popular societies took root. Appealing to the more radical trends in the American Revolution for authority, these heterogeneous groups called upon the people to awaken to their condition. By education and enlightenment, as well as by vigilance over and concern for government, liberty was to be preserved.

Ironic as it may seem to modern eyes, the first society to appear in the 1790's was organized by the Germans in Philadelphia. It was called the German Republican Society and must have been planned the last of March or the first of April, 1793, for by April 13 Freneau's *National Gazette* announced the formation and publication of its first circular.[1] This society was inspired by the Muhlenbergs, especially by Peter—"A stern republican," who was "ever on the side of the people, and unhesitating and undeviating in his opposition to all aristocratic measures." [2] It issued a circular, the first and one of the best emanating from democratic societies and worthy of full presentation here:

In a republican government it is the duty incumbent on every citizen to afford his assistance, either by taking part in its immediate administration, or by his advice and watchfulness, that its principles may remain uncorrupt; for the spirit of liberty, like every virtue of the mind, is to be kept alive only by constant action. It unfortunately happens that objects of general concern seldom meet with the individual attention which they merit, and that individual exertion seldom produces a general effect; it is therefore of essential moment that political societies should be established in a free government, that a joint operation may be pro-

---

[1] It is to be noted that this society was formed at least six weeks before the arrival of Genet. Talk of organizing such societies began as early as the summer of 1792, before Genet had even been chosen as ambassador to the United States. See the *Norwich Packet*, Connecticut, Aug. 9, 1792. Some have written that the Pennsylvania Democratic Society was the first, appearing on July 4, 1793. If this were true, Genet could have stimulated the formation of the clubs. See Scharf and Westcott, *History of Philadelphia*, I, 474.

Scherger (*The Evolution of Modern Liberty*, p. 27) advances an interesting argument to show that German barbarians who helped overthrow the Roman Empire had a keen sense of individualism. From his study of the *Germania* of Tacitus, he concludes that modern liberty stems from these freedom-loving barbarians who hated cities, regarded taxpaying as a form of serfdom, and elected democratically their own chieftains. The revival of the Roman idea of the omnipotent state stifled this freedom, according to Scherger.

[2] Muhlenberg, *The Life of Major-General Peter Muhlenberg*, p. 332.

duced, which shall give that attention and exertion so necessary for the preservation of civil liberty. The importance and truth of these reflections have operated on a number of Germans in this city, they have therefore thought fit to associate themselves in a society under the name of the German Republican Society of Philadelphia. The German character has hitherto languished in America, owing to the inattention of the Germans to objects of government and education; it is high time they should step forward, declare themselves independent of other influence and think for themselves. Ignorance not only excludes us from many enjoyments in life, but renders us liable to imposition, and to judge of an evil and its extent we should have a mind cultivated by education, added to our own, or the experience of others; hence the necessity of instruction and information in a government where every citizen should be capable of judging of the conduct of the rulers, and the tendency of the laws. The society wishes to impress the importance and advantages of education upon the minds of their brethern throughout the state. To be respected men should be virtuous, but to be capable of fulfilling a republican duty and of serving our country, we should connect wisdom with virtue. There is a disposition in the human mind to tyrannize when cloathed with power, men therefore who are entrusted with it, should be watched with the eye of an eagle to prevent those abuses which never fail to arise from a want of vigilance. Jealousy is a security, it is a virtue in a republic, for it begets watchfulness; it is a necessary attendant upon a warm attachment to our country.

The society wish to call the attention of their countrymen to affairs of state; they wish to inspire them with jealousy to guard them against every encroachment on the equality of freemen. As the faithful administration of government depends greatly upon a judicious delegation made to offices dependent upon the people, it is a common duty to give this every attention; we shall therefore comprehend this in our plan, and we shall take the liberty, occasionally, to offer our opinions, and shall take a peculiar pleasure in receiving a free communication of sentiment from you on this subject. . . .

Thus we have in as concise manner as possible, pointed out the views of the society, and we hope for your concurrence and assistance in giving the Germans that station which their industry, their integrity, and their patriotism merit; any communications which you have to make, you will please address to the President of the German Republican Society of Philadelphia. As we have in our constitution provided for the admission of members at a distance by the title of honorary and corresponding members, you will please inform us if you wish to be considered as one of our body, that we may enroll you accordingly.

With our best wishes for your private as well as public happiness, we are—

By the order of the society,
HENRY KAMMERER
Vice-President

April 14th.

This long circular of the German democrats contains the basic principles of the societies subsequently organized, namely, the maintenance of vigilance concerning the actions of governmental officers, the search for self-improvement through increasing political education, and the correspondence with other societies of a similar nature to insure a unified viewpoint.

"A Customer" of the *National Gazette* had seen the circular when it appeared in German in the *Philadelphische Correspondenz*, April 9, 1793. He wrote Freneau asking him to print an English translation in his paper. His letter closes with a significant paragraph:

It would be to the advantage of Pennsylvania and the union if political societies were established throughout the United States, as they would prove powerful instruments in support of the present system of equality, and formidable enemies to aristocracy in whatever shape it might present itself. *May the example of the German Republican Society prove a spur to the friends of equality throughout the United States.*[3]

Some years before, Benjamin Franklin had offered a friendly criticism of the German Americans, saying they were too isolated in their group loyalty and that they should increase their interest and activity in the new republic. Now the tables were turned: the Germans set the example in political organization for other Americans to follow.

---

[3] *Aurora and General Advertiser*, April 15, 1793 [italics mine]. This was the paper of Benjamin Franklin Bache, who reprinted the entire story of the German Republicans from Freneau's *National Gazette*. Both Bache and Freneau became active members of subsequently formed democratic societies.

The records do not reveal whether the citizens of Norfolk, Virginia, were influenced by the Germans "in and around Philadelphia." Late in May a Norfolk and Portsmouth Republican Society appeared. On June 3 the "Standing Committee" met and adopted the declaration of the association, which all members were expected to sign:

We the undersigned citizens, declare as our unalterable opinion, that the blessings of a just, mild and equitable government can only be perpetuated by that pure spirit of Republican vigilance to which (under favor of the Supreme Governor of the Universe) we owe our present political ease, tranquillity and happiness.

That the inattention which many of our fellow citizens discover toward the dearest rights, privileges and immunities of freemen, is to us a matter of serious concern and regret. That the excellence of a mild representative government (affording an example of the happiness of equal liberty) will excite jealousies in the mind, and be painful in the sight of tyrants and their abettors; it does therefore behoove men who are experiencing the blessings of liberty, to be ever on the guard against the machinations of those enemies to mankind.

That the imaginary security into which we have been lulled, by our remote situation from the combined despots of Europe and other considerations, may have the most fatal tendency; if not to destroy our independence as a nation, at least to sap the foundation of that glorious fabric upon which our liberties rest——our free and excellent constitution. That it becomes Republicans at all times to speak their sentiments freely and without reserve; but more particularly at this alarming period, when we behold the Tyrants of the world combined, and every engine of despotism employed in making a grand effort to crush the infant spirit of freedom, recognized by our brethren of France, whose virtuous exertions (in a cause so lately our own) we cannot as men and as Republicans behold with indifference, or contemplate without a mixture of sympathy and admiration.

That it is the truth, not less notorious than it is to be lamented, that in the bosom of our own country we have men whose principles and sentiments are opposed to all free governments, that such are just objects of suspicion.

That strongly impressed with these sentiments, we have conceived

it to be our interest, but more particularly our duty, to form this association, for the purpose of strengthening the bands of Union, and of cherish-
ing Republican sentiments, manners, morals, and associations.

By order of the Standing Committee,
T. NEWTON, Jun. President.[4]

The third popular society to appear during the second administration of Washington proved to be the most influential of all. In the
first place it was organized in Philadelphia, "the primum mobile of
the United States," a city that "from habit, from necessity and from
local circumstances, all the states view . . . as the capitol of the
new world." [5] Furthermore, this society enlisted a brilliant slate of
American leaders, including David Rittenhouse, considered as second only to Benjamin Franklin in wisdom and scientific knowledge;
Charles Biddle, prominent Quaker merchant; Dr. George Logan,
farmer and politician; Alexander J. Dallas, Secretary of State in
Pennsylvania; and Peter S. Du Ponceau, erudite lawyer. Because
the national government was established in Philadelphia, thereby
making it necessary for representatives from every state in the union
to gather there, this society was in a position to inspire and lead a
great social movement. Regardless of the fact that democratic societies antedated this one, it was not until the Democratic Society of
Pennsylvania sent out its circular urging the formation of societies
in every section of the nation that the movement assumed unity and
real momentum. Other societies, such as those in Vermont, Kentucky,
and South Carolina, copied its organizational pattern; these and
others used its comprehensive statement of principles as a guide in
writing their own constitutions. Members of the national legislature from the various states joined the organization and took part
in its program. Although the vitriolic remarks by William Cobbett
about these societies were usually inaccurate, he was right when he
called this "the mother society." [6]

---

[4] *Virginia Chronicle*, June 8, 1793.

[5] Benjamin Rush to Noah Webster, Feb. 13, 1788, in the Noah Webster Papers,
New York Public Library.

[6] Cobbett [Playfair], *The History of Jacobinism: Its Crimes, Cruelties and Perfidies*, II (Appendix), 18.

The constitution of the Philadelphia society is too long to re-produce in full here,[7] but its first circular, sent to county and state leaders throughout the land, states its major principles:

We have the pleasure to communicate to you a copy of the constitu-tion of the Democratic Society in hopes that after a candid consideration of its principles, and objects, you may be induced to promote its adop-tion in the county of which you are an inhabitant.

Every mind, capable of reflection, must perceive, that the present crisis in the politics of nations is peculiarly interesting to America. The European Confederacy, transcendent in power, and unparalleled in iniquity, menaces the very existence of freedom. Already its baneful operation may be traced in the tyrannical destruction of the Constitu-tion of Poland; and should the glorious efforts of France be eventually defeated, we have reason to presume, that, for the consummation of monarchical ambition, and the security of its establishments, this country, the only remaining depository of liberty, will not long be permitted to enjoy in peace, the honors of an independent, and the happiness of a republican government.

Nor are the dangers arising from a foreign source the only causes at this time, of apprehension and solicitude. The seeds of luxury appear to have taken root in our domestic soil; and the jealous eye of patriotism already regards the spirit of freedom and equality, as eclipsed by the pride of wealth and the arrogance of power.

This general view of our situation has led to the institution of the Democratic Society. A constant circulation of useful information, and a liberal communication of republican sentiments, were thought to be the best antidotes to any political poison, with which the vital principles of civil liberty might be attacked; for by such means, a fraternal con-fidence will be studiously marked; and a standard will be erected, to which, in danger and distress, the friends of liberty may successfully resort.

To obtain these objects, then, and to cultivate on all occasions the love of peace, order, and harmony; an attachment to the constitution and a respect to the laws of our country will be the aim of the Demo-cratic Society.[8]

---

[7] It may be found in Hazen, *Contemporary American Opinion of the French Revolution.*

[8] Cobbett [Playfair], *op. cit.,* II (Appendix), 20–21.

The important elements in the circular letter and constitution of the Pennsylvania Democratic Society are the emphases: to "cultivate a just knowledge of rational liberty"; to uphold the sovereignty of the people in the right to keep a constant check upon public servants, with the right to alter the form of government; and to enlighten the citizens upon the meaning and responsibilities of a representative government. This constitution, which was drafted by Alexander J. Dallas, secretary to Gov. Thomas Mifflin and later prominent in national politics, was adopted on July 3 by the society. The group requested that it be published in the newspapers.[9] It was the most widely circulated of all the democratic societies' constitutions. Many of the Federalist presses reprinted it, before they adopted the general policy of boycotting news of the popular associations. Thus a national movement got under way, stimulated by the central "mother society" whose members Cobbett branded as "butchers, tinkers, broken hucksters and trans-Atlantic traitors."[10]

[9] *The Federal Gazette*, July 15, 1793; Hazen, *op. cit.*, p. 193. In Charleston, Philadelphia, New York, and other cities there were French Benevolent and Patriotic Societies formed to support the French Revolution. These, together with the democratic clubs, have been unfairly lumped together and tagged "Jacobin Clubs." Some Americans, notably Dr. George Logan and Robert Goodloe Harper, were members of both groups, which may account for the confusion. Genet was at one time president of the French "Friends of Liberty and Equality" in Philadelphia, but his name does not appear in the extant minutes of the Democratic Society. These French clubs are more truthfully "Jacobin Clubs," while the democratic societies, as will be pointed out later, were primarily concerned with critical American problems. See the minutes of the "Friends of Liberty and Equality" (in French) in the Pennsylvania Historical Society. A rough draft of its constitution, with corrections by Genet, is in the Genet Papers, Dec., 1792. A clause states that this society shall not interfere in the affairs of the states, but will fraternize with the citizens and remind them of the reciprocal interests of the two nations. By Feb. 3, 1793 (Genet Papers) this Society of Liberty and Equality was recruiting for the French army and was calling the French Benevolent Society, of which Peter S. Duponceau was a member, traitorous and aristocratic. See also *The North Carolina Journal*, May 22, 1793, for a statement of purpose of the French Patriotic Society. Childs, *French Refugee Life in the United States, 1790-1800*, p. 148, says that the Société française des Amis de la Liberte et de l'Egalite was a real Jacobin Club in America. She says they may be compared with the Democratic Societies which "have at times been attributed to French influences."

[10] Cobbett, *A Little Plain English Addressed to the People of the United States*, 1795, p. 70. While Washington, Pennsylvania, and Lexington, Kentucky, followed the suggestion of forming a society, Hanover County, Virginia, turned down the proposal, saying it was sympathetic, but feared that branched societies would create faction and discord; *American Daily Advertiser*, Aug. 12, 1793. That the cir-

A month later two important societies appeared, one, the Kentucky Democratic Society at Lexington, and the other, the Republican Society of South Carolina, meeting at Charleston.[11] Around the first Kentucky organization were two satellite democratic societies, one in Scott County, meeting in Georgetown, and the other in Bourbon County, meeting at Paris, Kentucky.[12] An offshoot of the Charleston club was the Democratic Society of Pinckney District. Throughout the nation spread these organizations, interrelated by committees of correspondence. Forty-one such popular groups were organized between March, 1793, and the election of Thomas Jefferson in 1800. A complete list of all those that have been uncovered by an examination of the records of each state from Maine to Georgia reveals:

POPULAR SOCIETIES ORGANIZED IN THE THIRTEEN STATES
BY 1800

1793

1. Philadelphia, The German Republican Society
2. Norfolk, Virginia, The Norfolk-Portsmouth Republican Society
3. Philadelphia, The Democratic Society of Pennsylvania
4. Lexington, Kentucky, The Democratic Society of Kentucky

cular of the Pennsylvania Society spread throughout the states is further indicated in Judge Jonathan Sayward's diary, which is preserved in the library of the American Antiquarian Society. At his home in York, Maine, he entered in his diary for Feb., 1794, the statement that he had read the masterly declaration, which must have carried conviction. Sayward, however, was opposed to the "self-created clubb."

[11] *The Kentucky Gazette*, Aug. 31, 1793. John Bradford, the printer of the *Gazette*, suggested the formation of the Kentucky Society. At its first meeting it ordered a circular to be sent out to other counties in the state, inviting them to form societies and correspond. A bound volume of manuscripts entitled "The Republican Society of South Carolina" is in the Boston Public Library. It contains thirty-seven pieces, sixteen in English and twenty-one in French, mostly letters to Mangourit, the French consul. They are of great historic interest and value, though not all of them are related to the Republican Society. They should be considered as an addition to Frederick Jackson Turner's work on the papers of the French consuls. This collection makes clear that the Charleston democratic club *did not* join the Paris Jacobins, even though it did, through Mangourit, address the National Convention. It was the French Patriotic Society that petitioned for membership in the Jacobin Clubs.

[12] *Kentucky Gazette*, Nov. 2, 1793; Harry Innes Papers, Vol. XIX, no. 104 in the Library of Congress.

   5. Charleston, South Carolina, The Republican Society of South
Carolina
   6. The Scott County Democratic Society (Kentucky) [13]
   7. The Bourbon County Democratic Society (Kentucky) [13]
   8. The Democratic Society of Pinckney District (South Carolina) [14]
   9. The Republican Society of Ulster County (New York) [15]
*10. The Republican Society of New Haven (Connecticut)
 11. Boston, The Massachusetts Constitutional Society

1794

 12. New York, The Democratic Society
 13. Newark, New Jersey, The Republican Society [16]
 14. Washington, North Carolina, The Democratic-Republican Society
*15. Fayetteville, North Carolina, The Committee of Correspondence
*16. Mingo Creek, Pennsylvania, The Society of United Freeman
 17. Washington, Pennsylvania, The Democratic Society [17]
*18. The Republican Society at the Mouth of the Yough (Pennsylvania)
 19. Greenville, South Carolina, The Madisonian Society [14]
*20. Pendleton, South Carolina, The Franklin or Republican Society [14]
*21. Norfolk, Virginia, The Democratic Society [18]
 22. Baltimore, Maryland, The Republican Society
 23. Newcastle, Delaware, The Patriotic Society
*24. Carlisle, Pennsylvania, Committee of Correspondence

* Societies, fifteen in all, not mentioned in the lists compiled by Luetscher, *Early Political Machinery in the United States,* chap. ii; Woodfin, "Citizen Genet and His Mission," pp. 490–91, n.; or Miller, "The Democratic Clubs of the Federalist Period," pp. 45–46.

[13] Branches of the Democratic Society of Kentucky.
[14] Branches of the state-wide Republican Society of South Carolina.
[15] Related to the Democratic Society of New York.
[16] A "Patriotic Society" in Newark is not considered a popular society in this study. Its purposes were nonpolitical and "for promoting objects of public utility." Among its activities were prison relief and reform, poor relief, protection from fire, raising money for yellow-fever victims, and the like. Its members were merchants and conservative ministers. See Wood's *Newark Gazette,* Oct. 9, 16, 1793, and Jan. 22, March 19, 1794.
[17] A Branch of the Democratic Society of Pennsylvania.
[18] In July, 1794, this society was organized at Norfolk, where a Republican Society already existed. Why, cannot be discovered. The statements of purpose of the new organization are more radical than that of its predecessor (*South Carolina State Gazette,* July 25, 1794).

25. The Columbia County Democratic Society (New York) [19]
26. Portland, Maine, The Republican Society [19]
*27. Mt. Prospect, New Jersey, The Political Society
28. Wytheville, Virginia, The Democratic Society
29. Dumfries, Virginia, The Democratic-Republican Society
30. The Chittenden County Democratic Society (Vermont)
31. The Addison County Democratic Society (Vermont)
32. The Rutland County Democratic Society (Vermont)
*33. The Second Society of Rutland County (Vermont) [20]
34. Northumberland, Pennsylvania, The Democratic Society
*35. Shawangunk, Ulster County, New York, The Democratic Society

1795

36. St. Bartholemew's Parish, South Carolina, The Republican Society
37. Lancaster, Pennsylvania, The Republican Society
*38. The Essex County Democratic Society (New Jersey)

1797

*39. Philadelphia, The True Republican Society

1798

*40. Norwalk, Connecticut, The Republican Society
*41. Stamford, Connecticut, The Republican Society
*42. Norfolk, Virginia, The Constitutional Society

It is important to note the various names used by the popular societies. Evidently among their heroes were Madison and Franklin. "Republican" called to mind the Pennsylvania state constitutional struggles, the new France, and the societies started by Thomas Paine in that country. The name "Constitutional" was familiar to the critical period and reminded also of the patriotic societies of Great Britain. "United Freemen," which was used by the Irish in Western Pennsylvania, doubtless was suggested by the United Irish-

---

[19] This society was inspired by the Massachusetts Constitutional Society.

[20] Two societies were organized in Rutland County, Vermont. One met usually at Fairhaven or Castleton and the other at Middletown. The Vermont societies were more closely tied up with New York as a focal point.

men, the reform organization of Ireland. The mother society originally was to be called "The Sons of Liberty"; Genet suggested the name "Democratic Society." [21] Many societies, especially those along the more radically minded frontier fringe, took the name of their prototype.

Documentary evidence is not sufficient to establish the existence of other democratic societies, which were said to have formed at many other places. *The Connecticut Courant* for September 24, 1794, names additional societies in Virginia. In this active republican state there were doubtless others, which, because there was no printer in the neighborhood or because they were so small a unit of the larger pattern, do not seem to have registered themselves for the student of history. An attempt was made to form a society in Bennington, Vermont, as evidenced by an announcement in Anthony Haswell's newspaper, *The Vermont Gazette*, February 28, 1794, but whether or not the effort was realized remains unknown. It is never mentioned again in the press, nor are there any records of its meetings. A society was believed to have organized at Vasselborough, Maine, and well it might have, considering the republican complexion of the community.[22] But it is not recorded in the extant Maine newspapers of the period, nor do the papers of the neighboring Portland Republican Society make any reference to it. Citizens of Pittsburgh, Pennsylvania, held popular meetings, toasted the Rights of Man, the free use of the Mississippi River, and the return of the western posts, but there is no basis for Fisher Ames' listing it as having a Democratic Society.[23] Hugh H. Brackenridge read to the assembled delegates, from neighboring communities, letters from "the people of Kentucky" regarding western interests. These delegates passed resolutions supporting the contentions of the westerners and sent them to the Philadelphia and Kentucky Democratic Societies.[24] So far as it is known, there was no permanent organiza-

[21] Minnigerode, *Jefferson, Friend of France*, p. 220.
[22] For the strong democratic influence around Vasselborough, see Robinson, *Jeffersonian Democracy in New England*, maps.
[23] *Annals of the Congress of the United States*, Third Congress, pp. 927–29.
[24] *The Pittsburgh Gazette*, July 6, 1793, April 5, 1794; McMaster, *A History of the People of the United States*, II, 177.

tion formed. Rather it was one of the innumerable town meetings of the time, which were often referred to as Democratic societies and as such opposed by conservatives. The chief difference between the two was that the town meeting was organized temporarily, to deal with an immediate, pressing issue, while the Democratic Society had a more permanent basis and dealt with a platform of issues.

The Juvenile Republican Society of New York is worth no more than mention here. It met on July 4, 1795, toasted religion without superstition, a free press, the Rights of Man, and "Less respect to the consuming speculator, who wallows in luxury, than to the productive mechanic who struggles with indigence." [25] But apparently it died stillborn.

Another type of association akin to the popular societies is "The Society for Free Debate." Such a club existed throughout the decade in New York City and was under the influence of democratically minded leaders. It welcomed both the high officer of government and the lowly shoemaker to its forum.[26]

A popular society near Wytheville, in western Virginia, called "The Society of Whigs," seems to have existed since Revolutionary days. Although not active and not connected with other societies, it did revive to some extent in 1793, and it is of importance to note that this original Revolutionary society also defended the cause of France, urged Washington to fulfill our treaty obligations with that country, and requested active assistance "to our republican allies." [27]

The Tammany Societies of the 1790's, scattered like the Democratic Societies throughout the states, could well be considered in the category of popular societies. In their unity by correspondence, they presented a formal organization of the so-called "lower class" of American citizens. Their original purpose, however, seems to

[25] *The American Daily Advertiser*, July 10, 1795. This is the only reference to this juvenile organization.

[26] *The Baltimore Daily Repository*, Oct. 18, 1793; Johnston (ed.), *The Correspondence and Public Papers of John Jay*, p. 238.

[27] Arthur Campbell to George Washington, Miscellaneous Letters, Department of State, May 29, 1793, in the National Archives. The Whig Societies as progenitors of the democratic societies will be discussed in chap. ii.

have been primarily a friendly, benevolent one, perhaps as an offset to the more aristocratic Society of Cincinnati. Not until falling
under the influence of the democratic societies did they become
forthright political clubs.[28]

[28] The minutes of the meetings of the New York Tammany Society are in the
New York Public Library. Tammany first thought of itself as the Sons of Liberty.
By 1794 it was debating important current issues and upholding the same positions
as the New York Democratic Society. In fact, every member of the Democratic Society whose name is known, was also a member of the Tammany Society. The author has omitted special attention to the Tammany Societies, although they are mentioned here and there through this study. Source materials on them are rare, but
they might well be the object of special study by a patient investigator. Tammany
Societies existed in Virginia, Rhode Island, North Carolina, Pennsylvania, New
York, and doubtless elsewhere. Their toasts on festive occasions were ultrademo-
cratic in nature; see, viz., American Daily Advertiser, May 13, 18, 1794; Kilroe,
Saint Tammany and the Origin of the Society of Tammany or Columbian Order in
the City of New York, p. 193.

Chapter Two

POPULAR SOCIETIES AS SOCIAL FORCES

Solitary opinions have little weight with men whose views are unfair, but the voice of the many strikes them with awe.

From a resolution of the GERMAN REPUBLICAN SOCIETY, 1794

CRITICS AND OPPONENTS of the democratic societies have too readily dismissed them with a statement that they were mere replicas of the French Jacobin clubs. Many have said that they were inaugurated by Genet, the French ambassador; others, that citizens of French birth in this country set them on foot; while still others have seen the pernicious influence of "French gold" bribing certain Yankee rapscallions to form such organizations. These erroneous conceptions of the societies have persisted from the time Federalist opponents propagated them for political reasons down to many of the most recent productions of present-day historians.[1]

---

[1] Gibbs, *Memoirs of the Administrations of Washington and Adams*, p. 134; McMaster, *A History of the People of the United States*, II, 175; Hildreth, History *of the United States of America*, IV, 425; Schouler, *History of the United States of America*, I, 298–99. Federalist opinion on the rise of the clubs is reflected in numerous statements in that party's press in 1794; Wood's *Newark Gazette*, Oct. 15, 1794, contains the following example:

"A New Chapter—Political

"1. This is the book of the generation and downfall of Jacobinism.

"2. Brissot begat the Jacobin clubs of Paris. The Jacobin clubs of Paris begat Genet, and his French brethern:

"3. Genet begat the Democratic Societies in America; the Democratic Societies begat the Pittsburgh Rebellion and its consequences:

"4. The Pittsburgh Rebellion begat an armament of 15,000 men:

To accept uncritically the Federalist explanation of the appearance of the clubs as due to French intrigue of some variety or other leaves us with oversimplified and superficial conclusions. The democratic societies had a broader setting, as broad, in fact, as the social philosophy of Locke and Rousseau, which permeated much of Europe and America in the eighteenth century. Nor can the societies be divorced from the powerful social movements of the last quarter of the eighteenth century. These shook the thrones of the kings in all lands and caused "unholy hands" to grip more firmly the ruling scepter. That the clubs were modeled after the French Jacobins, then, is only partially true. One must add that they were also modeled after certain English societies and that both the English and French popular clubs were influenced by American Revolutionary organization. Let us trace the interrelationships of this world social labyrinth more carefully.

The genealogy of the popular societies of the eighteenth century reveals a forebear in England by the name of "The Revolution Society." In order to commemorate the Glorious Revolution of 1688 this society was organized. Its adherents were inspired by "the great Mr. Locke's" defense of that revolution. It proved to be the mother society of England, and in fact, of all democratic societies. The organization had become quiescent long before the American and French Revolutions, but these latter events brought it new life. It hailed the new republic and "the citizens of the world," who were activated after a century by the principles of 1688.

What were these principles? According to the Revolution Society they were these: that all civil and political authority comes from the people; that the abuse of power justifies resistance; and that the right of private judgment, liberty of conscience, trial by jury,

---

"5. The armament of 15,000 men will beget an expense of near two million dollars, of which all the people of the United States must bear a proportion:

"6. The expense will beget an attention of the people to the rise and origin; and

"7. That attention will beget the detestation and downfall of Jacobinism are eight generations.

"Thus endeth the first political chapter."

For the acceptance and perpetuation of the biased Federalist propaganda, see the new *Dictionary of American History*, ed. by James Truslow Adams, which even discusses the democratic societies under the heading of "Jacobin Clubs."

freedom of election are sacred and inviolable.[2] These are precisely the main planks in the platforms of the so-called "Jacobin Clubs" of America in the 1790's.

The idea of encouraging the formation of like societies and corresponding with them was lacking in the Revolution Society. In the 1780's English democrats saw the results of associated popular organizations such as the American committees of correspondence. In 1792 these Englishmen, as we shall see, began corresponding with the various Constitutional Societies of their own country and the Patriotic Societies of France.[3] With the appearance, therefore, of the American democratic societies in 1793, both English political philosophy and American Revolutionary techniques can be seen clearly in the background.

Certain indigeneous characteristics of the post-Revolutionary popular organizations can be traced in the Sons of Liberty, in the Associators, and in the committees of correspondence. In fact, the popular association itself was used in colonial times, even before the days of the stamp men and the regulators, as an instrument to protest and to take action on undemocratic measures. The appearance of the Sons of Liberty in 1765 gave rise to the committee of correspondence, which knit the popular groups into a more powerful unit. Often spoken of as "The Associated Sons of Liberty," their united efforts were successful in bringing about the repeal of the Stamp Act, the enforcement of the nonimportation agreements, and the boycott on English tea.[4]

Vigilance was the watchword of the Sons of Liberty. They recog-

[2] *The Correspondence of the Revolution Society in London, with the National Assembly, and with the Various Societies of the Friends of Liberty in France and England*, pp. 1–3.

[3] *Ibid.*, p. 11. See also Philip A. Brown, *The French Revolution in English History*, for a brilliant discussion of all the popular societies and their leaders in England. The National Archives in Washington has an invitation sent "To the American Ambassador" by "The Society for Commemorating the Glorious Revolution of 1688, when the People of England expelled a Tyrant and Seated on the Throne William II, A Prince of their own Choice," inviting the ambassador to the banquet in celebration of that event in 1792. Across the top of the invitation are the words "Universal Freedom," and just below a figure holding the Bill of Rights. (Notes from Great Britain, Vol. III, Department of State.)

[4] Davidson, "Sons of Liberty and Stamp Men," *North Carolina Historical Review*, IX (1932), 50.

nized the necessity of checking counter-Revolutionary activities and of preserving the gains made in the fight for freedom. Often it was imperative to work secretly. The mails were intercepted; only upon a special messenger or upon the new system of intervisitation of members from the different clubs could reliance be placed.[5] Therefore necessity made them secret, for vigilance would be impossible if members were easily identified. These organizations, which were composed largely of artisans and mechanics, preserved their watch over government well into the postwar era.[6]

The democratic societies took as a heritage from the Sons of Liberty the committee of correspondence, the technique of associating together for action, and the system of visitation. As has been noted in the preceding chapter, the Philadelphia democrats thought of themselves as Sons of Liberty; the Liberty Pole was a common symbol to both groups.[7] In many cases Liberty Boys became highly honored members of the later societies. Benjamin Edes, William Eustis, and William Cooper, Revolutionists of '76, were leading members of the Massachusetts Constitutional Society. Cooper, in fact, was president.[8] In New York, Udney Hay and Henry Rutgers were both erstwhile Sons of Liberty, and both prominent leaders of the Democratic Society.[9] This was the case in all the societies es-

---

[5] Leake, *Memoir of the Life and Times of General John Lamb*, pp. 2–14.

[6] Morais, in *The Era of the American Revolution*, ed. by Morris, pp. 269–89.

[7] Long before the brilliant analysis of symbols was presented by Sigmund Freud, Joel Barlow had discovered a Freudian explanation for the Tree of Liberty. In his notebook he traces it back to a phallic symbol arising out of the worship of Osiris in the Nile country. Next it was adopted by the Romans for the worship of Bacchus, then called Liber, and symbolized freedom for the bacchanalia. In England it became the May Pole, and in America the Liberty Pole. The French then took it over as the Tree of Liberty. The Liberty Cap, Barlow finds, originated from the same source. It symbolized the head of grain growing from the abdomen of Osiris, or the head of the impregnating phallus. The red cap was used in Rome to denote a freed slave, whence it got the name "Phrygian" cap. Thence it appeared in France and America as the *bonnet rouge*, or Cap of Liberty, which all good democrats wore on festive occasions. See "Genealogy of the Tree of Liberty," Joel Barlow's Notebook, Box 4 of the Barlow Papers in Harvard University; also Preble, *Origin and History of the American Flag*, pp. 134–36.

[8] Correspondence of the Sons of Liberty, 1766–83. New York Historical Society. Also *Boston Gazette*, Jan. 20, 1794.

[9] The papers of John Lamb, Box 1, reveal the names of many Sons of Liberty, including those mentioned above. The *New York City Directory for 1794* gives the names of the officers of the Democratic Society.

tablished in 1793 and in 1794. Each had its Revolutionary heroes, who held the highest offices in the organization.

Likewise the point of view of the two bodies was similar. In defending the right of the people to act against oppressive rule, the Sons of Liberty of Rhode Island wrote, "When tyrannic and oppressive measures make their approaches upon the subjects of civil government it becomes not only suitable but even indispensable Duty, resolutely to combine for the defence of their Rights." [10] This encouragement of the citizens to use vigorous efforts to preserve their rights was also the rallying cry of the societies in the 1790's. If the delegated authorities should turn their powers against the good of the people, explained the Sons of Liberty, "a plain opposition to the unjust force and usurpation is justifiable and exceedingly honorable." [11] Likewise, the Democratic Societies if necessary, would follow their predecessors and adopt extreme measures to preserve their liberties. Because of these parallels it seems quite evident that the patriotic societies of the 90's were a recrudescence of the organized spirit of '76.

Not only did the Sons of Liberty leave successors in America, but they also made an impact upon the growth of popular government in England and elsewhere. Nicholas Ray, in London, writes to the New York organization in 1766, saying that he was disappointed that it intended to dissolve, but adding: "I think it necessary to assure you that the continual account we had of the Sons of Liberty through all North America had its proper weight and effect." Ray suggested that these Liberty Boys form a permanent group to "commemorate the deliverance of March 18th," calling it "The Liberty Club." [12] This letter was answered by Isaac Sears, John Lamb, and others. They explained that such clubs were formed only when a crisis demanded them; that they would postpone the organization of such a group "until the time seems more eligible." They closed by assuring "all our good friends on your side of the

[10] The New York Sons of Liberty, March 19, 1766. Lamb Papers, Box 1, New York Historical Society.
[11] Ibid.
[12] Lamb Papers, July 28, 1766. March 18 was the day of the Stamp Act Repeal.

water" that they appreciated the help and sympathy extended to the Sons of Liberty.[13] About the same time John Wilkes, another Englishman who openly defended the American colonies in the 1760's, corresponded with the Boston societies. A London Patriotic Society was formed, which wrote to John Adams that "Your cause and ours is the same." [14] By 1776 two other popular societies in England were lending support to the American cause. One, "The Supporters of the Bill of Rights," elected Adams to membership and defended a free press and parliamentary reform; the other, "The Constitutional Society," raised money to send to the widows and children of Concord and made Benjamin Franklin the bearer of the gift.[15]

This interplay between popular movements on both sides of the Atlantic tended to make them, in organization and program, more and more alike. Each copied from the other, and Herbert M. Morais in his recent study properly says that the committee of correspondence, an indispensable instrument of the Sons of Liberty, was taken over from America by France and England.[16] The most important characteristic of all democratic societies was the committees of correspondence, and these were derived not from England or the Jacobin clubs of France, but from their own colorful background in colonial history.

Throughout the critical period from 1765 to the close of the American Revolution, a great variety of popular associations appeared. Besides the Sons of Liberty and their committees, which Jared Sparks more than a century ago credited with the successful prosecution of the Revolutionary social change,[17] the "Regulators" of North Carolina should be mentioned. They, like the democratic societies later, criticized the taxing system, the too-exalted courts, and their overpaid officials. They, too, formed semimilitary associations around the local militia, to unify their protests and, if necessary, act upon their demands.[18]

---

[13] Leake, op. cit., p. 36.
[14] Dora M. Clark, British Opinion and the American Revolution, pp. 154–55.
[15] Ibid., p. 158.   [16] Morais, in Morris, ed., op. cit., p. 272.
[17] Sparks, Life of Gouverneur Morris, I, 30 ff.
[18] Foote, Sketches of North Carolina, p. 53.

Nor was this all. In Charleston, South Carolina, the Non-Importation Association coöperated with Boston Sons of Liberty in opposition to the Townshend Acts. This association was led by Christopher Gadsden—the "Samuel Adams of the South"—and appealed to some planters, but chiefly to small merchants and mechanics, who joined its ranks.[19]

Elsewhere "Patriotic" societies were not uncommon. One in Pennsylvania was organized for the purpose of giving a vote and representation in the Assembly at Philadelphia. Its method was to vote *en bloc* at elections.[20] Another, in Connecticut, entitled itself "The United Company" and petitioned the Assembly in 1776 to relieve the tax burdens of the poor and to remove exemptions from lawyers and the clergy. "The want of fifty shillings never ought to be the criterion which distinguishes a Bondman from a Son of Liberty," [21] it declared. It also reprobated war profiteering.

The Revolutionary committees around Philadelphia had common features with the Democratic societies. Charles Thomson, secretary of the Continental Congress, said the committees kept the people informed from the capital by passing information to a county committee, thence to a district committee, and from there to popular meetings.[22] Subsequent organizations used the same system. So effective were these committees that the first Congress recognized their value and recommended their formation throughout the colonies. Like all popular meetings of the time, they met at courthouses to discuss issues and to form a united opinion which they freely circulated. They were Revolutionary agencies of government under the control and direction of leaders genuinely sympathetic to the masses.[23]

[19] Leila Sellers, *Charleston Business on the Eve of the American Revolution*, pp. 203–4.

[20] *Pennsylvania Gazette*, Aug. 19, 1772.

[21] *To the Honorable General Assembly of the Colony of Connecticut, to Be Holden at Hartford in May, 1776. The Memorial and Petition of a Numerous Body of the Inhabitants of Said Colony, Known by the Name of the United Company.* This rare item was recently acquired by the John Carter Brown Library and was called to the investigator's attention through the kindness of Dr. Lawrence Wroth, Librarian.

[22] Selsam, *The Pennsylvania Constitution*, pp. 66–67.   [23] *Ibid.*, p. 68.

Important to Pennsylvania history, too, are the Associators. Beginning as military associations composed of mechanics and artisans, they also formed along county lines. All of their officers were elected by themselves, at frequent intervals. They objected strenuously, therefore, to an attempt of Congress to violate their democratic procedure by appointing brigadier generals over their heads. These Associators took an active part in elections and in 1776 resolved to support only members of their own organization for the state assembly. They were the united power defending the extremely democratic constitution framed by Pennsylvania, at the convention, over which Benjamin Franklin presided, in 1776.[24] Around Philadelphia too, the Germans formed Associator groups, calling themselves "The Whig Associators" and meeting at the German Lutheran School House.[25]

The Whig clubs, like those of Boston and Baltimore, and "The Marine Anti-Britannic Society" of Charleston, in common with the popular societies a decade or more later, were concerned with the ferreting out and exposing of pro-English citizens and counter-Revolutionary plots. The Baltimore Whig Club in 1777 ordered a Tory printer, William Goddard, to "leave town by tomorrow morning and the country in three days," and, should he have refused, "he will be subject to the resentment of a *Legion*." Goddard answered by ridiculing the membership of the club, publishing their names and professions—sailors, haberdashers, tailors, and watchmakers—and asked how a man who was only fit to "patch a shoe" could have the temerity to attempt to patch the state. The governor and the house of delegates passed resolutions against bodies of men who acted without authority. Despite this support, Goddard found it better, after a personal call by a committee of the club, to quit Baltimore.[26]

---

[24] Selsam, *The Pennsylvania Constitution*, pp. 102–3. The Delaware Patriotic Society referred to themselves as Associators in their constitution, *Delaware Gazette*, Aug. 27, 1794.

[25] Selsam, *op. cit.*, p. 138. Also *Pennsylvania Packet*, Nov. 11, 1780.

[26] "Papers Relating to the Whig Club," April 8–17, 1777, in Maryland Miscellaneous (1771–1838), Library of Congress. It is worth noting that Goddard, while sneering at the humble occupations of the members, mentions David Rittenhouse as a "son of Esculapius." Rittenhouse was the first president of the mother Democratic Society in Philadelphia. For the Whig Club see also Goddard, *The Prowess of the Whig Club*.

A similar society in Boston called itself "The Free and Independent Whig Society of Observation." Its declared purpose was to assist the civil magistrates, to support the general welfare, and to keep an eagle eye on Tories returning to Boston. Like the later democratic societies, it appointed committees to observe and report the actions taken by representatives in government. In fact, Benjamin Edes and William Cooper, Sons of Liberty and members of the Constitutional Society, were likewise active in this popular organization.[27]

The Anti-Britannic Society of Charleston despised any persons having anything to do with the English while they occupied the city and it prevented such persons from joining the club. Although this society was a seamen's aid organization for the purpose of offering relief to widows and orphans of sailors and of taking the leadership in erecting a marine hospital and seminary, it was also probably responsible for some of the direct action taken against Tories at the time. Its leaders were far-famed democrats who later became involved with Citizen Genet in some insurrectionary plots.[28]

One would certainly expect to find patriotic societies in Virginia during this tempestuous period, and so there were. "The Society for the Preservation of Liberty" gave as its *raison d'être* exactly what its name implied. The society met in 1784 and resolved to oppose faction and ambitious innovations in the form of government and, at the same time, to communicate and print such facts as would better explain the form of government. Among its leaders was an array of famous names—Madison, Monroe, Henry, John Taylor, the Pages, and the Lees. John Breckinridge, a member, was later to become president of the Kentucky Democratic Society.[29]

Like Boston and Baltimore, Philadelphia had a Whig Society in 1777, dedicated to precautionary vigilance against internal enemies of a British leaning. It corresponded with individuals and with other

[27] The manuscript constitution and minutes of the "Free and Independent Whig Society of Observation," 1778–80, are in the Boston Public Library.

[28] *South Carolina State Gazette*, April 22, 1784.

[29] J. G. de Roulhac Hamilton, "A Society for Preservation of Liberty, 1784," *American Historical Review*, XXXII, 550–52. An original broadside of this society is in the library of the University of North Carolina.

societies, called town meetings, and insisted that Tories guilty of opposing the new government be brought forward for arrest. Among its leaders were Charles Willson Peale (president), David Rittenhouse, and Thomas Paine.[30] The greatest concern of this society was the defense of the Pennsylvania constitution of 1776 from the attacks of wealthy and conservative classes who liked it no better than they liked the Articles of Confederation for the national government. Later the club changed its name to "The Constitutional Society" and pledged its determination to defend the democratic governmental system to the last.[31] Two years later the citizens of Germantown formed a similar group.[32]

The principles and articles agreed upon by the members of the Constitutional Society approach even nearer those of the democratic societies than did the Sons of Liberty. In the first place, these Philadelphians proposed their plan of organization as a model for "Lovers and Supporters of Civil Government in other Parts of the State." They hoped their plan would bring about a confederation of the entire state, just as in 1793 David Rittenhouse and his cohorts envisaged a unity created by correspondence on a national scale. Furthermore, the principles of the two practically coincide. Both were disturbed by "the decline of civil government in the old world." Both laid the blame on "remissness" and lack of vigilance concerning government. Both societies appealed to the Declaration of Independence as their guide and inspiration and felt that willful men were attempting to encroach upon its guarantees. Though the Constitutional Society lacked a definite committee of correspondence in its organizational plan, it did have a sense of "party" unity. One of its articles reads,

We will, as a "party" support men and measures which will promise happiness and prosperity to the state, no matter who originates them. . . . We will not support men and measures merely because of formal connection.[33]

[30] *Pennsylvania Gazette*, April 9, 1777. Peale, *Charles Willson Peale and His Public Services during the American Revolution*, pp. 11–13.
[31] *Pennsylvania Gazette*, March 26, May 21, 1777.
[32] *Pennsylvania Packet*, July 15, 1779.
[33] *Pennsylvania Gazette*, April 28, 1779. These principles and articles should be compared with those of the Democratic Society of Philadelphia.

Every social movement has its counteraction, and the Constitutional Society did not escape this law of history. Opponents of the Pennsylvania constitution, who did not favor its popular one-house legislature or its article assuring legality to societies of the people,[34] formed the "Republican Society." The leaders were Richard Bache, George Clymer, Robert Morris, and the more conservative merchants and traders of the state. They held that they were equally opposed to British tyranny and popular tyranny. By the latter these men referred to the single-house legislature, the election of judges, and the general recognition of wide control by the mass of the people.[35] With the broadside and newspaper the Republican Society kept up a relentless barrage against the constitution and in favor of calling a convention to modify it.[36] The discussions were long and bitter, with the Constitutionalists representing in general the farmers and mechanics, and the Republicans defending the interests of the rich merchants. To the former, men like Robert Morris were monopolists or "engrossers," who were directly responsible for high prices and hard times.[37] The merchants, on the other hand, resented a system of government which allowed "any character to rise into power . . . and there are some of us who think not so meanly of ourselves as to dread any rivalship from those who are now in office." [38] The Constitutional Society was successful in upholding the constitution of 1776 until 1789, when the assembly adopted resolutions that delegates be chosen for a convention to form a new constitution, to be patterned after that of the national government.[39] Franklin, Paine, and Rittenhouse were defeated.

[34] In their defense, the Constitutionalists cited Benjamin Franklin as authority that the one-house legislature was the safest and best. They added that Franklin's opinion was worth more than that of the combined opposition. (*Pennsylvania Gazette*, March 31, 1779). The article in the state constitution justifying popular societies reads "that the people have a right to assemble together, to consult for their common good, to instruct their representatives, and to apply to the legislature for redress of grievances, by address, petition, or remonstrance." (Scherger, *The Evolution of Modern Liberty*, p. 200).

[35] "Address to the Citizens of Pennsylvania," *Pennsylvania Gazette*, March 24, 1779.

[36] *To the Citizens of Pennsylvania* . . . , a broadside filed under "Republican Society" in the John Carter Brown Library.

[37] Sellers, *The Artist of the Revolution*, pp. 193–97.   [38] *Supra*, n. 32.

[39] Scharf and Westcott, *History of Philadelphia*, I, 454–55.

Long before Washington stigmatized the democratic societies as "self-created," that phrase was used by the opponents of these earlier clubs.[40] Aware of the political power they wielded by their unified action and conscious of their ability to act, if necessary, through their semimilitary personnel, it is no wonder that they were feared and bitterly opposed by the conservative classes. Daniel Leonard, "an able Tory" of Massachusetts, said in 1772 of the committee of correspondence in general:

This is the foulest, subtlest, and most venomous serpent ever issued from the egg of sedition. I saw the small seed when it was implanted; it was a grain of mustard. I have watched the plant until it has become a great tree.[41]

Opinion such as these continued and grew stronger, until twenty years later leading Americans were using equally vitriolic language against any popular organization of a similar nature.

The issues involved in the adoption of the national Constitution caused a wider disturbance of popular feeling than the constitutional issues within the state of Pennsylvania. Prominent leaders and patriots of the war were not satisfied with the new instrument of government. Melancton Smith, an officer-to-be of the New York Democratic Society, wrote that conditions were not so hopeless under the Articles of Confederation and that the evils had been overdrawn.[42] Pennsylvanians, issuing broadsides in English and German, voiced their resentment against the convention's exceeding its powers by totally abolishing the Articles. Furthermore, they criticized the speed and force used in the efforts to procure ratification.

As for the document itself, some common objections were that it proposed a too-expensive government, that legislative bodies were not chosen annually, that the judiciary and the Senate could prevent the expression of the public will, that too great scope existed in internal taxation, and, above all, that it lacked a bill of rights to

---

[40] *South Carolina State Gazette*, May 6, 13, 20, 1784.

[41] Hosmer, *The Life of Thomas Hutchinson*, p. 238. For examples in the 1790's, see *infra*, chap. viii, n. 1.

[42] *An Address to the People of the State of New York*, by a Plebeian [Melancton Smith]. Jensen's important study, *The Articles of Confederation*, should be consulted in connection with this chapter.

protect the citizens in freedom of the press and speech and against
the danger of a standing army.[43] Spokesmen for the farming interest opposed the Constitution because it contained no "Agrarian
Law," no limitation upon individual wealth in land or trade. One
such writer felt the Constitution should deprive the very wealthy
from holding office or voting, for "luxury destroys popular government, equality preserves it." [44] Patrick Henry, of Virginia, wrote
John Lamb, "I am satisfied four-fifths of our inhabitants are opposed to the new scheme of government." [45] There is no way of
being certain whether or not Henry overstated the case, but it is
clear that the opposition was widespread and strong.

Out of this turmoil sprang another genie to torment the lives of
men with an opposite political intent. John Lamb, after the Constitutional Convention presented its work, set about writing letters
to Aedanus Burke, of South Carolina, Timothy Bloodworth, of
North Carolina, George Mason and Patrick Henry, of Virginia,
Joshua Atherton, of New Hampshire, and others, in which he suggested the immediate formation of republican societies to oppose
the ratification of this constitution. "All these [men]," Lamb wrote,
"entered very zealously into the scheme and concurred in representing the great body of the people of their respective states, as being
determinedly hostile to the adoption of the Constitution." [46] Sometimes referring to themselves as "Republican Committees," at others
as the "Society of Federal Republicans," the anti-constitutionalists
insisted upon a bill of rights as imperative for the new system. That
this movement ever congealed into formal societies before ratification by the requisite number of states is a matter of doubt. So rapidly
was the ratification procedure pushed that John Lamb's correspondence hardly had time to take effect. Rawlins Lowndes, of South Carolina, and Richard H. Lee, of Virginia, both wrote that the suggestion
for the formation of societies had come too late. Lowndes added

---

[43] *Objections to the Constitution.* Broadside, Sept. 29, 1787, New York Public
Library.

[44] P. Lewis to Joseph Nicholson, July 29, 1789. Nicholson Papers, Library of
Congress.

[45] Henry, *Patrick Henry, Life, Correspondence and Speeches,* p. 342.

[46] Leake, *op. cit.,* p. 306.

that had there been more time great weight could have been brought to bear, while Lee speaks of his surprise at the sudden change of mind of so many people so soon after "a cruel war for liberty." [47]

After the ninth state had accepted the new order, the combined forces of those who opposed, added to those who, like Jefferson and Monroe, favored it as "good, but not perfect," joined to demand a bill-of-rights amendment.[48] In order to facilitate this, republican societies were organized. George Mason consented to act as chairman of the Virginia society, and Patrick Henry made a suggestion for spreading its influence, which the democratic societies used with great effect a few years later. He wrote, "Perhaps the organization of our system may be so contrived as to include lesser associations dispersed through the state." [49]

In New York, Lamb was chosen president of the Republican Society and Melancton Smith and David Gelston, who were soon to become activists in the Democratic Society, were among its members. Fraunces's Tavern was the meeting place, where on October 30, 1788, they appointed a committee of correspondence to address other states, as well as counties within New York, asking them as "friends of equal liberty" to form societies, to elect men who would support an amendment to the Constitution, and to facilitate communication and free discussion throughout the country. For vice president of the United States they favored George Clinton, whom they relied upon to support this amendment.[50]

A state-wide meeting was called at Harrisburg, Pennsylvania, to endorse the steps taken by the New York society. Albert Gallatin attended, but even more significant, Blair McClenachan, the firebrand president of the Philadelphia Democratic Society in 1794, was unanimously elected chairman.[51] A patriotic society in Virginia,

[47] Leake, *op. cit.*, pp. 307–13.
[48] Thomas Jefferson to James Monroe, Aug. 9, 1788. Monroe Papers, 1787–90, New York Public Library.
[49] Henry, *op. cit.*, p. 343.
[50] Leake, *op. cit.*, pp. 320–23, 326. The minutes of "The Society" beginning Oct. 30 and running through Nov. 13, 1788, are in the Lamb Papers, Box 5, New York Historical Society.
[51] The *Pennsylvania Gazette*, Sept. 17, 1788. It is difficult to follow Purcell, in

about which little is known, except that it was organized in 1788 "to instruct our delegates," was doubtless a part of this general movement. Bushrod Washington, in accordance with Patrick Henry's suggestion, wished to establish similar societies throughout the state, but he was advised by George Washington against participating in such plans.[52]

That popular societies were a commonly used social force in America is further indicated by Shays's Rebellion. Here the farmers united in semimilitary, semipolitical bodies, called themselves "Regulators," and convened in the taverns to discuss their problems and to make plans. Daniel Shays, as one student of him has rightly said, was a part of a broader movement to secure justice, if necessary, by revolutionary means.[53]

The famous "Political Club" existing in Danville, Kentucky, from 1786 to 1790 should also be mentioned here as an important social force. Sometimes called "The Saturday Night Club," its program consisted largely of debates and discussions on critical current affairs. At its first meeting it chose for debate the most important problem that was to stir the Kentucky Democratic Society into forms of direct action, namely, the opening of the Mississippi to the westerners. It had much to do with separating Kentucky from Virginia and in framing the first constitution of the new state. As to the Federal Constitution, the Danville clubbists held that it must have a bill of rights. Other significant positions which they took were opposition to capital punishment, except for murder or trea-

his valuable book *Connecticut in Transition, 1775–1818*, p. 228, when he writes that anti-Federalism cannot be considered as a forerunner of Republicanism. Despite the fact that anti-Federalists became the leaders in Jeffersonian democracy, he writes that there is "no binding link between them." Cf. Beard, *Economic Origins of Jeffersonian Democracy*, in which the author traces, with a wealth of supporting evidence, the organic relation between the two.

[52] Corbin, *The Unknown Washington*, pp. 318–20. It is worthy of note that Washington opposed the popular societies long before they were associated with Genet and the French Revolution. Corbin asserts that Washington did not think the people competent to judge larger national issues.

[53] Dyer, "Embattled Farmers," *New England Quarterly*, IV (1931), 460–81. Crane, "Shays' Rebellion," *Proceedings of the Worcester Society of Antiquity*, V (1881), 62–63, speaks of the farmers gathering under Shays's leadership into town meetings and forming committees of correspondence.

son; the right of citizens to expatriate themselves.[54] and the be-
stowal on Congress of the power to prohibit slavery after 1808.
Members of this club who were to become leaders in the democratic
societies of the state were George Muter, Thomas Todd, Baker
Ewing, and James Brown.[55]

Finally, we get hints of societies as late as 1791, in the exciting
diary of Samuel Shepard, a frontier Indian fighter. In an entry for
September 10, 1791, he writes: "I became a member of a political
society for the first time." This notation was made at his home in
Georgetown, Kentucky.[56] From the foregoing it is obvious that the
popular society was a social force and an indigeneous phenomenon
in early America.

The reciprocal influence of English popular democracy after the
Revolution of 1688, and American social action during the 1760's
has been commented upon in this chapter. Each contributed to the
other important elements in the emerging concepts of democratic
control. This interaction was not confined solely to these two countries. France also felt the impress of English and American thought
and action, not to mention other peoples of the western world.
France, in turn, as will be brought out in subsequent pages, placed
its contribution on the altar of world democratic thinking. The influence of English thought upon France has been carefully followed
by C. H. Lockitt.[57] He points out how dependent France was, before the French Revolution, upon the leading social thinkers of
England, citing the extent to which translations of Hume, Gibbon,
and Adam Smith were circulated in France.

Other authorities have detected the strong impact made by the
American Revolution upon the French. *Common Sense*, the master-

[54] The importance of the attitude on expatriation is that it aids in understanding the actions of patriotic Americans who accepted commissions from Genet to
serve in the French cause. These Americans did not consider themselves as disloyal
to their country, especially when they were fighting for a sister republic.
[55] Speed, *The Political Club, Danville, Kentucky, 1786–1790, passim.* Also in
John Mason Brown, *The Political Beginnings of Kentucky,* pp. 109–10.
[56] "The Diary of Sam'l Shepard, 1787–1796," MS, the Massachusetts Historical
Society. This is an interesting and informative diary of one of Anthony Wayne's
militiamen.
[57] Lockitt, *The Relations of French and English Society, 1763–1793,* chap. v.

piece of Thomas Paine, was as widely read in France as in America,
according to Samuel Deane.[58] Bernard Faÿ and George Scherger
have indicated still other factors to be considered, such as Benjamin
Franklin's printing in France of the Declaration of Independence
and the radical state constitutions of Pennsylvania and Massachusetts; Brissot's writing on America's recognition of the rights of
man; Mirabeau's giving America the credit for turning the eyes of
the world toward freedom; and Condorcet's pointing out the appearance in Virginia of the first "declaration of rights" in the world.[59]
A conservative German authority, F. J. Stahl, writing in 1854, gave
America this credit: "The French Constituent Assembly was en-
tranced with the philosophical procedure of North America and
imitated it with the greatest exaggeration." [60] Of even greater
pertinence is the fact that all these authorities state that the Jacobin
clubs of France, as revolutionary instrumentalities, were inspired
from America. "A Republican" writing in the *Independent Chronicle*, December 8, 1794 recognizes that the Jacobins were but counterparts of the committees of correspondence, that their first and real
name was the "Breton Committee," later called "The Revolutionary
Society," "Friends of the Constitution" and "Friends of Liberty
and Equality" respectively. Finally the full power of the thinking
and action which England and America had inaugurated swept
over France and rebounded, to threaten the more conservative social
orders established by its prime movers.

Enthusiasm for the principles of Liberty, Equality and Fraternity,
although reverberating through Ireland, Germany, Poland, Switzerland, Holland, and America, disturbed most of all the financially
powerful upper classes of England. Even the liberals (Whigs), who
were frightened by the extremes of democracy pursued by the
French, were afraid the popular societies were stirring and inciting
the lower classes. Most to be feared was the infecting of the regi-

---

[58] Woodfin, *op. cit.*, p. 20 n. Also chap. i, *passim.*

[59] Scherger, *op. cit.*, pp. 208–14.

[60] *Ibid.*, p. 257. The democratic societies were aware that France had copied
from American Revolutionary techniques; for an example see the statement of the
Wythe, Va. society at a July 4 celebration. *American Daily Advertiser*, Aug. 2,
1794.

ments, such as the Scots Greys and the The Guards, with the virus of "Jacobinism." Thomas Paine, patron of the societies, was distrusted because of his writings, which were making the farmers restless and "causing mischief." [61] At banquets and festivals toasts were drunk to world revolution, George Washington, and Thomas Paine. One much-applauded toast was: "Revolutions may never cease, while the cause of them exists!" [62] The Revolution Society assumed new life and a hundred others sprang up to advocate, in varying degrees, the birth of liberty in the neighboring country.

There was ample basis for revolutionary excitement, because in 1793 England was in a state of economic depression. Bankruptcies were frequent, commerce was at an ebb, money was scarce because banks were not willing to put funds into circulation. Furthermore, the tinners and miners around Cornwall and the "subterranean gentry" in general were demanding bread and were on the edge of revolt. It was an ideal period for a declaration of war, with the cities of Manchester and Birmingham already "turning plough-shares into swords." [63] Social unrest was at a peak, and the resultant class antagonisms were particularly marked and sharp.[64] The soil for the seeds of the popular societies was well tilled.

[61] Lockitt, *op. cit.*, pp. 112–14. Joel Barlow, though less influential than Paine, was a member of the London Constitutional Society and was writing in defense of democratic ideas. W. P. Hall, *British Radicalism, 1791–1797*, p. 124.

[62] Thomas Mullett, of Bristol, England, to Horatio Gates, Nov. 24, 1791. Gates Papers, Library of Congress.

[63] Nathaniel Cutting to Wm. Shippen, Vol. VII, June, 1793, Shippen Papers, Library of Congress. W. P. Hall, *op. cit.*, has a helpful discussion on English economic conditions at this period. See especially pp. 11–45.

[64] Birley, *The English Jacobins from 1789 to 1802*, pp. 29–30. Contrast between the Rich and the Poor in Great Britain (n.p., c. 1793), British Broadsides, No. 271, Library of Congress. This reads:

"The rich live in splendid houses, in unbounded luxury, dissipation, and extravagance.

"The poor live in miserable hovels, in want of coals, food, clothing, and every comfort, and are forced to work ten hours a day merely not to starve.

"The rich keep horses, carriages, hounds, and whores.

"The poor cannot even keep themselves.

"The rich have all the places and pensions.

"The poor have all the tythes and taxes, which ultimately fall upon the laborers of the land.

"The rich are proud, insolent, unfeeling, and debauched.

"The poor are humble, broken-hearted, and hopeless.

"The rich may get drunk, frequent brothels, and do as they like.

The fertile soil nourished popular societies into sudden full bloom. The Revolution Society began holding its meetings more often than an annual celebration of 1688.

Le banquet de London Tavern compta cette année-là nombre d'hommes éminents, parmi lesquels des membres de Parliment. La vieille société fut transformée: William et Mary et l'année 1688 furent éclipsés par Thomas Paine en 1791.[65]

The London Corresponding Society and the Constitutional Societies of Scotland, the more radical wing of the movement,[66] set

---

"The poor are sent to Bridewell for the slightest irregularities, and cannot do what they like.

　　　　　　　　　　. . .

"The rich are armed,
"The poor must not even carry a gun.

　　　　　　　　　　. . .

"The rich are called honorable gentlemen and noble lords.
"The poor are called Seditious Rascals, idle Vagabonds.
"The rich are called persons of rank,
"The poor are rank and file.
"The rich are named but not numbered.
"The poor are numbered but not named.

　　　　　　　　　　. . .

"The rich are in robes,
"The poor are in rags.
"The rich are represented,
"The poor are misrepresented.
"The rich do not work at all,
"The poor do all the work.
"The rich get commissions and employments before they will fight in any cause.
"The rich have many friends,
"The poor have no friends.
"The rich are people of fashion,
"The poor are the Swinish Multitude.
"The rich wear stars,
"The poor wear scars.
"The rich are for continuing the war,
"The poor are anxious for peace.
"The rich will not make peace,
"The poor must perish."

[65] Conway, "Thomas Paine et la revolution dans les deux mondes," *La Revue hebdomadaire*, VI (May 26, 1900), 221.

[66] The Revolution Society, The Society for Constitutional Information in London, and The Friends of the People were all of a more conservative type. The latter, for example, favored reform "without a French republican direction." Erskine, *A View of the Causes and Consequences of the Present War with France*, p. 11.

about to unify discontent and to usher in sweeping reforms; the
first was known as a poor man's reform club. It opposed the heavy
burden of taxes, the deprival of civil liberties guaranteed in the
Bill of Rights and the Magna Carta, and the war against the republic of France. Insisting that the common people be permitted
to express their will in the halls of government, the club opened its
membership to all workingmen, thereby introducing the reform
movement into a new layer of society.[67] Moreover, this society, in
its addresses, urged the formation of like groups everywhere, with
which it could carry on a correspondence. This universal plan was
to include France, Ireland, Germany—every country where the
struggle for liberty was in process; it appealed to "citizens, soldiers
and sailors of all nations, empires, kingdoms and states." [68] In a
dilemma between the desire for vast change on the one hand, and
a policy of nonviolence on the other, the Corresponding Society's
principles were enmeshed in inconsistencies which favored both
revolution and reform; nonviolence and militancy. If necessary,
the society would fight for liberty; passive resistance was an argument of slaves. Walter P. Hall, student of English radicalism in
this period, believes that the societies were secretly arming, in spite
of assertions of mere reform and nonviolence.[69]

The Constitutional Societies, meeting throughout England and
Scotland, affirmed the principles of the London Corresponding Society and joined with it in favoring peace and internal reform instead
of war and continued injustice. Active societies appeared at Norwich, Manchester, Sheffield, and Edinburgh, each united by correspondence with London. They sent long petitions and resolutions
for their London colleagues to present to the King or to Parliament.[70] They also addressed communciations to the Jacobins in
France and sent personal representatives. Manchester, for example,
sent James Watt, son of the inventor, and Thomas Cooper, who
later became a famous refugee in America.[71] The club at Sheffield,
anxious to improve the thinking of the people, had printed a

---

[67] P. A. Brown, op. cit., p. 56.   [68] The *Diary* (New York), Feb. 26, 1794.
[69] *Op. cit.*, p. 209.   [70] *South Carolina State Gazette*, Oct. 3, 4, 1794.
[71] Alger, *Englishmen in the French Revolution*, pp. 45–48.

pamphlet entitled *The Spirit of John Locke*. Its introduction contains this interesting statement:

Citizens, Edmund Burke, the Knight Errant of Feudality, declared in the House of Commons that "Locke's Treatise on Civil Government was the worst book ever written." We are certain it needs no further recommendation.[72]

In the same spirit many others printed and circulated Paine's *Rights of Man*, an activity which Paine himself supported by donating the royalties on his writings to the use of the constitutional societies.[73] With principles basically like those of the American popular clubs, it is no wonder that Walter P. Hall has referred to the English organizations as "democratic" and "patriotic" societies,[74] nor is it difficult to follow Philip Brown when he says that the English societies were not copied from French models, but that the Jacobins were probably founded in imitation of English precedents.[75]

Critics and friends alike proclaimed the organizations as giving voice to "another class of people." Thomas Hardy, of the London Corresponding Society, wrote that the French Revolution had brought the rank and file into politics in England, that it had given voice to tradesmen, shopkeepers and mechanics.[76] Opponents looked with askance on common people addressing one another as "citizen" and assembling under the "tree of liberty." Nor did they favor Richard Lee, the republican printer, circulating Rousseau and hundreds of little pamphlets called "Political Dictionaries." [77] When miners rioted and sang democratic songs, the societies were blamed for the uprising, for were not their assemblies "composed of the lowest type . . . to agitate propositions or to discuss subjects of a

---

[72] *The Spirit of John Locke on Civil Government, Revived by the Constitutional Society of Sheffield*, Miscellaneous Pamphlets, Vol. VIII, Library of Congress.

[73] British Broadsides, No. 271, May 18, 1792. Library of Congress.

[74] *Op. cit.*, p. 182.   [75] P. A. Brown, *op. cit.*, p. 68.

[76] *Ibid.*, p. 70. The Library of Congress has the best collection of materials on the London Corresponding Society, including the following from which references have been taken: *Address of the London Corresponding Society; The London Corresponding Society's Addresses and Regulations*, Duane pamphlets, Vol. LXXXII, No. 4; *To the Parliament and People of Great Britain.*

[77] Richard Lee, *Account of the Proceedings of the Meeting of the London Corresponding Society.*

most alarming nature?" Moreover, *The Rights of Man* taught the artisan and mechanic to despise the system under which he lived, "institutions venerated by his ancestors," to criticize the administration and to plot sedition.[78] When the suggestion came in 1794 to hold a general convention, composed of representatives from all the associated societies, the *status quo* was truly threatened and the upper classes sought more effective measures for subduing the subterranean gentry.

Across the Irish Sea revolutionary seeds had taken root. Here too, according to a broadside addressed "To the People of Ireland," the common men were told by those who were attempting to "fleece" them of their property that they should not delve into politics. According to the broadside, these privileged characters felt that the poor did not need light, but were to be docile followers. The authors of the broadside emphasize, however, that the poor are the bulwark of society, making the shuttles fly and the corn grow, and without whom the rich could not live. Therefore, the poor should learn their rights and should be conscious of those who would keep them in darkness.[79]

In 1791 this sentiment congealed about a society named by Wolfe Tone "The Society of United Irishmen," which first appeared in Dublin, then Belfast, and spread throughout Ireland. In a letter written to The Friends of the People in London, the United Irishmen stated:

The title which you bear is a glorious one, and we too are the Friends of the People. If we be asked "Who are the people?" we turn not our eyes here and there, to this party and to that persuasion, and cry "Lo! The People," but we look around us without impartiality or predilection, and we answer, the multitude of human beings, the living mass of humanity associated to exist, to subsist and to be happy.[80]

As the United Irishmen supported and circulated *The Rights of Man,* they also held that the rights should apply to all sects and

---

[78] *A View of the Relative State of Great Britain and France at the Commencement of the Year 1796.*
[79] *Delaware and Eastern Shore Advertiser,* Sept. 6, 1794.
[80] *Proceedings of the Society of United Irishmen of Dublin,* p. 26.

denominations of Irish; that Ireland should be democratic and independent; and that France should be defended in her struggle for freedom. Each society appointed or elected a Committee of Correspondence, which not only kept in touch with local and county organizations, but also wrote and received information from the Constitutional Societies of England and Scotland. They had the idea that an international brotherhood might develop from a unity of the democratic societies all over the world.[81] True to form, men with counter ideas slurred "the blasted Jacobin society" as "incendiaries" and "seditionists," and, that failing, turned to the persecution of the leaders. Whole books were written in Ireland to refute "revolutionary democracy" and the theories of Rousseau, just as Burke, in England, and Hamilton, in America, attacked these same theories.[82]

As it spread in all directions, the French Revolution shook not only the British Isles but also Germany, Switzerland, Italy, Poland, and even more distant points. In Mainz and Hamburg, Germany, liberty poles were erected, celebrations held in honor to those who stormed the Bastille, and protests entered against joining the combination of powers attempting to thwart France. Frederick, who "squeezed his subjects for taxes," [83] was opposed. Hamburg accordingly organized "The Philanthropic Society" for the purpose of corresponding with republicans of all countries and spreading democracy in northern Germany and Holstein.[84] James Lyon, in his *The Scourge of Aristocracy*, October 15, 1798, tells the story of the loss of democracy in Switzerland. He explains that in the thirteenth century the people met once each year and chose their governors in a democratic fashion; now they were ruled by an aristocratic

---

[81] Jacob, *The Rise of the United Irishmen, 1791–1794*, pp. 66–78, 201–9; chap. vi is especially helpful on the relations between English, Scottish, and Irish societies.

[82] For critics of the Irish movement see *Ibid.*, pp. 214–21; Knox, *Essays on the Political Circumstances of Ireland*. Knox charges the Irish societies with aping the Jacobin Club of Paris and with being a part of the Illuminati, both of which were common charges brought against American societies.

[83] *Virginia Chronicle*, Jan. 12, 1793. Gooch, "Europe and the French Revolution," in *The Cambridge Modern History*, VIII, 773, 775.

[84] Jacob, *op. cit.*, pp. 205–6.

junto, which persecuted popular leaders like Frederick Caesar de la Harpe. Lyon sympathized with the aid France was giving to attempts at Genevan independence. Not so David Chauvet, who wrote Albert Gallatin saying that a body of levelers, instigated by France, was inciting insurrection by means of popular clubs. At one club, he wrote, the members drank from a common cup, "the gift of J. J. Rousseau." [85] The tremors of revolt spread further.

Certain Italian provinces felt the vibration, and established popular societies.[86] Poland, in the throes of a partitioning, heard the appeal of Kosciusko for "civism," and for organizing to supply not only arms and men, but also grains and food supplies in the fight for freedom.[87] In far-away Martinique and Guadeloupe popular societies cropped up,[88] as well as in Spanish Louisiana (New Orleans), and Montreal, Canada. The Montreal "Patriotic Club" was alleged to have led the uprising against British soldiery in the spring of 1793. It called its 200 members the Friends of Liberty and Equality. Before opening meetings, the assembly sang revolutionary songs; afterwards they held discussions and passed resolutions against the government banning news of the progress of France.[89]

Writers, contemporary and modern, have stimulated an awareness of the world democratic sweep. An anonymous German critic of the time, whose writings were reprinted in the *City Gazette* (Charleston), summarizes its comprehensiveness:

This rage of liberty, at present so generally spread throughout Europe, this revolt of nations against their sovereigns, the insulting writings which are addressed to them, this credulity of every kind, which has become so frequent, all these political fermentations are the effects of a fanatical

---

[85] [Chauvet] *The Conduct of the Government of France towards the Republic of Geneva*, pp. 7–8.

[86] *New York Journal*, Sept. 9, 1796.

[87] Miscellaneous Letters, March 24, 1794, Department of State; in the National Archives.

[88] Mangourit, *Mémoire de Mangourit*, p. 28.

[89] Elijah W. Lyon, *Louisiana in French Diplomacy*, p. 67, for the New Orleans Club. *New Hampshire Gazette*, July 2, 1793, and Henri Merière, "Observations on Canada," in Affaires Étrangères, Correspondance Politique, États-Unis, Supplement, Juin 12, 1793. This was written by Genet's principal agent in Canada.

philosophy, which is propagated by a herd of pretended philanthropic writers who have all the same end in view. The writers disseminate every day their poisons throughout all the states of Europe. They have obtained the notice of the world in most nations, and above all in Germany. The public opinion is in their hands. Their names for the most part, celebrated, or rather, famous; their poverty and their pride, their impudent loquacity and effrontery, all their arts and all their intrigues, joined to their secret associations, serve to propagate everywhere their destructive principles and to give them a fatal influence.

It is, therefore, time to give another direction to the public opinion. . . . Otherwise all the thrones of Europe are in danger of being buried in their own ruins, or of falling, by a democratical license into the most horrible anarchy and confusion.[90]

The resurgence of American Revolutionary feeling must be placed against this background and setting. As Max Lerner has well stated,

The wheelings and turnings of Federalists and Republicans were not only the maneuverings of propertied groups and the agrarian-labor masses for salvaging or hemming in the consequences of the Revolution; they were part of a world-wide movement of social struggle fought out in France and England as well as in America. For the history of this period can be written adequately only if it is seen as world history.[91]

Given this setting, we are ready to proceed to "the wheelings and turnings" of the American "social struggle."

[90] The *City Gazette* (Charleston), July 4, 1792.
[91] Lerner, "John Marshall and the Campaign of History," in *Columbia Law Review*, XXXIX (1939), p. 409.

Chapter Three

THE DEMOCRATIC SPIRIT
OF '76 AWAKENS

These little whirlwinds of dry leaves and dirt portend a hurricane.
FISHER AMES, commenting upon the "mobocrats"

THE *cordon sanitaire* to prevent expansion of revolutionary ideology was not, as yet, a perfected device in the closing years of the eighteenth century. The winds of the French revolutionary storm swept across the waters of the Atlantic to create commotion in the thoughts of certain of America's most eminent leaders and thousands of her citizenry. The extent of the disquiet has been carefully pointed out by such students as Charles Hazen, Howard Mumford Jones, and Bernard Faÿ.[1] Every conceivable method available to the people of that day was called into service to spread information concerning the development of affairs in France. Broadsides were headlined "Vive la Republique," newspapers carried columns entitled "News from France," personal letters containing comments were given to the printers, travelers were cross-examined, and recent visitors to the new republic were expected to divulge all they knew. Liberty poles, down since our own days of turmoil, went up again. American and French flags appeared together in the taverns and ordinaries, where sumptuous feasts celebrating recent successes of the French were held. Numerous citizens donned

[1] Hazen, *Contemporary American Opinion of the French Revolution;* Jones, *America and French Culture;* Faÿ, *The Revolutionary Spirit in France and America.*

the *bonnet rouge*, symbol of free men, and wore it on all occasions. Slurring remarks about France were challenged and made the issue of a free-for-all brawl in the streets. Not even America, although itself only recently in the throes of violent social change, was to escape the world-resounding impact of the French Revolution.

From the day of its birth Americans welcomed their sister republic. Now there were two free nations; America no longer stood alone to face a hostile world. Collective security was essential to the preservation of democracy, and as early as 1791 the friends of Samuel Adams wrote to him of the importance of the successful outcome of the French experiment. If France should fail, America could not withstand alone.[2] Conscious that victory across the water was essential for ultimate victory elsewhere, the democrats grew increasingly ardent until they made this argument a major tenet of every "statement of principles" propounded by the democratic-republican societies. The opportunity to hail France was by indirection equally an opportunity to criticize the forfeitures suffered by popular democracy at home.[3]

This thesis may be supported by comments of contemporaries, both liberal and conservative. Benjamin Franklin Bache, grandson of Franklin and according to Channing, "inheritor of his prejudices," recognized the changes induced in American politics by the French Revolution. He wrote, "The national character, which had almost taken form before the successes of the French were known, is refermenting and will no doubt take a shape less inauspicious to liberty and equality." [4] George Hammond, British minister, bemoaned that the "discontents" in the United States had received encouragement from French affairs, and wrote to Grenville that the

pernicious principles of the French Revolution have found here a soil adapted to their reception. The dangerous notion of equality of rights

---

[2] Mrs. Catherine Macauly Graham to S. Adams, March 1, 1791, Samuel Adams Papers, New York Public Library.

[3] Maude H. Woodfin in her thesis, "Citizen Genet and His Mission," has caught the significance of the pro-French feeling. She says that the feasts for Genet were more of a protesting by Americans of the policies of their government than an honoring of "the citizen" (p. 237).

[4] Benjamin Franklin Bache to Richard Bache, Feb. 4, 1793, in Bache Papers, owned by Franklin Bache, of Philadelphia.

. . . has confirmed the prevailing opinion that the constitution may be changed or altered without danger or inconvenience at popular will or caprice.[5]

Charles Nisbet, defender of the British system and Pennsylvania college president, was disturbed at the "madness of the country" over French successes. He expected to hear of Captain Shays getting his army together again.[6] Col. Eleazer Oswald, Revolutionary warrior, returned from fighting with Doumouriez for France. He felt that our democracy was weighed in the balance and found wanting. With the red cockade on his head, he went about New York and Philadelphia stirring the populace and reminding them of threats to their liberty.[7] Oswald was an active member of the democratic societies in both these cities. Many democrats thought they noted a decline in zest for the annual celebration of the Declaration of Independence. "A citizen" expressing himself through the medium of the New York Journal, June 22, 1793, raised a pertinent question when he asked why the Fourth of July was not more widely celebrated.

Republicans became solicitous over the sudden realization of the lethargy toward the preservation of liberties into which the people had fallen. This lethargy was permitting the democratic gains made in '76 to slip gradually through their fingers. News of the progress of France called all this back and set up a frame of reference by which our gains and losses in democracy could be sharply compared.

With the arrival of Edmund Charles Genet, the first minister from a republic, the emotional temper of most Americans reached its apogee. Everywhere he was welcomed with enthusiasm and applause. Jefferson wrote, "All the old spirit of 1776 is rekindling." [8] In words very like those of Jefferson, Genet admitted his mission

[5] Letter dated March 7, 1793, in the Archives of Great Britain, Public Records Office, United States, Foreign Office 5, Vol. I, No. 5. Hereafter referred to as British Archives, F.O.5. The transcripts in the Library of Congress were used.
[6] Charles Nisbet to Wm. Young, March 16, 1793. Nisbet Letters, New York Public Library.
[7] Leake, Memoir of the Life and Times of General John Lamb, p. 345.
[8] Jefferson to Monroe, May 5, 1793. Monroe Papers, New York Public Library.

to be the revival of America's revolutionary sentiments.[9] William E. Dodd summarizes the sweep of events: "The leaven of the American Revolution was working mightily in every country in the civilized world, and Americans began to stand awe-stricken at the havoc they had done and were doing still." The upshot, he adds, was that the conservatives of this country drew back and crystallized the reaction, while the radicals held to the Declaration of Independence.[10] It would seem to be apparent that right here at home could be found the causes underlying the more superficial Francophile bombast of the time.

The leaders of the day were especially sensitive to the dissension arising in the new American republic. Many of them expected peace and concord—a democratic millennium, forever free from internecine strife and party faction. As early as 1791, William Maclay, a keen observer, of pronounced democratic sympathies, confided to his journal:

There is a system pursuing, the depths of which I can not well fathom, but I clearly see that the poor goddess of liberty is likely to be hunted out of this quarter, as well as other quarters of the globe.[11]

Jefferson wrote to Mazzei of the arising of "an anglo-monarchico-aristocratic party," and Washington feared that internal dissension would "ruin the goodly fabric" of the nation.[12] There was trouble brewing. It appeared that the adoption of the Federal Constitution had not allayed certain important social irritants of long standing. In fact, it almost seemed to add to their aggravation.

What were the recurrent threads of discontent which ran through the social fabric? In the 1790's influential men persisted in favoring, if not a king, at least a centralized power or aristocracy equivalent to that of kinghood. Joseph Dennie, Federalist and printer

---

[9] Woodfin, op. cit., p. 25, n.

[10] Dodd, The Life of Nathaniel Macon, p. 58. As late as 1798 societies were organizing to "revive the republican spirit of '76," viz., Republican Society of Norwalk, Conn. (New London Bee, April 4, 1798.)

[11] The Journal of William Maclay, p. 261.

[12] The Writings of George Washington, ed. by Ford, XII, 175.

for American conservatives, favored a limited monarchy, patterned on the British constitution.[13] He thought America "bleak" and wished that he might serve a king "in the sunshine of a court." He named as his friends John Adams, John Fenno, of the *Gazette of the United States*, Christopher Gore, Samuel Dexter, and Timothy Pickering; these, he added, were sympathetic with the British governmental system.[14] That England looked with approval upon this tendency in America and encouraged its progress is partially revealed in a letter written by a Canadian neighbor, Gen. J. G. Simcoe, to Governor Clark, August 20, 1792.[15] He wrote that if "Congress should adopt a Prince of the House of Brunswick for their future President or King, the happiness of the two nations would be interwoven and united." He added that this is worthy of Great Britain's attention, since "many of the most temperate men of the United States" have contemplated it "and which many events, if once systematically begun, may hasten and bring to maturity."

To this evidence may be added the secret interviews between Hamilton and Hammond, representative of a limited monarchy; the widely printed writings in 1793 of William Willcocks, spokesman for Hamilton and who subscribed his signature with "God bless the colonies"; Oliver Wolcott's statement that a single despot was a refuge from "the despotism of the many"; and the strong leanings toward an autocratic government of Rufus King and Henry Knox.[16] There would seem to be a basis for the warnings voiced by

[13] Joseph Dennie to his parents, April 25, 1793. Dennie Papers in Harvard University.

[14] J. Dennie to his mother, April 24, 1795, April 26, 1797. Dennie Papers. Surprisingly enough, Dennie lists among his friends Mrs. Perez Morton (Sarah Wentworth), the wife of a prominent leader of the Massachusetts Constitutional Society. She, however, was pro-English and encouraged Dennie's literary abilities and aided him financially.

[15] British State Papers, Colonial Correspondence, Canada 1789-98, Vol. LXI. Transcripts, Library of Congress.

[16] For Hamilton's confidences with Hammond, see Hammond to Grenville, April 2, 1793, F.O.5, Vol. I, No. 11; July 7, 1793, F.O.5, Vol. I, No. 16. Here in secret code Hamilton is named as Hammond's informer. For Willcocks, see Willcocks to Genet, Nov. 5, 1793, Genet Papers. Hamilton was suspected of giving direct aid in Willcocks's tirades against the democratic societies, *New York Journal*, Feb. 11, 1795. George Gibbs, *Memoirs of the Administrations of Washington and Adams*, p. 515, for Wolcott statement. Dunbar, *A Study of "Monarchical"*

Maclay and others, that a counter-revolution to subvert popular government was altogether possible. At least one could conclude with Jefferson that a party "not numerous but wealthy and influential" was attempting to influence the tone and principles of the Constitution so as to lead to something very different from what many Americans conceived to be the spirit of republican government.[17] The democratic societies sounded the alarm and rose as an antithesis to this tendency.[18]

Democrats perceived monarchical tendencies in the financial maneuvers of the new government. Distrust of these existed from the very beginning, and it was early suggested that frequent inquiry be made into the conduct of public officers.[19] But it was not until 1790, when Hamilton proposed his Funding and Assumption System, that voices everywhere were raised in a chorus of dissent. William Manning was one of the first to object. He wrote a letter to the state legislature of Massachusetts, February 6, 1790, giving his reasons against those who wanted "valuable" money in order to

Tendencies in the United States from 1776 to 1801, emphasizes frontier plots to set up kingly government, but does not stress the aristocratic leanings she finds in Hamilton, King, and Knox. See especially chap. vi. John Beckley, Clerk of the House and Jefferson's faithful informant, said that while he was in New York in the year of 1793 Sir John Temple, a strong English republican, showed him a letter from Sir Gregory Page Turner, M.P. from a borough of Yorkshire, which said the English considered Hamilton, King, and Smith, of South Carolina, as main supports of British interest in America. Hamilton, not Hammond, was their effective minister. Turner advised these men to go ahead and change the government, for if the anti-Federalists came to power, they could find asylum in England. Beckley said that Grenville also confirmed this in another letter. See Thomas Jefferson's Papers, Vol. LXXVII, I.15082, Library of Congress. Men like West, Bignall, and Courtnay, of Charleston, S.C., were, in their aristocratic St. George Society, drinking toasts to the King of Britain in 1793; see *Columbian Centinel*, May 15, 1793. Even the Federalist, Charles C. Pinckney, could not approve Wm. L. Smith's monarchical leanings; see C. C. Pinckney to Thomas Pinckney, Oct. 5, 1794, in Pinckney Papers, Library of Congress.

[17] Thomas Jefferson to Harry Innes, May 23, 1793, *Writings*, VI, 266.

[18] The commoners, like William Manning, wanted an organization to counterbalance the influence of the Society of Cincinnati. One such wrote, "I am now fully persuaded that it [the Cincinnati] originated with Hamilton with a view to secure the influence of the military officers to seport [sic] an aristocratical faction of which he is the head in order to the Enterduction [sic] of Monarchy which I am much against." See "My thoughts on Sincinnatus Socity," Misc. Papers (Cincinnati Society), transcript in the New York Public Library.

[19] *New York Journal*, Oct. 30, 1788.

buy cheap, to make their salaries worth more, and to collect high rents.[20] "An American Farmer" reputed to be George Logan, of Philadelphia, composed the *Letters Addressed to the Yeomanry of the United States Containing Some Observations on Funding and Bank Systems*.[21] He objected to those "who had speculated in the certificates given for services rendered by the meritorious citizens," thus creating an inequality among the people and an enormous debt which would increase taxes and make them burdensome to the farmer and the mechanic. His other objections were to the excise law and the growth of a financial aristocracy in America.[22]

Though the taxes on tobacco and sugar pinched certain manufacturers such as the democratic Thomas Leiper and Jacob Lawerswyler, it was the tax on whisky that raised the greatest resentment, especially in the frontier regions.[23] Long before the people there had heard of developments in France, or of the arrival on our shores of the first republican ambassador from the Old World, they were aroused by the excise and the presence of the hated excisemen. Albert Gallatin, John Smilie, and David Bradford had all taken part in mass protest meetings. One held in August, 1792, adopted the principle of the boycott, refusing to have intercourse with any and all excisemen. Interestingly enough, three years later in Congress, when the discussion of the Whiskey Rebellion and Democratic So-

[20] Wm. Manning, "Some Proposals for Making Restitution to the Original Creditors of Government," Manning Papers, Harvard.

[21] This was published in Philadelphia in 1793.

[22] An "Anecdote" characteristic of the contemporary feeling against speculators reads: "I met a fat plump-faced speculator the other day, staggering under a heavy canvas bag. With true Yankee freedom, I asked him what he had in his bag. 'The Grace of God,' replied the wag. 'Ah,' said I, 'I have often heard of that article, but never saw it in a bag.' By this time he had flipped his hand into the bag and taking a dollar, 'There,' he said, 'Dei Gratia, Carolus III is stamped upon the face of every dollar in the bag." I was surprised to hear a speculator say he had the Grace of God, especially such a load as to stagger under it, but upon explaining himself my surprise ceased and I smiled. He had cleared three hundred dollars that morning by the sale of public paper. He was too much pleased with the abundance of his grace to stand discussing nice points, and we parted." (The *Oracle of Dauphin*, July 22, 1793.) Fee, "The Effect of Hamilton's Financial Policy upon public Opinion in New Jersey," *Proceedings of the New Jersey Historical Society*, L (1932), 35, confirms the statement that Hamilton's actions were partially responsible for the rise of popular societies in that state.

[23] Callender, *A Short History of the Nature and Consequence of Excise Laws.*

cieties was at white heat, Gallatin justified this action with a shrewd reference to the refusal of The Republican Society of conservative merchants in Pennsylvania, opposed to the radical state constitution of 1776, to accept any offices under a government with which they disagreed.[24] With every conceivable method of protest, short of violence itself before 1793, the ingenious mind of the westerner tried to gain repeal of the odious excise. He failed and in failing thought the central government was careless and inattentive to the lack of money and markets in the West. East and West alike were stirred, not because the principle of taxation was undemocratic, but because the excise seemed unfair. It fell heaviest upon those who had already lost on the Funding and Assumption measures. The newly created debt was directly reminiscent of the debt held over the people by the monarchical system which all had hoped to overthrow by gaining freedom. A poem of the day expresses the current feeling:

> Tax on tax young Balever cries,
> More imposts, and a new excise,
> A public debt's, a public blessing,
> Which 'tis of course a crime to lessen.
> Each day a fresh report he broaches,
> That spies and Jews may ride in coaches,
> Soldier and farmer dont dispair,
> Untax'd as yet are earth and air.[25]

But the money policies inaugurated by the new government were not the sole occasions for resistance. In the midst of the Revolutionary War militiamen as well as members of the Continental line

[24] Gallatin, *The Speech of Albert Gallatin*, p. 6. A manuscript outline of this speech is in the Galatin Papers, Vol. XV (1795), in which the author names the society to which he refers as the "Republican Society."

[25] John Malcolm to Horatio Gates, March 24, 1790, Gates Papers, New York Public Library. The anti-Semitic reference is unusual for republican literature of this period. It is found a number of times in Federal writings; for example, an article signed "Slow and Easy" in The *New York Journal*, Dec. 19, 1795, is critical of the Jews, like Jacob Montagnie, of New York, and Israel Israel, of Philadelphia, in the democratic societies. Israel is also derided as "a Jewish tavern-keeper" by the Federalist, Charles Nisbet, in a letter to Charles Wallace, Dec. 11, 1797; Nisbet Letters, New York Public Library. Joseph Dennie speaks of himself as anti-Jewish in a letter to his mother, May 20, 1800, Dennie Papers.

had felt themselves mistreated in regard to fair payment of wages. Afterwards, soldiers and farmers alike lost, to speculators buying up governmental promises-to-pay at a few cents on the dollar, what compensation they had earned. In 1794 the predicament of the common soldier with regard to pay persisted and gave impetus to the militia companies forming the nuclei for democratic societies. The militiaman saw in the inequality of remuneration an aristocratic tendency which favored the "few" officers at the expense of the "many" citizen soldiers. "A private soldier" complained of the low wages paid to privates while captains received more than twelve times as much. He said, after seeing this in the paper, that he was sure of some mistake in printing, for a captain could not stop more bullets nor was his life so precarious as that of the guard. A sharp retort by "A Friend of Good Government" called the objector "an audacious, impudent scribbler," to which the soldier answered, "I see I must not speak evil of the 'chosen few.'" He added sarcastically that at the present rate of pay the militia would all be generals, colonels, and captains, who would "make Governor Simcoe and his banditti of tawny devils, negroes, and British scamper away."[26]

In the light of these social clashes one can appreciate the comment of the traveler, Wansey, who said that men holding aristocratic principles of any form were not popular in the villages of America.[27] Whether the questions were centralized power, taxation, class favoritism, or others of the antidemocratic practices, they all were the ferment in which the societies sprang up and flourished. As Alexander J. Dallas, himself a society organizer, stated it, the clubs, products of a revolutionary democracy

instead of wishing, deprecated change; for the change they most feared was that retrograde one into which the supposed monarchical theories and habits of certain eminent statesmen might gradually glide. What in Europe was represented as subversive could here be, in reality, only progressive and conservative.[28]

---

[26] Wood's *Newark Gazette*, June 18, July 16, 1794.

[27] Wansey, *An Excursion to the United States of North America in the Summer of 1794*, p. 207.

[28] G. M. Dallas, *The Life and Writings of Alexander J. Dallas*, p. 223.

Upon these very objections the democratic societies built their platforms and unified the widespread sentiment against speculation,
favoritism, and heavy taxation.

Another thread which may be traced as a factor giving rise to
the popular societies and fanning the spirit of the revolutionary
days was the increasing economic rivalry with England. The South,
particularly, turned strongly republican after the war because of
the debts owed to the mother country.[29] The attempt to collect these
by Federalistic agents pushed the issue into the realm of politics
and made Virginia a leader in anti-English movements. The ani-
mosity grew more bitter, with the Americans insisting on the right
to trade freely in all the ports of the world where Yankee clippers
called. England sought to limit Yankee trade and rising carrier
capacity, seeing them a threat to her own supremacy. The British
Orders in Council of June and November, 1793, which declared
that products carried by neutral ships to French and West Indies
ports to be contraband, set anti-English fires burning all up and
down the American seacoast. A large and vocal group of merchants,
prospering by a rich trade with the Indies, raised a protest loud
enough to bring Madison's embargo proposals to the floor of Congress.[30] By striking at the economic security of an influential trader
group, Parliament unwittingly gave leadership to a long-standing
discontent which underlay the societies. Furthermore, seamen as
well as traders looked upon England's agreement with the Barbary
States and the release of the latter's pirate ships into the Atlantic
as directly aimed at American shipping.[31] All this, added to the cap-
ture and impressment of sailors, created retaliatory emotions in the
bosoms of prosperous merchants as well as in the brawny chest of
the poorest seaman. This situation was sufficient to encourage a rapid
formation of democratic societies throughout the United States in
the early months of 1794.

England's warring with France further inflamed the feelings

[29] Beard, *Economic Origins* . . . , p. 245.
[30] Cf. Luetscher, *Early Political Machinery in the United States*, p. 38. This
author feels the British Orders in Council were directly the cause of the spread of
democratic societies in 1794.
[31] Callender, *The History of the United States for 1796*, p. 180.

of those in America sympathetic, for economic as well as ideological reasons, to one or the other of the two combatants. The Federalists, geared in their financial schemes with the relatively stable England and distrusting the "extremism" of Francophile enthusiasts, were accused of conniving with the British to destroy democracy everywhere. Men like Hamilton, Sedgewick, Cabot, and King advocated stern measures and even war against France in order to put a check to "Jacobinism." [32] George Hammond, British ambassador, reported to his superior that he was doing everything in his power to bring about a breach between France and the United States.[33] He noted the prevailing hostility to Great Britain, which he said pervaded the whole of the United States.[34] The republicans, on the other hand, recalled the writings of Benjamin Franklin in defending their pro-Gallic position and had the following circulated by "the patriotic printers":

This powerful nation [France] continues its friendship for the United States. It is a friendship of the utmost importance to our security, and should be carefully cultivated. Britain has not yet well digested the loss of its dominion over us; and has at times some flattering hopes of recovering it. Accidents may increase those hopes, and encourage dangerous attempts. A breach between us and France would infallibly bring the English again on our backs; and yet we have some wild beasts among our countrymen, who are endeavoring to weaken that connexion.[35]

Now that France had become a republic there could no longer be any question among the republicans as to which nation deserved loyalty and support. Besides, it offered Americans freedom to enter its ports for trade—a privilege England did not grant, even going so far as to obstruct the United States trade with France.[36]

[32] George Cabot to King, March 21, 1798; Sedgewick to King, Jan. 20, 1799. King Papers, Vol. XLI, New York Historical Society; Alexander Hamilton Papers, Vol. XXVII, No. 3818.
[33] Hammond to Grenville, Aug. 10, 1793, F.O.5, Vol. I, No. 17.
[34] Ibid., May 8, 1794. F.O.5, Vol. IV, No. 18.
[35] Pittsburgh Gazette, Dec. 14, 1793.
[36] "Commerce between the United States and the French Colonies in the West Indies." This is a manuscript dated 1793, without author, in the New England Historical and Genealogical Society.

Moreover, if Americans aided France in subduing England, could they not demand the release of the western military posts, held by England in violation of the treaty, since the Revolution? Up and down the frontier fringes small farmers and those with landed interests were certain that the British were inciting and aiding the Indians in repeated attacks upon the border settlements. Both Generals St. Clair and Wayne had said their armies encountered white warriors among the Indians.[37] The landed men saw this policy cramping their avaricious expansion, while for the squatter and the rentee it was a matter of self-preservation. Thus from North to South, according to William Findley, western landowner, the people favored stern measures against Britain. He favored the seizure of Niagara, which would cut off Detroit and check English influence in the West, asserting at the same time that the people of Vermont were ready and willing to join in such an enterprise.[38] Hugh H. Brackenridge, another western landowner of prominence, saw a solution in a direct alliance with France, for "If kings combine to support kings, why not republics to support republics?"[39] Behind his altruism and internationalism was the antipathy for the nation whose interests in the great West rivaled that of his own. Landed men, like these, became the leaders in the democratic societies, aiding and abetting the illiterate frontiersman to form organized protest against a Federal government which seemed to shilly-shally with western problems.

From all appearance, with pressure from England on the seacoast and frontier, America was caught in a vice. It is little wonder that a spot map locating the popular societies shows them hugging the Atlantic in the east and the fringe of civilization on the west. Loud were the protestations of the people against the Anglophile complexion assumed by the ruling Federalists, and long were the cries for sending "riflemen and hardy woodmen" to France for assist-

---

[37] Callender, *Sedgewick and Company, or a Key to a Six Percent Cabinet*, p. 45.
[38] William Findley to A. Addison, April 30, 1794. Nisbet Papers, Darlington Library, University of Pittsburgh. These papers, for the most part written by an arch-conservative, Nisbet, are fascinating and of great value to historians. To date they have not been published.
[39] Hugh H. Brackenridge, *Gazette Publications*, p. 275.

ing Citizen Genet and for defending America by aiding the French.[40]

In all this social restlessness, societies were proposed as early as 1792 and actually appeared the following year. Where clubs did not spring up, the town meeting was in evidence. The newspapers of the day are replete with stories of meetings where the citizens gathered at the county courthouse and passed resolutions upholding the right of the people to assemble and discuss issues; to expect a "fair and honest interpretation" of the constitution, as explained at the time of adoption; and to show their attachment to France.[41] In other words, as one meeting stated, they were convened to consider the "subjects that agitate the public mind." [42] Travelers in America were impressed by the political agitation which they found in all parts of the country. The Frenchmen, Bonnet and La Rochefoucauld, noted the interest in politics and the avidity with which the newspapers were read. Mazzei, of Italy, heard much political talk and said the Americans reasoned even more on public affairs than in the days of the Revolution.[43] And John Drayton added that he found the farmers reading "religious books, the public laws, and the newspapers." [44] Evidently the public mind was awake and widely concerned about the critical issues of the day.

The instrumentalities necessary to give unity and direction to so-

[40] A Boston paper in 1793 called for volunteers to serve in the French army. The *National Gazette*, July 21, 1793, responded with the statement that a corp of riflemen would soon rendezvous in Providence for that purpose. See Affaires Étrangères, Vol. XXXVIII, Part I. Jefferson shared the prevailing conception that in case France were conquered the combined kings would move against the United States. *Writings*, ed. by Ford, VI, 265–66.

[41] Meetings with the same sentiments were held at Richmond, Fredericksburg, and Charlottesville, Virginia. *American Daily Advertiser*, Dec. 3, 4, 1793. The files of the *Independent Chronicle* (Boston), the *New York Journal*, and the *Aurora* (Philadelphia) for the years 1792–94 are especially useful for tracing the innumerable meetings at county courthouses and in the towns in all sections of the country.

[42] *Columbian Mirror and Alexandria Gazette*, Oct. 5, 1793.

[43] Sherrill, *French Memories of Eighteenth Century America*, pp. 249, 251, 254. Thomas Cooper found the American farmers not ignorant and as many newspapers circulating here as in France. *Some Information Respecting America*, pp. 44 ff.

[44] John Drayton, *Letters Written during a Tour through the Northern and Eastern States of America*, pp. 65–67.

cial restlessness were at hand. One might mention the increase in post-office service during the decade. In 1776 the country had but 28 such offices to aid in the dissemination of information by letter. By 1790 there were 75, or in fourteen years about three times as many. But, most phenomenal of all, in five years, 1790–95, they increased to 453, or sixfold! [45] So sharp a rise in communication must indicate a social stirring of significance. Again, one might allude to the role of the innkeeper. Here was a contemporary news broadcaster who was as effective, within the range of his voice, as the modern prototype. These innkeepers were usually well-informed men, many of them former Revolutionary soldiers who had now assumed a position of respect and leadership in the community.[46] Their profession drew around them travelers from far and wide, who came bearing knowledge of affairs elsewhere. Also an informed tavern owner attracted the news-hungry to stop frequently for "a drap" of whisky and made his quarters the ideal spot for democratic societies. It is not surprising, then, to find social life centering around the taverns and ordinaries, in the form of public meetings, polling, disputations, and business transactions.[47] Nor is it startling to find men like Jonothan Walker, at Canaan, New York, Israel Israel, in Philadelphia, or Patrick O'Flinn, at Wilmington, Delaware, as examples of the many tavern owners who were active leaders in the popular clubs. Doubtless there were Federalist innkeepers, too, whose political complexion followed that of their patrons. No matter what their politics, their locale was a unifying force for eighteenth-century society.

By all odds the greatest vehicle of the time for conveying "useful knowledge" was the newspaper. Mention has already been made of the extent to which the press was followed. Within the decade under

[45] McMaster, *A History of the People of the United States*, II, 59, n. The author is aware of the centralization of the postal system in this period, but, as Channing points out (*History of the United States*, IV, 6), such an increase may also indicate that ideas were circulating and that the country was more socially alert.

[46] Sherrill, *op. cit.*, p. 221; H. M. Brackenridge, *Recollections of Persons and Places in the West*, p. 65; Cooper, *op. cit.*, p. 111.

[47] Pomerantz, *New York, An American City*, p. 154; Harpster, "Eighteenth Century Inns . . . ," *Western Pennsylvania Historical Magazine*, XIX (1936), 15; Weld, *Travels*, p. 84. This traveler notes the long political arguments that went on in the rural taverns.

consideration four outstanding democratic printers were issuing sheets of first importance to the anti-Federalist cause. These were Thomas Adams, of Boston; Thomas Greenleaf, of New York; Philip Freneau, in New York as well as in Philadelphia; and Benjamin Franklin Bache, in the Quaker City. Lesser lights from all sections of the country joined "the big four" in the attack on Federalist policy.[48] Bache, whose paper was first announced by broadside in 1790, and Freneau, whose *Gazette* had the people aroused and the opposition worried by the beginning of 1793, were the leaders in the fray.[49] Freneau's paper, especially, received wide circulation, not only by subscription but also by the webwork of letterwriting practiced at the time. Jefferson, in his letters to Joseph Fay,

[48] Since the press and the democratic societies are so closely related, the writer presents the following list of printers who were definitely known to be members of one or more of these political clubs. In compiling the list the author collaborated with Donald E. Stewart, of Columbia University, who is working on a doctoral dissertation on propaganda and the press from 1790 to 1800, and is indebted to him for help in identifying several printers in this list. Only those whose names have been found definitely as members of a society are included here. Strong suspects, such as Thomas and Abijah Adams, of Boston, are not listed, for there is no source material to prove membership. *New York:* Philip Freneau, David Denniston; William Keteltas, Naphtali Judah, Thomas Greenleaf, John Fellows; *New Jersey:* Aaron Pennington (Newark); *Kentucky:* John Bradford (Lexington); *North Carolina:* Caleb D. Howard (Fayetteville), Dr. John Sibley (Fayetteville); *Delaware:* Robert Coram; *Pennsylvania:* William Dickson (Lancaster), Henry Kammerer, Eleazer Oswald, Robert Cochran, Robert Aitkin, John Israel, James D. Westcott, Benj. F. Bache; *South Carolina:* Thomas B. Bowen, John Markland, John Miller (Pendleton); *Vermont:* Prosper Brown.

[49] In the New York Historical Society's fine collection of broadsides is one announcing Bache's paper. (Broadsides, 1790, Group I.) For Freneau's influence, see Fisher Ames to Geo. R. Minot, Feb. 20, 1793, Ames Papers. Cf. Marsh, "Philip Freneau and His Circle," the *Pennsylvania Magazine of History and Biography*, LXIII (1939), 47. Here it is stated that Freneau's paper was widely read in small villages in all parts of the country. One might well take issue, however, with Marsh's efforts to separate Freneau from his more radical friends, Thomas Paine, Genet, and William Duane, whom Marsh terms "brawlers" (p. 59). The article admits (p. 46) that Jefferson broke with Freneau. That the poet-printer criticized Washington and was in turn called "that rascal Freneau" is brought out in the interpretation by Pattee, ed., *The Poems of Philip Freneau*, I, lxi. Besides his membership in the democratic societies and his daring to question the Washington policies, Freneau defended Paine's *Age of Reason* and refused to join in the tirades against Fries Rebellion. See Robert Slender [Freneau], O.S.M. (One of the Swinish Multitude) *Letters on Various Interesting and Important Subjects* (Philadelphia, 1799). In contrast to Marsh, see also H. H. Clark, ed., *The Poems of Freneau*, Introduction.

of Vermont, enclosed copies of the *National Gazette*.[50] Hancock and Samuel Adams, by the same method, distributed Freneau's sheet in Massachusetts.[51] In the distant backwoods of South Carolina this printer was not unknown and without influence, for there he troubled the Tory, William L. Smith, who assured the people that this paper was "packed with lies." [52] Genet soon recognized the value of the press for his purposes and instructed his consuls to use the gazettes in order to counteract enemies.[53]

The popular societies found a democratic press indispensable for the educational purposes they had in mind, and the strongest societies arose where a printer was at their beck and call. We find in the remarkable collection of the Republican Society Papers, Portland, Maine, that this club encountered difficulty because it lacked aid from the local press. It had to appoint a messenger to deliver announcements of meetings to the homes of members the day before convening,[54] and to depend upon news from society members, like Samuel Hewes, in Boston.[55] The Rev. Hezekiah Packard attributes the alien and sedition laws to the fear of the influential press. He stated:

The sentiments conveyed in newspapers have an amazing influence upon the minds of people at large. Happy would it have been for the United States if those printing presses, which have been squeezing out seditious sentiments, had been long ago crushed by the power of our national authority.[56]

---

[50] Fay to Jefferson, May 7, 1793. Jefferson Papers, Vol. LXXXV, No. 14735, Library of Congress.

[51] Jefferson, *Writings*, ed. by Ford, VI, 134.

[52] Alexander Hamilton Papers, Vol. XIX, No. 2566, Library of Congress. For the presence of the *National Gazette* in far western Virginia, see Wm. McKinley to Genet, Oct. 8, 1793, Genet Papers.

[53] *Affaires Étrangères*, Vol. XXXIX, Part II.

[54] Republican Society Papers, Aug. 7, 1794, Maine Historical Society. The writing in this collection is shot with typical William Manning spelling—"A True Cappy," "committy," "spetial," and "no sparots" to be used during meetings. It reveals, also, the dependence of the democratic party upon some "larned person," like a printer, to assist in editing its materials for publication.

[55] *Ibid.*, a "Democrat" [Samuel Hewes] to David Bradish, March 2, 1795.

[56] Hezekiah Packard, *Federal Republicanism Displayed in Two Discourses*, p. 35.

If a writer like Bradford, in Kentucky, or Ebenezer Bushnell, in Connecticut, should carry in his paper rather detailed news of the English constitutional societies and the French patriotic clubs, it might well stimulate the formation of like organizations in this part of the world.[57] This very thing happened. The press played a major role in the process that gave rise to the American societies.

As these organizations made their appearance, some sprang up following a sociological pattern of diffusion from a central point of impetus. By referring to the spot map (see frontispiece) and the footnotes to the listing of the various clubs in chapter i, the reader will be able to trace this pattern more easily. The national center, of course, was Philadelphia. Here the congressional representatives from the far corners of the nation gathered to carry out their official functions. Those ardent democrats among them, such as Caesar A. Rodney, or John Bird, were members not only of their local organizations, but also of the one in the capital city.[58] This factor tended to head the entire movement in Philadelphia. Then, too, each state in its key city had a democratic society which was considered "coextensive with the state," from which radiated district or county societies, as the case might be.[59] These lesser organizations were an integral unit of the larger state organization, and the town or parish organizations were subgroups of these.[60] The rise of the societies, in a general way, followed this scheme, starting with the top at Philadelphia, spreading to the state capitals, and fanning out from there into the hinterlands.

To the critical student of social relationships this generative pattern for a social movement is much too pat. There were significant exceptions, and the exceptions in sociology are of the greatest impor-

[57] The *Kentucky Gazette*, March 30, 1793; *Connecticut Gazette*, Aug. 2, 1792; *Pittsburgh Gazette*, Jan. 25, 1794 carried a full article on The London Corresponding Society. These are a few of the innumerable instances of printers giving space to European patriotic clubs.

[58] Names of the Philadelphia members were derived from a partial collection of the original minutes of the Democratic Society of Pennsylvania, preserved in the Historical Society of Pennsylvania.

[59] See Article 1 of the constitution of the Philadelphia Society.

[60] For example, see the publication of the Washington, Penn. society in the *American Daily Advertiser*, Jan. 31, 1795, which reads "That part of the Democratic Society of Pennsylvania established in the county of Washington."

tance, although often the most difficult to explain. Mention has been made of the German Republican Society and the society in Norfolk, Virginia, both of which antedated the so-called "mother society," and yet always considered themselves popular societies coöperating in advancing the same ideals. Among others which one might say were spontaneously generated and independent were the Committee of Correspondence of Carlisle, Pennsylvania,[61] The Political Society of Mt. Prospect, New Jersey,[62] and The Society of United Freemen at Mingo Creek, Pennsylvania.[63] The Carlisle people stated, in a set of unprinted resolutions, marked by poor writing and orthography, what they considered the "grievances of the farmers"—namely the selling of land in the interior in quantities to big companies, the funding and assumption system, the excise taxes, and the low pay of militiamen. Resolutions numbers five and eight are worthy of attention. They read:

5. That it be recommended to our fellow citizens throughout the United States who concur with us in sentiment respecting the measures of government complained of, to assemble in a peaceable (constitutional) manner, communicate with each other and present their collective sense thereof to Congress in such manner that redress may be obtained and the effusion of blood with which we are now threatened, be prevented.

6. That a committee be appointed by this meeting for the purpose of corresponding with our fellow citizens in other parts of the United States upon the subjects complained of and that it be the duty of this committee to prepare a remonstrance to be offered to the people of this county to be signed and presented to Congress praying a repeal of the excise laws.

From these statements one may see the elements familiar to popular societies in general. Nor was the Society of United Freemen, better

[61] For sources on this society, see its resolutions for Aug. 29, 1794, in the Rawle Papers, "Insurrection in Western Pennsylvania," Vol. I, Historical Society of Pennsylvania.
[62] Wood's *Newark Gazette*, March 26, 1794.
[63] Rawle Papers, Vol. I, Feb. 1794. The reader will find in these papers a fragment of the minutes of this society, together with a partial list of its membership. Cf. William Miller, The Democratic Societies and the Whiskey Insurrection," *The Pennsylvania Magazine of History and Biography*, LXII (July, 1938), 345. Miller draws a distinction between the Mingo Creek Society and democratic societies in general. These minutes reveal that both fall into the category of popular societies.

known as the Mingo Creek Association, different in character and purpose from the others. It objected to the same prevailing practices of the Federalist administration as did all the others and, like them, urged the formation of similar societies in other districts *to promote constitutional knowledge* and to guarantee the rights of man to all people.[64] It was organized in February, 1794, and was the first of the popular organizations to appear in Western Pennsylvania. These, and certain others in the list presented in chapter i, were outside the orbit of the Philadelphia society and its direct radiating impulses. They were, none the less, vestiges of Revolutionary days, with committees of correspondence, and in a real sense democratic societies.[65]

Sectionalism was another factor which must be considered in discussing the configuration assumed by these organizations. Already distant rumblings of the Civil War could be heard in the economic and social clashes that arose between North and South. Disunion talk was heard and fostered by men of the Essex Junto in Massachusetts.[66] Oliver Wolcott, of Connecticut, believed that the major dissatisfaction really centered in the southern states and that the arguments against the general government were like those used against the adoption of the Constitution.[67] It was not uncommon to hear comparisons between "northern aristocracy" and "southern democracy" and to feel the rivalry that existed at this early date.[68] Broadsides appeared which tended to intensify the feeling and the spirit of competition.[69]

Slavery, of course, was the paramount issue, with the northerner

[64] Rawle Papers, Vol. I, Feb. 1794. John Holcroft, alleged to be "Tom the Tinker," was a member of this club.

[65] Mt. Prospect, New Jersey, and The Committee of Correspondence of Fayetteville, North Carolina, are other cases in point. For the latter, see Affaires Étrangères, Vol. XL, Part VI, April 18, 1794.

[66] Taylor, *Disunion Sentiment in Congress in 1794*, Introduction, pp. 12–14.

[67] Wolcott to Joel Barlow, June 10, 1794, Barlow Papers, Box 2, Harvard.

[68] In reading through the Sedgewick Papers for the two years, 1793–95, in the Massachusetts Historical Society, one is impressed with the many references to North-South rivalry.

[69] A broadside dated April 7, 1792, was an effort of John Broome, president of the New York Chamber of Commerce, to get the farmers to bring clean wheat to the market so that it could demand prices equal to those obtained by the southern states. Broadsides, New York, No. 112. Library of Congress.

constantly reminding the "democrat" of the South of his flagrant inconsistency. Typical is this Federalist jibe from Rutland, Vermont, "May Virginia slave drivers cease to theorize on the Rights of Man till they cease to tyrannize over their sable brethren." [70] Many anti-slave citizens of the South were stung by these shafts of censure. Men like John Bradford, organizer of the Kentucky Democratic Society, placed the criticism at the feet of southern slave owners like Washington. Bold leader that Bradford was, he reprinted and cir-culated a letter written to Washington by an Englishman who crit-icized the President for holding slaves and at the same time favoring democracy in theory.[71] This southern dichotomy was exploited to the full by northerners who wished to suppress the growing ideas of "rational liberty." The Yankees flaunted their consistency and boasted of the fact that a Negro had been elected town clerk by "a decided majority of votes" in a northern town.[72]

Because of the basic differences in their economic and social out-look, these two sections of the young republic, one primarily agri-cultural and the other commercial and finanical, began to divide. In the light of this breach, the democratic societies of the middle states and the South proved to be the strongest and the most radical. With the exception of the five Vermont clubs and the district of Maine club, all in a frontier locale and not a part of the commercial East, there was only one society of any importance in New England in 1794. In the same year there were twelve in the middle states and seventeen in the southern.

But the country was divided vertically as well as horizontally by sectionalism. Here geography made one of its well-known impresses on the story of America, by the rib of mountains dividing the wealth-ier, established, class-oriented East from the poorer, changing, rough-and-tumble West. Each of these sections developed divergent culture patterns, as sharply marked as the North-South distinctions. Travelers in the western country presented an almost unanimous reaction to the crude social characteristics of these people. Popular

---

[70] The *Norfolk Herald*, March 26, 1799.

[71] Rushton, *Expostulatory Letter to George Washington of Mt. Vernon, on His Continuing to Be a Holder of Slaves.*

[72] The *Carlisle Gazette*, Aug., 1793.

amusements were drinking, gambling, and cards. Fights were a free-for-all in which eye-gouging, as one of a number of body mutilations, was not uncommon. Houses were of logs, daubed with clay, and taverns were uniformly poorly equipped and vermin-infested.[73] The women, although said to be in general more polished than the men, were still, as one author has said of Matthew Lyon's wife, a bit coarse.[74] Liancourt was probably too conditioned by the frippery of court life to appreciate the burly frontiersmen, when he wrote:

This class of inhabitants are, by the report of every individual that is not one of themselves, the very worst set of men in all America, and perhaps in the whole world. The sentiments, and even the very idea of honesty and humanity are unknown to them. They are all a ferocious plundering banditti.[75]

In spite of their uncouth manners, which might readily be misunderstood by visitors bound by conventionalities and unaccustomed to the personalities of a frontier environment, the western settlers practiced a frankness, generosity, and sincerity which have often been minimized for the lesser virtues of etiquette. Also the nature of their lives stirred in them a questioning attitude. Isaac Weld wrote that they were full of all sorts of questions,[76] while Wansey, bearing him out, comments that "the printers of newspapers succeed generally very well, particularly in the backcountry, for they are all great newsmongers."[77]

The basic differences were, however, political and economic. These very differences, as we shall see later, split the societies wide open. From Maine to South Carolina the grievances of the westerners were much the same, including the distance from state capitals, where the judicial system centered; the allotment of large tracts of land to easterners of wealth, which often deprived the settler of his claim or caused expensive adjudication at a distant point; the lack of

[73] Ashe, *Travels in America*, p. 172. Thomas Cooper, *op. cit.*, pp. 29 ff.

[74] Matthew Lyon collection (letters written chiefly about Lyon in 1858) in the Vermont Historical Society. James, *Three Years among the Indians and Mexicans*, pp. 295–96.

[75] La Rochefoucauld-Liancourt, *Travels through the United States of North America*, IV, 528.

[76] Weld, *Travels*, p. 171.   [77] Wansey, *op. cit.*, p. 80.

a circulating medium of exchange; the control of the legislatures by wealthy men of the East; high salaries of lawyer representatives in Congress; unequal taxation; and the deprivation of an adequate defense against the Indians.[78] Prices on goods from the East seemed exorbitant when it required "a good tract of land of four hundred acres, for a rifle gun and a horn of powder." Salt, a necessity, as well as sugar and coffee, were equally high.[79] On the other hand, their own products, because mountains and rival Spanish and English traders cut off their markets, were worth little. Flour in Philadelphia sold for twelve dollars a barrel, in Pittsburgh for three.[80]

Given this situation, it is no wonder that protest and organized resistance appeared. The Society of United Freemen arose to object to the rule of the East, whose interests, it believed, were not with the uplanders, but with England. These men, it insisted, treated the people of the West exactly as Britain dealt with the colonies—ignoring petitions, taxing, and dragging citizens off to be tried in distant courts.[81]

A panacea for most of these ills seemed to be to gain one of the rivers, Mississippi or St. Lawrence, as an outlet for the products of the western farmers. This same plea, it might be added, played into the hands of land speculators and fur traders so that it soon became the *cause célèbre* of the entire West. In Vermont the question was the use of the St. Lawrence River. Vermonters had no outlet for their growing trade, with an angry New York on one side and a rivalrous, unfriendly Canada on the other.[82] Alexander Moultrie,

[78] *Address of a Convention of Delegates,* . . . (Portland, Me., 1795); *An Address to the People of South Carolina by the General Committee of the Representative Reform Association* (Charleston, 1794). A series of newspaper debates went on between "Appius" and "Americanus" in South Carolina, concerning the nature of "equality," as it related to up-countrymen as against low. The Charlestonians opposed talk about "an equality of condition" instead of "equality of rights," for this would, they knew, "strip wealth of its advantages." The *City Gazette,* Oct. 24, 31; Nov. 26, 1794. See also Robinson, *Jeffersonian Democracy in New England,* p. 43; Turner, *The Significance of Sections in American History,* p. 137; Snowden, ed., *History of South Carolina,* pp. 509–13.

[79] Veech, *The Monongahela of Old,* p. 38.

[80] Callender, *American Annual Register for 1796,* p. 30.

[81] Rawle Papers, also Buck, *The Planting of Civilization in Western Pennsylvania,* p. 467; Ferguson, *Early Western Pennsylvania Politics,* p. 49.

[82] Burt, *The Old Province of Quebec,* pp. 452–53.

leader in the Republican Society of South Carolina, wrote Genet a long letter in 1794 stating in glowing terms his faith in and prophecy for American expansion into the Mississippi region. This country had now become, he said,

the grand nursery of the growing strength and future athletic power of America. Here will be her riches, here her population and here her weight in the great scale of political influence.

The low country, he added, was degenerating, its soil was being depleted, and it was governed by a "mercantile aristocracy of the most poisonous kind," while in the West there was more social and friendly equality and fewer restraints. The farmers were free, they could think for themselves, for "no implicit faith governs [their] minds." When trade was opened up there, "riches like a flood will move into the Atlantic and a second Mediterranean will surpass the old one," for it would be "the garden of a new world and on the mouth of the Mississippi will arise the great Emporium of the new age." The furs, naval stores, grain and cattle—raw materials of the new territory—"will give useful employments and lucrative industry to the manufacturers and traders of the old; they will reciprocally and by active and reactive energy, advance the happiness and glory of each other." [83]

Though these dreams of a balanced economy never came true, they do indicate in a colorful way the deepest concern over the opening of "the river" on the part of the back-countrymen. It was the primary plank in the emerging platforms of the popular societies from Western Pennsylvania southward. For almost ten years the question had been in agitation, with no results. The time had come for more stern measures and positive action, which to these people meant the resurrection of the old Revolutionary instruments—organized bodies of the people. Accordingly, the Franklin Society in western South Carolina, supporting itself in its organizational resolutions by an appeal to the traditions of '76, upheld the right of freemen to proceed outside the confines of the United States, without

---

[83] Moultrie to Genet, Jan. 9, 1794. The Genet Papers. For a good description of the western country and the importance of Mississippi trade for the grain products of the West, see de Lezay-Marnezia, *Lettres ecrites des rives de l'Ohio*, p. 52.

punishment.[84] The reason for so doing was to work in behalf of revolt in Louisiana against Spain, thereby gaining the mouth of the coveted Mississippi. The Democratic Society of Kentucky and its county satellites took a stronger position, insisting that the eastern interests were ignoring their plight, and the time had come for direct action on the part of the West.[85] Washington, Pennsylvania, chimed in with the same tune; appeal for government aid had been ignored and evidently eastern America intended to keep the West in poverty. If the general government would not act, it went on, this society would not be answerable for any consequences "of our own attempts" to take territory.[86] Popular was the idea of aiding France and becoming its ally, for France would help in ousting English and Spanish on the western rivers.[87]

Of equal moment in the sectionalist contentions of the period was the question of the hated whisky tax, which the men of the West attributed directly to Hamilton's financial policies. It caused "a discontent of a threatening aspect," said William Findley, not only because it was "draining money to the eastward," but also because it enraged people who felt they were exploited by a system they did not understand.[88] Whisky in the West was almost a measure of value, a medium of exchange used in place of scarce money. It sold for approximately twenty cents a gallon, whereas in Philadelphia it brought almost three times as much. Yet the excise tax fell equally, at seven cents a gallon, on East and West.[89] It was to be expected

[84] The *City Gazette*, June 30, 1794.

[85] John Breckinridge, president of the Lexington society, wrote the famous remonstrance on the Mississippi question. Breckinridge Papers, Vol. IX, No. 1531, Library of Congress. Also, The *Kentucky Gazette*, Oct. 12, Nov. 16, 1793; July 12, 1794.

[86] Petition, March 24, 1794, in Misc. Letters, Department of State, National Archives.

[87] The *Pittsburgh Gazette*, Jan. 18, 1794. Frontier opposition to the Neutrality Proclamation was based on the hope that supporting France would eventuate in a free Mississippi. The West looked upon the neutral position as being sponsored by seaboard traders, who feared loss to themselves, should trade shift to the gulf ports. Wm. McKinley to Genet, Oct. 8, 1793, Genet Papers, Library of Congress.

[88] Wm. Findley to Alexander Addison, Feb. 10, 1792, Nisbet Collection, Darlington Library, University of Pittsburgh.

[89] Boucher, *A Century and a Half of Pittsburgh and Her People*, p. 301; Crumrine, *History of Washington County, Pennsylvania*, p. 265.

that within the category of "Aristocrat" the backcountry placed excise officers and wealthy men.[90] To be hustled off to Boston, Philadelphia, or Charleston for evasion of the hated tax, to bear the
expense of the trip, finally to be tried in eastern courts by those not
one's peers, was to call back memories of colonial injustice, and to
raise widespread and bitter resentment. The democratic societies fed
on this resentment.

A third major contention of the western country was the failure
of the central government, in the hands of pro-English Federalists,
adequately to protect the settlers on the frontier. Back of the Indian
depredations were seen the hands of Spain and Britain, making every
effort to staunch the first seepings of what was to become "manifest
destiny." General Simcoe, of Canada, noted the tendency of the
United States to "act" and "push on," [91] as likewise did Baron de
Carondolet, of Spain. The latter admitted that his country must use
the same policy of arousing the Indians against America as that of
Lord Dorchester; in fact the two countries must reach a secret agreement on this point.[92] The frontiersman caught the brunt of this in-
citement of the red men, and the land speculators and Indian traders
felt an economically impossible constraint. These men raised the cry
that the various state as well as the national administrations were
not lending sufficient protective aid to their western brethren.[93]
Hence they must act upon their own initiative.

Samuel Hammond, member of the Republican Society of Charlestown, and his brother Abner, partners in the Indian trading company of "Hammond and Fowler," proceeded to act. With the aid of
his friend Mangourit, Genet's astute consul in Charleston, Ham-

[90] Wilson, ed., Standard History of Pittsburgh, Pennsylvania, pp. 668–74.
[91] General Simcoe to Hammond, July 5, 1794, British Archives, F.O.5, No. 4.
Spain also opposed the penetration of American economic rivals into the Mississippi
area and sought to use the Indians as a barrier to expansion. Genet to Jefferson,
July 2, 1793, in French Legation Letters, Department of State, National Archives.
[92] Carondolet to Duke de Alcudia, Spanish Letters, Clark MSS, Vol. XLIIa.
Draper Collection, University of Wisconsin. Also McLaughlin, "The Western
Posts and the British Debts," American Historical Association, Report, 1894,
pp. 413–44.
[93] Phineas Pierce to Governor Clinton, May 5, 1794, in the New York Historical
Society. Gov. Henry Lee to Benj. Biggs, March 26, 1793, Biggs Papers, Draper
Collection (5NN38).

mond planned to destroy the Indian trade of the English firm of "Panton, Leslie and Company." This was to be accomplished by bribing the Indians to a greater extent than Spain did and by an armed force to wipe out

Panton and Leslies Stores at St. Johns and St. Marks and the intercepting as much as possible their future supplies. The former might easily be affected by a party of Indians who could be engaged for the purpose, or by a detachment of Our Own Horse at a proper season.[94]

To men like Hammond and the American fur traders, protecting the frontier had a deeper significance, namely that of overcoming English traders and monopolists who found it to their interest to defend the Indians against the Yankees.[95] It is no wonder the defeat of St. Clair in 1791 was bemoaned as a "Columbian Tragedy" and considered "the most shocking that has happened in America." [96] Such a setback for the land-hungry, the ambitious trader, and the settler inexorably pushing westward created a general distrust of the sincerity of "our Eastern Rullers."

British finance was controlling the East. Of this the frontiersmen were certain. William Hartshorne, a traveler from New York to Detroit in 1793, claimed to have overheard a statement of Simcoe's which bore proof that the popular societies were right in sensing English financial controls over eastern America. Simcoe said to an American:

I know the disposition of your people,—what signifies that Pidgeon House (pointing to a fort)? I know you can take it. It is not in the strength of the place that I put my dependence, but it is in this, that we have Boston, New York and Philadelphia in mortgage for your peaceable behavior.[97]

---

[94] Hammond to Mangourit, March 3, 1794. Charleston Republican Society MSS. Also *American Historical Association, Report, 1897,* p. 572.

[95] Stevens, "The Northwest Fur Trade, 1763–1800," *University of Illinois Studies in the Social Sciences,* XIV (No. 3), 407–610. See also "Papers Relating to the Georgia-Florida Frontier, 1784–1800," *Georgia Historical Quarterly,* Vol. XXIV (1940), Nos. 1, 2 and 3.

[96] Columbian Tragedy, broadside, 1791, in the New York Historical Society.

[97] William Hartshorne, "Diary of a Journey from New York to Detroit," 1793. Photostat in the New York Public Library.

Whether or not British control in the East was as dominant as the westerners believed is subject to some doubt. But the constraints upon the men of the West were real and called to their minds almost analogous troubles in 1776.

Chapter Four

THE ANALYSIS OF MEMBERSHIP

In the lowliest stations and amidst the obscurest paths, the choicest germs of intellect are often doomed to wither and to languish unnoticed and unknown.
    TUNIS WORTMAN, leader in the New York Democratic Society

SOME HISTORIANS may have looked upon the democratic societies with a jaundiced eye. They may actually have been conditioned by the aristocratic point of view. This may account for the scathing comments they have made about the societies and their members. A study of these organizations from contemporary sources and along lines more recently developed reveals interesting and significant detail. For example, in this chapter, we shall consider the members of the societies and show that it is caustic, unfair, and "aristocratic" to label them demagogic, unscrupulous, and insincere.

Let us look at the occupations represented by the membership of two of the most active clubs—The Democratic Society of Philadelphia and The Republican Society of Charleston, South Carolina:

Number and percentage of the members of the Philadelphia and Charleston popular societies whose occupations could be identified from city directories of 1794 *

	PHILADELPHIA		CHARLESTON	
	Number	*Percent*	*Number*	*Percent*
Identified	206	64.4	77	67.6
Unidentified	114	35.6	37	32.4
Total	320	100.0	114	100.0

* These data were secured from the partial collection of the minutes of the

Occupations of the members of the two societies

	PHILADELPHIA	CHARLESTON
Doctors	6	5
Merchants *	30	12
Maritime group †	21	7
Public Officials ‡	13	4
Lawyers	6	8
Craftsmen §	103	34
Teachers	7	5
Financiers ¶	5	2
Printers	6	3
Innkeepers	9	1
Planters	0	6
Total	206	77

Different interests represented in the two clubs, as indicated by the percentage of the known membership in certain occupations

	PHILADELPHIA	CHARLESTON
Craftsmen	32.8	30.0
Merchants	9.3	10.5
Maritime group	6.5	6.1
Public Officials	4.1	3.5
Miscellaneous: Printers, Lawyers, Doctors, and so forth	11.7	17.5
Unidentified	35.6	32.4
Total	100.0	100.0

Philadelphia society, which gave 320 names, and the "Correspondence of the Republican Society of South Carolina," which revealed the names of 114 of its members. The names of the "unidentified" did not appear in the directories. The investigator found no complete listing of the membership of any of the popular societies.

* Includes manufacturers, brewers, tobacconists, refiners, and so forth.

† Includes all those connected with maritime activities, such as ship captains, carpenters, riggers, wrights, and boat builders.

‡ Includes city and state officials and employees.

§ Includes tanners, blacksmiths, saddlers, painters, shotmakers, tailors, cordwainers, carpenters, hatters, boot and shoemakers, makers of spinning wheels, ropemakers, silversmiths, coppersmiths, hucksters, scriveners, coachmakers, bricklayers, engravers, ironmongers, and bakers.

¶ Includes brokers and factors.

As might be expected in the case of Philadelphia, governmental officials ranked in fourth place, after the seamen; while in Charleston the legal profession ranked third (7 percent), with the naval interests in fourth place. The six leading classifications of the members of these seaboard societies were craftsmen, merchants, seamen, lawyers, governmental officials, and the teachers and doctors as a group.[1] The "unidentified," those whose names were not found in directories, must surely have been of the so-called "lower order" of men. More than a third of the membership falls in this category.

A different occupational picture would be presented by the trans-Allegheny organizations. Although there is no extant list of a western society long enough to be of sampling value, we do know that the officers of these clubs were men of extensive landed property—men who lived and moved and had their being in terms of the land they could acquire and sell.[2] On the other hand, the body of the clubs on the frontier was comprised of small farmers, settlers, and rentees. This we gather from the evidence already cited on frontier objections to the trends of the day, namely antiland speculation, the payment of what seemed to be exorbitant rents, the excise, and the criticism of lawyers hired to defend the rich against the poor farmer.[3] These were the complaints of the poor settler.

[1] Brinton concludes from his study of the French Jacobins that they came from the "middle class"—citizens "prosperous and biologically fit in their environment." His classification of occupations may be compared with that of the democratic societies given here. His rankings are: artisans, 28 percent; shopkeepers, 17 percent; occupations not given, 12 percent; peasants, 10 percent; followed by lawyers, and civil servants. See his "The Membership of the Jacobin Clubs," the *American Historical Review*, XXXIV (July, 1929), 740.

[2] Cases in point are the following members of western clubs: John Breckinridge and Richard Henderson, in Kentucky; Alexander Smyth, in Western Virginia; John Baker, in Maine; David Redick, in Western Pennsylvania; and Udney Hay, in Vermont.

[3] Further evidence on this statement is deduced from the number who were members in the western clubs. Not all of them could have been gentlemen farmers. Pendleton, S.C., had 400 members (*City Gazette*, June 30, 1794); Lexington, Ky., had more than 200 (Breckinridge Papers, Vol. XI, No. 1741). At a meeting on Jan. 28, 1795, 84 attended the meeting of the Chittenden, Vermont, society, and this was only part of the total membership (*Vermont Gazette*, Feb. 6, 1795). The stoutest opposition to the excise was from small farmers, see, for instance, Ferguson, "Albert Gallatin," *Western Pennsylvania Historical Magazine*, XVI (1933), 190. Alexander Smyth of the Wytheville, Va., Democratic Society, was known as a spokesman for the settler as against the land company. See Smyth's *Speeches*, p. 44.

At first glance this mixture of "haves" and "have nots," and of high and low in social status, may seem to present a hopelessly tangled picture. While one may recognize that the motives for joining these societies of protest were diverse and in a specific sense beyond the recovery of the historian, one can bring some order out of chaos by better understanding the group frictions of the day. Birds of the same economic or social feather flock together; so too, the "gregarious democrats," as they were called by Jabez Fitch,[4] had certain broad issues of self-interest around which they rallied. By tracing some of the principal concerns of the groups from which the popular societies drew members, more insight into the motley membership may be gained.

First of all there was a group of merchants who were independent of Britain and whose success or failure was not dependent upon English prosperity. They were a prosperous, well-to-do group of traders, preponderantly of the southern states, who saw their bread buttered thickly by trade with France and the French islands in the West Indies.[5] In contrast, New England was full of Anglophile merchants, who had hidden their real sympathies during the Revolution or had returned to America after the war was over.[6] Naturally, these would argue against France, favor neutrality, and turn America toward England. The former group noted France purchased almost three times as much flour as did England, and had been doing so since Jefferson's negotiations with that nation in 1786.[7] France bought tobacco and rice, too, while England had a

[4] See July 4, 1796, in the diary of Jabez Fitch, Society of Mayflower Descendants, Boston. This Jabez Fitch has been confused with a man of the same name from Greenwich and Stamford, Conn. They are entirely different. The Vermonter was a Federalist, while the one from Connecticut was a fiery democrat and leader in the Republican clubs of his state.

[5] Winterbotham, *An Historical, Geographical, Commercial and Philosophical View of the United States of America*, III, 213. The *Vermont Gazette*, Dec. 25, 1795, gives a comparative list of the trade advantages with France as against those of England.

[6] Callender, *History of the United States* . . . , p. 45; Morison, *Maritime History* . . . , p. 169; La Rochefoucauld-Liancourt, *Travels*, p. 278.

[7] For flour purchases from the two countries from 1786–88, see Alexander Hamilton, *Works*, ed. by Lodge, III, 427, 428. Jefferson gained much credit for opening markets for our agricultural products in France; see Will Hunter to Jefferson, March, 1790, Jefferson Papers in the Massachusetts Historical Society.

heavy duty on "the weed," and had not been buying our rice.[8] With the outbreak of war in Europe, market prices advanced sharply, except those of wheat, rice and tobacco, which did not rise a copper.[9] In this state of affairs came news that France needed and intended to buy even more supplies from the United States. Before the arrival of Genet, with his ambitious plan to collect the debt America owed France and buy necessities with it, consuls had been directed to procure horses, cattle, grain, fodder, and so forth for their country.[10] But Genet really gave the traders an itching palm, and the flour merchants, in particular, vied with one another to obtain the most favorable consideration. France was in need, the merchants argued, and America abounded with supplies.[11] The sensible thing was, then, to aid Genet in his request for debt payment. Although this failed, shipments of flour and military stores for France were going out from Baltimore, Philadelphia, Norfolk, and Charleston to such an extent that it disturbed the British minister, who promised to make every effort to stop it.[12]

The attempt on the part of England, through Orders in Council, to halt American trade with France and the West Indies fanned the flame of pecuniary desire and caused it to flare up into positive, heated pro-French declarations. Attacks on ships carrying produce called forth violent denunciation from American merchants and alienated even those who had been denouncing Genet's actions in this country.[13] When matters reached this white heat, the democratic societies looked as good to men like John Swanwick or Stephen Girard, in Philadelphia, David Gelston, in New York, or Thomas Newton, in Norfolk—all West Indies merchants—as the commit-

[8] James to John Schoolbred, May 4, 1795, Schoolbred Letterbook in the Charleston Library Society.

[9] This is according to Jefferson, who was much concerned about the prices of agricultural commodities in 1793. Jefferson Papers, Vol. XCII Item 15, 876.

[10] The Genet Papers, June 6, 1793.

[11] The Jefferson Papers, Vol. LXXXV, Items 14760, 14771, and 14796, reveal the rivalry among Virginia merchants, who thought Jefferson could secure for them the agency for handling of Genet's flour to France.

[12] British Archives, F.O.5, Vol. IV, No. 30.

[13] Charles C. Pinckney to Thomas Pinckney, March 29, 1794, Pinckney Papers, Box "B," Library of Congress. Also Le Roy to King, March 30, 1794, and John Alsop to King, April 8, 1794, King Papers.

tees of correspondence had looked to Hancock and Otis in critical
pre-Revolutionary days. Swanwick, who engaged in banking, philan-
thropy, and education, as well as in trade, was one of Philadelphia's
wealthiest citizens.[14] He dared take issue in defense of his democratic ideas, with the master of invective, William Cobbett.[15] This
was not the only time merchants took pen in hand or stepped to the
rostrum to assume the leadership in the democratic-republican clubs.

Other groups which found it to their interest to lend support and
leadership to the societies were those of certain manufacturers. Notable among these were makers of iron implements, who from colonial days had suffered from English competition. In Vermont burly
Matthew Lyon and Ironmonger John Burnam manufactured iron
agricultural tools and nails. In a series of press articles, signing himself "A Farmer," Lyon pleaded for the development of American
iron, pottery, and glass industries. He opposed the trading of our
wheat for foreign manufactured goods, pointing out that our streams
could turn wheels and our hills were full of ore and that therefore we
could produce cannon, anchors, and such, cheaper right here at
home.[16] His arguments and proposals for a duty to be levied on imported nails was vigorously attacked. Then it was that James Witherell, president of the Rutland County Democratic Society, came
forward to defend the position of Lyon.[17] A similar picture is derived from southwestern Virginia, in Wythe county. Here society
members were also involved in the production of iron from the
neighboring ore beds. Walter and Joseph Crockett, of the family of
the famous David, and Alexander Smyth, all three leaders in the

[14] All these merchants were officers of societies. David Gelston wrote Governor
Clinton, Sept. 8, 1794 (Misc. MSS, New York Historical Society): "These repeated and aggravated insults look as though the British were determined to
plunder and rob us on our coasts until they have taken everything we have and
then laugh at us, as it is said by them we have not spirit to resent any insult
offered." Also Gelston to Clinton Sept. 8, 1794, Misc. Letters, Department of
State. See further, The *New York Journal*, Nov. 26, 1794, Aug. 8, 1798. The last
gives Swanwick's obituary. Also Wharton, *Salon Colonial and Republican*, p. 73.
[15] Swanwick, *A Roaster; or, A Check to the Progress of Political Blasphemy*.
[16] Crockett, *Vermont: The Green Mountain State*, p. 514; The *Farmers Library*,
Oct. 14, 1794.
[17] *Ibid.*, Oct. 21, 1794.

local popular society, were interested in the Wythe iron works.[18] Forges in upper South Carolina, near Pendleton, were owned and operated by the Tate family, whose members aided Genet and fostered republican clubs.[19] Advertisements in the newspapers of 1794 almost urged the people to "Buy American." Metal buttons, for example, were advertised as being equal to or better than those brought over from England.[20] These manufacturers were in direct conflict with the influential New England trader, who was importing articles ready-made. One of these, Stephen Higginson, of Boston, belittled American manufacturers as "of no consequence" and did all in his power to impede the political progress of Dr. Charles Jarvis, Constitutional Society leader, who spoke in behalf of protecting "our infant industries." [21]

Likewise, producers of snuff, tobacco, and sugar joined the democratic movement. These objected to the excise on such commodities, and claimed that if it were not removed these industries would collapse and Americans would again be subject to the ruinous British competition. In a memorial to Congress in 1794 the tobacco manufacturers claimed there were twenty-seven of them in Philadelphia alone and that Pennsylvania manufactured half the tobacco of all the states. If this business should be destroyed, distress and unemployment would follow.[22] The sugar refiners passed resolutions in the same spirit.[23] Signers of these memorials and resolutions are on the membership rolls of the Democratic and True Republican Societies in Philadelphia. Among the tobacconists were William Wat-

[18] See a lease signed by Patrick Henry, Walter Crockett, and others in 1786, McGavock Papers, Folder 22, William and Mary College Library; also Whitman, *The Iron Industry of Wythe County.*

[19] Drayton, "A View of South Carolina," pp. 151, 152. There were iron works in Kentucky, too, in 1794; Hubbard Taylor to J. Madison, Madison Papers, Vol. XVII, No. 34, Library of Congress.

[20] The *Delaware and Eastern Shore Advertiser,* May 28, 1794. A button manufacturer, Samuel Post, was a member of the Philadelphia Club.

[21] The *Independent Chronicle,* May 4, 1795. That friction over manufacturing competition was felt in England as well as in America is indicated by a broadside from the former country which says England is pleased with American interest in land speculation, as it diverts Americans from manufactures; see British Broadsides, Jan. 1792, No. 271, Library of Congress.

[22] The *American Daily Advertiser,* May 6, 1794.   [23] *Ibid.,* May 12, 1794.

kins and Thomas Leiper; while the refiners were Jacob Lawerswyler, vice president of the German Republican club, Christopher Kucher, treasurer of the German club, Jacob Morgan and Isaac Pennington, members of the Philadelphia society.[24] Doubtless these men were responsible for introducing resolutions passed by the two Philadelphia organizations condemning excise taxes and pledging devotion to the American manufacturing interests.[25]

Particularly in the West, but not by any means exclusively so, there were society members whose all-absorbing interest and security was the land bonanza. "Such a deluge of land have been tumbled upon the people, that it may literally be said they are struggling with the atlas upon their backs," wrote E. D. Turner, land agent, to his employer, Winthrop Sargeant in 1796.[26] Speculation ran riot. Fortunes mounted for those with the capital to buy vast blocks of mother earth and retail it in small portions to poorer settlers moving westward.[27] Broadsides in Europe and America announced half-million acre plots in Western Pennsylvania and Kentucky, which could be had for as little as twenty-five cents an acre and could be resold at the rate of from one to five dollars.[28] This was a neat profit for those who could play at the tables where America was bought and sold. Everybody who could, bought chips in this game, and prominent among them were members of the democratic societies, who discerned no incompatibility between hoarding land, collecting rents, and driving off "squatters," and at the same time indulging in high talk of equal rights and equal liberty.[29]

[24] All these names are found in the minutes of the Philadelphia society. The occupations of each were discovered with the aid of James Hardie, *The Philadelphia Directory and Register* (Philadelphia, 1793).

[25] *American Daily Advertiser*, April 14, May 13; the Mechanic Societies were concerned with the promotion of home manufactures, also Benj. Austin, of the Boston Democratic and Mechanic Society, spoke for infant industries; Minutes of the Society of Mechanics and Tradesmen, Sept. 3, 1788, Mechanics and Tradesmen Society Library, New York City.

[26] Sargeant Papers, Feb. 14, 1796, Massachusetts Historical Society.

[27] Gray, *History of Agriculture in the Southern United States to 1860*, pp. 638–39.

[28] British Broadsides, No. 271, Jan. 1792, Library of Congress; Mifflin Documents, Vol. XXIV, p. 36, in the State Library of Pennsylvania.

[29] In Kentucky were the big landowners John Breckinridge (Breckinridge to

On first consideration, it seems a bit strange that the landed gentry could find common cause with the settlers and dirt farmers within the confines of a popular society. How could David Redick, an officer of the Washington, Pennsylvania, society, fraternize with the poor settler? Redick, vast landowner, did his best to drive the settlers from his lands in the West, even suggesting the use of the militia.[30] Bitter disputes arose over the collection of rents.[31] In spite of all this, these men of opposing interests were brought together by certain other issues, such as the opening of the Mississippi, which would give markets for the farmer as well as release land for the speculator; [32]

Monroe, Aug. 12, 1798, Monroe Papers, New York Public Library); Richard Henderson, in the Transylvania Land Co. (Archibald Henderson, "Richard Henderson," *Tennessee Historical Magazine*, II [Sept., 1916]; also his "A Pre-Revolutionary Revolt in the Old Southwest," *Mississippi Valley Historical Review*, XVII [1930], 191; Robert Johnson (Johnson to Benj. Johnson, Nov. 18, 1795, Barbour collection, University of Virginia Library); Udney Hay, of New York and Vermont, an active supporter of Genet (Report of a Committee on Udney Hay's Letters, MS, 1792, in the New York State Library; also Hay to Regents of the University, Feb. 1, 1792, in the same library). Alexander Smyth and Daniel Sheffy, of Wytheville, Virginia, were in the Loyal Land Company (*Tyler's Quarterly Historical and Genealogical Magazine*, IV, 90–92); and John Montgomery, Jesse Evans, William Hay owned extensive lands (Will and Deed Books, Wythe County Courthouse). In Pendleton, S.C., the Loftons and Liddles, among others in the society there, executed big land deals (Anderson County, S.C., Deed Book B); in Maine an example would be the Bakers, especially John, Republican Society president (Washburn, "The Northeastern Boundary," *Collections of the Maine Historical Society*, VIII [1897], 41–50). James Sullivan and Perez Morton, of Boston, were interested in Maine and Mississippi lands respectively (Journal of the House of Representatives of Massachusetts, XV, 171, MS in the State Library). These are but a few of the many cases in which land speculators were members of the popular associations.

[30] Redick to Gallatin, April 20, 1796, Gallatin Papers, Vol. V.

[31] Benj. Dawson to Robert Carter, Nov. 6, 1797, in the Carter Papers 1700–1800, Virginia Historical Society. These papers contain many other instances of disputes between Carter's land agents and the rentees. George Washington wanted to sell his lands in Western Pennsylvania in 1795 because of the difficulty of collecting rents; see Washington to Israel Shreve, June 27, 1795, New York Public Library.

[32] Turner to Sargeant, Feb. 18, 1796. Here the agent Turner advises Sargeant to hold his land, for if the Mississippi should be opened speculation would accordingly increase. Richard Graham, whose land interest took him on long journeys into western Virginia and Kentucky, was disturbed about Spain "clogging trade" with her high duties. He adds, however, that the democratic societies are working on the difficulty; see Misc. Letters, Nov. 26, 1794, Department of State, National Archives.

the lack of frontier protection which discouraged both groups; and the excise, which tended to impoverish the West.[33]

There was a group of intellectuals—scientists, doctors, authors, printers, professional men—who gave their allegiance to the democratic cause. Many of them, from all parts of the country, were members of the American Philosophical Society, as well as of their local democratic clubs. Leading all these was David Rittenhouse, who as president of the Philosophical Society bore the mantle of Benjamin Franklin. His friends and colleagues in Philadelphia were Dr. James Hutchinson, Dr. William Shippen, Dr. George Logan, Alexander J. Dallas, Peter S. Duponceau, and John D. Sergeant. Outside the capital city were other friends and democrats, notably Dr. Absolam Baird; David Redick, and John Hoge of Washington, Pennsylvania; Dr. James Tilton, of Newcastle, Delaware; John Deas, of Charleston, South Carolina; and so on.[34] Bernard Faÿ has pointed out that the Philadelphia intellectuals in the American Philosophical Society, all old friends of Franklin, "provided the enthusiasm which stirred up the democratic faith of many people." [35] From the number of its leaders who were likewise spokesmen for democracy, it is not difficult to affirm the statement of Faÿ: Rittenhouse was one of the greatest scientists of his day, world-renowned, who dared uphold the Democratic Society, despite its unpopularity in certain influential circles.[36] He stands first among the leaders of a democratic and cultural movement.

[33] Werner, in his "War Scare and Politics, 1794" (*New York Historical Association, Quarterly Journal*, XI [1930], 328), indicates that the profits of land speculators were halted by Britain's actions. It should be added that also among the wealthier democrats of the day were those who had profited richly in the confiscation of Loyalist property. Matthew Lyon was one; Thomas Barker, Melancton Smith, and Wm. Boyd, of New York, were others. The last three were prominent members of the Democratic Society of their city. (Davenport, "The History of Vermont Politics," *The Vermonter*, VII, 379; Yoshpe, *The Disposition of Loyalist Estates in the Southern District of the State of New York*, pp. 113 ff.

[34] The names mentioned here are all found in the American Philosophical Society, *Proceedings* (Philadelphia, 1889), p. 83. An eight-volume travel book entitled *World Displayed* (Philadelphia, 1796) had as its first subscribers leading democrats of Philadelphia, Baltimore, and Western Pennsylvania. This would seem to indicate a community of intellectual interests in the democratic cause.

[35] "Early Party Machinery in the United States," *Pennsylvania Magazine of History and Biography*, LX (1936), 375.

[36] The *New York Journal*, July 5, 1796.

There was an impressive list of doctors, most of whom were interested in and lent their support to scientific projects of the day and who were also outstanding members of the "Jacobin clubs." These physicians had been trained at Edinburgh or Pennsylvania College to the humane and freedom-inducing naturalism of the Enlightenment. Corpulent, rotund James Hutchinson, a brilliant doctor, who served in the Revolutionary War, was one. He was one of the group of early experimenters who rode in John Fitch's steamboat, with Rittenhouse, Redick, Bache, and others.[37] Then there was Dr. William Thornton, architect, artist, inventor, opponent of Negro slavery, who thanked heaven that he lived "in this Age of Revolution, in this Age of Light and Reason." So ardent were his French sympathies that he worked out and sent to France some "hints" on effective warfare. These would rival the ingenuity of a Leonardo. A cannon ball, hot in the center, so that when it struck it would burst and scatter molten metal, was one device; a harpoon that could be shot at fleeing ships in order to retrieve them was another; a third was a kind of cartridge paper soaked in alum to prevent it from holding sparks which might ignite the powder when wadding.[38] Dr. George Logan was a democratic fugleman with versatile abilities. He wrote attacking the excise, saying America was mimicking the very system it broke from in '76.[39] Other writings of his were devoted largely to the encouragement of scientific agriculture and the promotion of agricultural societies.[40] As for Benjamin Rush, doctor, educator,

[37] Ruschenberger, *An Account of the Institution and Progress of the College of Physicians of Philadelphia*, pp. 60–66; Westcott, *The Life of John Fitch*, pp. 256 ff. Westcott says here that Fitch himself was an anti-Federalist and deist which prejudiced powerful people against him. Wm. Maclay was evidently not so impressed with the "puffing" James Hutchinson; he writes of the doctor coming in and talking so that "we were entertained with the belchings of this bag of blubber for half an hour. I took my hat and left them." *The Journal of William Maclay*, p. 379.

[38] Wm. Thornton Papers, Vol. I, June 12, 1794, Library of Congress.

[39] See an undated broadside written by Logan, in the Logan Misc. Manuscripts, Pennsylvania Historical Society.

[40] Logan, *Fourteen Agricultural Experiments to Ascertain the Best Rotation of Crops;* and *A Letter to the Citizens of Pennyslvania on the Necessity of Promoting Agriculture, Manufacturing and the Useful Arts*. Besides these, the Logan collection contains much manuscript material on the doctor's almost single-handed success in preventing war with France in 1798. His able wife, Deborah, wrote much of the extant materials on the colorful and useful life of Dr. George Logan.

antislavery proponent, supposition would make him a member of the Philadelphia Democratic Society. The name appears in the minutes of that society, but there was more than one Benjamin Rush in the city, according to Hardie's *Directory*. It could as easily have been the ship-rigger Rush as the famous Benjamin. Two clues, however, point to the doctor as the right one. First, Genet claimed that when he was ambassador, Dr. Rush gave him great attention and sympathy; [41] and secondly, Dr. Rush was not considered, according to Griswold, one of "the friends of Washington." [42]

It is not necessary to labor over suppositions, however, to prove prominent doctors to be democrats. We do it here only because of the eminence of Benjamin Rush. Outside Philadelphia the instances are impressive of physicians found on the Democratic Society rolls. Boston had eloquent, tall, bald Dr. Charles Jarvis, as well as the future governor, Dr. William Eustis, both of whom were prosperous traders, skillful politicians, and physicians, all rolled into one.[43] Ulster County, New York, had Dr. Charles Clinton, Dr. Elias Winfield, and Dr. Phineas Hedges.[44] The latter was a polished orator and author of *Strictures on the Elementa Medicinae of Doctor Brown* (Goshen, 1795), in which he offers a scholarly criticism of current medical theory.[45] In Columbia County, New York, there was the old Indian fighter, Dr. Moses Younglove, who is said to have been a pioneer in using isolation—the pest-house—for contagious diseases.[46] On the Vermont frontier lived Dr. James Witherell, carrying wounds from the war and memories from his days at

[41] Genet to [?], Oct. 19, 1828, in Misc. MSS G, New York Historical Society.

[42] Griswold, *The Republican Court*, p. 287.

[43] The Portland Republican Society Papers contain a letter from The Massachusetts Constitutional Society which gives nine names of Bostonian democrats. Among them are Charles Jarvis, Perez Morton, John Avery, Jr. and Benjamin Austin, Jr. See also Sullivan, *Familiar Letters on Public Characters and Public Events*, p. 26; cf. Robert A. East, "The Massachusetts Conservatives in the Critical Period," in Morris, ed., *The Era of the American Revolution*, pp. 352, 386; East indicates that Jarvis and Eustis were security-holders and conservative in the 1780's.

[44] *Rising Sun*, Jan. 11, 1794; Clearwater, ed., *The History of Ulster County*, p. 308. Koch, *Republican Religion*, p. 125.

[45] Hedges, *An Oration Delivered before the Republican Society of Ulster County*.

[46] *Western Star*, March 24, 1795; Simms, *The Frontiersmen of New York*, II, 82–84; Ellis, *The History of Columbia County, New York*, p. 313.

Valley Forge.[47] He was president of the democratic society in his neighborhood. Dr. James Tilton is well known to the citizens of Delaware as one who criticized the unsanitary conditions in the hospitals of the day, became surgeon general to the United States Army, and wrote discourses on diseases, human beings, flora, and fauna.[48] Edward Johnson, doctor, initiator of educational projects and mayor of Baltimore, is another example of the many that might be cited.[49] In concluding, we may say with Robinson that ministers and lawyers were monopolized by the Federalists; but the doctors, in general, were the "friends of freemen."[50]

To be mentioned among the intellectuals are the "patriotic printers" whose role as disseminators of information has already been emphasized. Not least among these was Benjamin Franklin Bache, grandson and protégé of the American sage, Benjamin Franklin. Like his grandfather, he had scientific leanings. It was Bache who persuaded J. P. Blanchard, the balloonist, to test a newly perfected barometer on his first ascension at Philadelphia in 1793.[51] Bache remained to the end of his days a warm friend of the oft-maligned republicans, Thomas Paine and Edmund Genet. For Paine, Bache distributed the *Dissertations on First Principles* and *The Age of Reason*. As for the French ambassador, he not only defended him to the end, but he went out of his way to pay the Genets a visit at their home on Long Island in July, 1795, where he received a "warm welcome" and had an "entertaining and instructive" time.[52] Because

[47] Hemenway, *The Vermont Historical Gazetteer*, II, 728–29.

[48] *Biographical and Genealogical History of the State of Delaware* (Chambersburg, Pa., 1899), pp. 1245–50.

[49] Coyle, *The Mayors of Baltimore*, p. 76. Had there been a Constitutional Society in Dedham, Mass. Dr. Nathaniel Ames would have certainly been a member. His brother, Fisher, was a lawyer and Federalist, while he was a doctor and Republican. As it was, Dr. Ames kept in close communication with his friend, John Avery, Jr., a leader in the Massachusetts Constitutional Society. For sources on these statements, see John Avery to Dr. Ames, Aug. 15, 1793; Fisher Ames to Thomas Dwight, April 17, 1800, in the Ames Papers; also see the racy diary of Dr. Ames, Charles Warren, ed., *Jacobin and Junto, or Early American Politics as Viewed in the Diary of Dr. Nathaniel Ames, 1758–1822*.

[50] Robinson, *Jeffersonian Democracy in New England*, p. 133.

[51] Blanchard, "The Journal of My Forty-Fifth Ascension," *The Magazine of History*, extra numbers, XVI (1918), 271.

[52] Paine to Bache, July 13, 1795, and Bache to his wife, July 19, 1795, Bache Papers.

of his democratic fervor and his loyalty to persecuted friends, Bache has unfortunately suffered some oblivion, and writers have chosen to believe with Fisher Ames that he was a "mean, lying, base-hearted puppy." [53]

The erudite Robert Coram, of Newcastle, Delaware, who gave his energies as a school teacher, librarian, writer, and printer, was among the democratic intellectuals. "In the death of this man," reads his obituary, "whose writings have been sometimes contradicted, but never refuted, Science and Philosophy have lost one of their brightest ornaments." [54] Among the intelligentsia of New York in the printing business were not only Philip Freneau, but also David Denniston, editor of *The American Citizen,* both leaders in the Deistical Society.[55] Thomas Greenleaf deserves more than mere mention here. He warned of the consequences of high rents, when all the "earnings of the people will get a deposit in the hands of a few" and poverty and misery would displace ease and happiness.[56] The first newspaper in Kentucky was published by John Bradford, who became a civic leader and chairman of the Board of Trustees of Transylvania University. Bradford and his friend Ned West, like Bache and Fitch, were pioneers in steamboat history. West and Bradford also experimented with perpetual motion. This sage printer was known by the sobriquet of "Old Wisdom." [57] One might also mention William Dickson, of Lancaster, Pennsylvania, a community booster and early muckraker, who exposed corrupt politics through the channels of his *Lancaster Intelligencer.*[58] Other influential men from the ranks of the printers could be noted in the popular societies, but we must pass on to a consideration of other intellectually prominent citizens.

[53] Ames to T. Dwight, Feb. 24, 1795, Ames Papers. When Seth Ames edited *The Works of Fisher Ames,* he deleted much of great historical interest in the letters.

[54] Conrad, *History of the State of Delaware,* I, 313; *Delaware Gazette,* Mar. 11, 1796.

[55] Pomerantz, *New York,* p. 129.   [56] The *New York Journal,* Feb. 12, 1794.

[57] Shane Interviews (No. 13CC211) in the Wisconsin Historical Society. Perrin, *The Pioneer Press of Kentucky,* p. 14; McMurtrie, *John Bradford, Pioneer Printer of Kentucky.*

[58] *Historical Papers and Addresses,* Lancaster County Historical Society, VIII, 72, 73.

As for the gentlemen of the bar and the cloth, there was a representative number of the first among the membership of the societies, even though many democrats thought lawyers should be anathematized.[59] Instances of preachers as members of the popular associations are rare indeed. In the long lists of the Philadelphia and Charleston memberships, there is no minister to be found. Exceptions, however, appear in Western Pennsylvania, where the Rev. David Phillips, a Baptist, was a member of the Society of United Freemen, and a leader of the "violent party" during the Whiskey Insurrection.[60] The Republican Society "in the forks of the Yough" convened at the Rev. James Findley's meeting house.[61] Whether or not the divine was a member of the club is not known, but he must have been at least sympathetic to permit an anti-excise convocation in his church. The only other minister found connected with the democratic societies was Thomas Tolman of Cornwall, Vermont.[62] A fine scribe and a well-educated man, he was the first pastor of the Congregational Church of Cornwall. In December, 1794, he was charged with being deistic when he failed to give satisfactory answers to the questions: Is the Bible the word of God? Is mankind naturally totally depraved? Was Jesus the son of God? In spite of his negative answers, he was "regarded as sane" but "dreadful and dangerous." Because he was informed on religion and could not be stigmatized as ignorant or insane, he was excommunicated and separated from the church body as "a corrupt and dangerous member," to be treated as "a publican and heathen." [63]

[59] Notable lawyer "citizens" were John D. Sergeant, son-in-law of Rittenhouse; David Bradford, whisky revolt leader; Thomas Lee, youthful Charlestonian; and Tunis Wortman, a man of outstanding intellectual capacities. Jesse Higgins, of the Patriotic Society of Newcastle, Del., a man described as having great powers of intellect, wrote a pamphlet entitled "Sampson against the Philistines," in which he attacked the legal profession. Attempts were made to suppress the writing, but William Duane published it in the *Aurora* (Conrad, *op. cit.*, p. 529). See the *New York Journal*, Jan. 12, 1793, for another expression of antipathy toward lawyers; and Manning, *The Key of Libberty*, pp. 33–34.

[60] David Phillips's name is found in "Insurrection in Western Pennsylvania," Rawle Papers, Vol. I; also in Letter to the Secretary of State of Pennsylvania, Aug. 17, 1794, Yeates Papers, Pennsylvania Historical Society.

[61] *Pittsburgh Gazette*, March 8, 1794.   [62] *Farmers Library*, Oct. 28, 1794.

[63] This material was taken from the original records of the First Congregational Church, Cornwall, Vt., and the writer is grateful to Edward H. Matthews, church

Any one of a number of other cultural leaders might be more fully commented upon, namely, John Hinckley Mitchell, the friend of the English scientists and democrats, Boulton and Watt; [64] Dr. John Willard, the husband of the educator, Emma Willard; [65] Donald Fraser, poet and teacher, who wrote an epithalamium for Edmund and Cornelia Genet; [66] John A. Graham, of Vermont; [67] Perez Morton; [68] Archibald Buchanan; [69] or William Keteltas.[70] All these were believers in the rights of man and took an active part in forwarding liberal principles by joining the popular societies.

Succeeding waves of immigrants had an effect upon the democratic clubs, often adding color and fieriness to the membership itself. Freedom-loving Irish came from across the sea to escape the aftermath of a thwarted revolution; Germans came to avoid the dictatorships of the Fredericks; French of high and low birth, who feared the uprisings in their native land and its West Indies Islands, arrived. Scotch and English came too. Many were willing to sell their freedom for a period, in order to gain a new start in America; others were induced to emigrate by land companies who wanted settlers on

---

clerk, for the courtesy extended him. Cf. Lyman Matthews, *The History of the Town of Cornwall, Vermont*, pp. 146, 147.

[64] Mitchell, ed., *The Mitchell Record; The Mitchell-Boulton Correspondence, passim.*

[65] The Willards will be discussed in a subsequent chapter.

[66] The Genet Papers, June 28, 1794.

[67] Graham, *A Descriptive Sketch of the Present State of Vermont.* Besides his writings, Graham is known for his activity in the Episcopal Church.

[68] The Genet Papers, Nov. 17, 1793. F. J. Lequoy, Genet's agent in Boston, describes Morton as "profound and methodical." Loring, *The Hundred Boston Orators*, pp. 129–30. Morton invested heavily in marine insurance and was interested in Mississippi lands, two powerful ties to the democratic movement. See "Papers Relating to Marine Insurance, 1789–1802," New England Historical Genealogical Society library; and *Memorial of the Agents of the New England Mississippi Land Company.*

[69] Buchanan, *An Oration Composed and Delivered at the Request of the Republican Society of Baltimore.* This man was likewise a forthright opponent of Negro slavery.

[70] Keteltas was a leader in prison reform and always evinced sympathy for the underprivileged and unfortunate. He got into considerable trouble with the courts and the state legislature in 1796 for defending two ferry boatmen whom he considered unjustly sentenced to "stripes and imprisonment." (*Rutland Herald*, April 4, 1796).

the frontier. Whatever the diverse reasons that brought them, the fact remains they came in great numbers, most of them poverty-stricken and dissatisfied.[71]

Every American locality felt the presence of the strangers, especially when the Irish and the Germans occupied certain sections of the urban environment and formed a so-called "lower class." [72] Great numbers, however, sifted into the backcountry, so that William Smith on his visit to upper South Carolina in 1793 remarked on "the strangest mixture of emigrants from other countries." [73] Smith was disturbed by the anti-Federalist sympaties of these backcountry Scotch-Irish; and Philip Livingston, in New York, claimed that the poor Irish and French alone, in the sixth and seventh wards of New York City, were sufficient to carry that center for Jefferson in 1800.[74] New England reacted against the favoritism of the democrats toward aliens. In 1795 Bostonians, led by Jedidiah Morse, disbanded an emigrant aid society and decided never to meet again.[75] Already, in Federalist eyes, the melting pot was not working, for immigrants were giving vent to "foreign" ideas.

Fifteen names in the Charleston membership list can be clearly identified as Frenchmen or "citizens of the United States born or descended of Frenchmen." [76] There were Abraham Sasportas, French Jew and an important merchant of the city; [77] Benjamin Legare, head of the Charleston Battalion of Artillery; [78] Capt. Jean Boutielle, of the privateer, "Sanspareille," who feted the republicans of the city in 1794; [79] and a number of lesser lights—craftsmen, includ-

---

[71] Faÿ, "Early Party Machinery in the United States," *Pennsylvania Magazine of History and Biography*, LX (1936), 375.

[72] Pomerantz, *op. cit.*, p. 659. In the twenty-five years preceding 1790 the population of Boston increased by less than 3,000, while in ten years from 1790 to 1800 it increased by 7,000. Hunt, *The Lives of American Merchants*, p. 149.

[73] Smith to Hamilton, April 24, 1793, Hamilton Papers, Vol. XIX, p. 2566. Library of Congress.

[74] Livingston to Jacob Read, Feb. 23, 1801, *Columbia University Quarterly* (June, 1931), p. 200.

[75] Amory, *Life of James Sullivan*, II, 95.

[76] *Federal Gazette*, April 30, 1793.

[77] Mangourit to Genet, March 6, 1794, Genet Papers.

[78] Legare to Mangourit, Feb. 6, 1793, "Correspondence of the Republican Society of South Carolina."

[79] *City Gazette*, March 27, 1794.

ing Penciel, the tinman; Anthony, the harnessmaker; Ranzier, the gunsmith; and Mattin, the tailor.[80] The brightest light among the French or French descendants in the Philadelphia Democratic Society is the erudite Peter S. Duponceau, Genet's lawyer, and one of the most profoundly learned men of his day.[81] Then there are Anthony Du Plaine, teacher; Peter Barriere, president of the French Patriotic Society; and others who could not be designated French aristocrats.[82] The Republican Society of Norfolk, Virginia, exchanged dinners with the French republicans of that seaport; [83] the same happened in Baltimore, where Paul Bentalou, Revolutionary hero serving under Pulaski, gave his loyalties to the Republican Society.[84] Among these people Genet found cohorts, and American democracy recruited some of its warmest advocates.

As for the Scotch and Irish, as early as 1780 Charles Lee wrote James Monroe:

We have neither Monarchy, Aristocracy nor Democracy; if it is anything, it is rather a Mac-O'-cracy by which I mean that a Banditti of low Scotch Irish, who are either themselves Imported Servants or the immediate descendants of Imported Servants, are the Lords Paramount. . . . God knows what is to become of us.[85]

The presence of these "Mac-O'-crats" was as strongly evident in the 1790's as in the 1780's. Broadsides defending the social importance

[80] *Aurora*, March 21, 1797, gives the names and occupations of French democrats mentioned here.

[81] Genet to Duponceau, Oct. 28, Dec. 23, 1793. The Duponceau Papers are in the Pennsylvania Historical Society.

[82] *North Carolina Journal*, May 22, 1793. Frances Childs, in her scholarly study of French refugee life in America (*French Refugee Life in the United States, 1790–1800*), has neglected consideration of the nonaristocratic elements in the picture. A rounded presentation should include the French Benevolent and Patriotic Societies, their leaders—Gayetan Aiguier, François Meurice, Paul Bentalou, Anthony Du Plaine, and others and their social and cultural influence as a result of their financial aid and ideological devotion to the French Revolution. Genet himself would be considered a refugee after 1794, and he was deemed worthy of election to The Mineralogical Society of Columbia College in 1799. See Geo. J. Warner to Genet, March 30, 1799, Genet Papers; also "Genet" in the *Dictionary of American Biography*.

[83] *Virginia Gazette*, Feb. 27, 1794.

[84] Bentalou wrote defending Pulaski against charges of inefficiency; see his *Pulaski Vindicated from an Unsupported Charge* and *A Reply to Judge Johnson's Remarks*.

[85] June 25, 1780, Monroe Papers, New York Public Library.

of the poor appeared in 1794, addressed "To the Men of Ireland." These sheets stated how gulled, misled, and mistreated the Irishmen were.[86] Probably the most famous of this ilk, though far from being a poor man, was the blustering, boisterous, red-faced Blair McClenachan, erstwhile Revolutionary patriot and at one time president of the mother Democratic Society.[87] Another was William Duane, who was the successor to Benjamin F. Bache as editor of the *Aurora* and who was charged with organizing United Irishmen in America and of desecrating a churchyard by nailing up petitions against the Alien and Sedition Acts.[88] Edward Lacey, hard-hitting, heavy-drinking president of the society of Pinckney District—a section settled by the Scotch-Irish from Pennsylvania,—was a stormy petrel on the frontier.[89] With him was Patrick McGriff, a man "quick to resent and as quick to forgive," also an officer of the Pinckney club.[90] So we might continue, naming any number of spirited Irishmen who might be termed the firebrands of the popular societies because of their fervency and activist spirit.[91]

The very existence of a German Republican Society, mentioned in chapter i, antedating other democratic associations, points to the strong support given the republican movement by some of the people of this nationality. The inhabitants of Lancaster, Pennsylvania, the population of which was three-fourths German, formed a republican society, one of many ways in which Lancaster imitated its neighbor Philadelphia.[92] David Rittenhouse was of this German stock, as also was Peter Muhlenberg, who through his activity in a republican society fought for the adoption of the Pennsylvania constitution of

---

[86] Broadside collection, 1794. Another broadside appealed to the Irish to enlist in service for France, see "They Steer to Liberty's Shore," Aug., 1793, Pennsylvania Broadsides, Library of Congress.

[87] Meigs, *The Life of Charles Jared Ingersoll*, p. 28; Griswold, *op. cit.*, p. 313.

[88] *Virginia Herald* (Fredericksburg), Feb. 19, 1799.

[89] Moore, *Reminiscences of York* [County, South Carolina], p. 2; and, by the same author, *The Life of General Edward Lacey*.

[90] The Sumter Manuscripts, Vol. XI, pp. 2–18, in Wisc. Hist. Soc.

[91] Woodfin, "Citizen Genet and His Mission," p. 184, gives further evidence of German and Irish support of the democratic cause.

[92] Kelsey, ed., *A Record of the Journal of Theophile Cazenove through New Jeresy and Pennsylvania*, pp. 73–74; *The American Daily Advertiser*, Jan. 26, 1795.

1790; [93] Henry Kammerer, the printer, was another; Michael Leib, the doctor, and George Forepaugh, carpenter, were others. These liberty-loving Germans, says James O. Knauss, were prominent as farmers, but did not restrict themselves to this pursuit. They were also millers, weavers, carpenters, wagon-makers, merchants, tradesmen, and manufacturers of musical instruments, iron, glass, and pottery.[94]

That people of English ancestry were in the American democratic movement goes without saying. The renowned names of Thomas Paine, Joseph Priestley, and Thomas Cooper are sufficient to remind the reader of the important role played by men of this nation. Paine, in the 1790's, was giving his support to the popular societies of England and France, and only indirectly to America. Priestley declined joining a New York political club, pleading the need for rest and study,[95] but through his writings no one can doubt where his sympathies lay. Cooper and Priestley planned a settlement, comprising 300,000 acres, on the headwaters of the Susquehanna River, to be settled by the "friends of liberty." [96] Although these plans did not mature, the two refugees located at Northumberland, where a democratic society appeared in 1795.[97] James Tytler, one of the compilers of *The Encyclopaedia Britannica*, came to these shores in 1794 to escape persecution for his writings on liberty.[98] These were among the more famous English democrats in America, who may or may not have been members. Of the membership of John Miller, one of several English printers who came to the United States in the last quarter of the eighteenth century we are certain.[99] He was an officer

[93] Woodfin, *op. cit.*, p. 183.

[94] Knauss, *Social Conditions among the Pennsylvania Germans in the Eighteenth Century, as Revealed in German Newspapers Published in America*, pp. 140, 160; also Faust, *The German Element in the United States*, I, 53.

[95] *Supra*, chap. iii.

[96] Knight, "Early Judges of Northumberland County," *The Northumberland County Historical Society Proceedings*, I, 38.

[97] *Aurora*, March 23, 1795. The writer does not wish to imply that Priestley and Cooper were members of this society. They may have been. Thomas Cooper was a most ardent member of the Manchester Constitutional Society before coming to America; see Knight, *op. cit.*

[98] Tytler, *The Rising of the Sun in the West*.

[99] Gilpatrick, "The English Background of John Miller," *Furman Bulletin*, XX (1938), 14.

of the Franklin Society of Pendleton, South Carolina, and wrote some of its most stirring anti-Federalist resolutions.[100]

The broad base of the pyramidic structure formed by the membership of the popular societies was composed of the so-termed "lower order" of society, the "swinish multitude," the "subterranean gentry."[101] Above them were the men with vested interests in land, a few large merchants, a greater number of smaller merchants, certain manufacturers, and tradesmen, and a group of the professional classes. But undergirding all these were the poor farmers, the artisans, the mechanics, and the sailors. These had carried the brunt of the war for freedom as common soldiers and members of the Revolutionary bodies, the Sons of Liberty.[102] Now in the 1790's they were suddenly awakened to the fact that the things for which they had sacrificed and fought were slipping through their fingers. A different land of liberty loomed before them than the one they had anticipated. This very situation spurred William Manning "to find out the real cause & a remidy" for the loss of free government.[103]

Manning was not alone in asking questions concerning the way in which America was moving. Other farmers were charging "the monied interest" with attempts to effect a silent revolution and to put the government into the hands of "the few," to delude the people, and to foster rivalries among the "labouring classes" in order to divide their concerted power. The "few" act "by a series of newspaper paragraphs and correspondencies, written by speculators, who have money and leisure for such performances, and who had rather write than work for a living."[104] The farmers fought the excise, land engrossing, high governmental salaries;[105] they favored a di-

---

[100] *City Gazette,* June 30, 1794; Oct. 28, 1795.

[101] The same descriptions, it is well to keep in mind, were applied to the members of the popular societies of England; see Robert Birley, *The English Jacobins,* p. 9.

[102] Schlesinger, *The Colonial Merchants and the American Revolution,* p. 72; Morais (*Deism in Eighteenth Century America,* p. 272) says the Sons of Liberty was "a lower class organization," made up of mechanics, artisans, and laborers, but led by merchants and lawyers. The same could be said for the democratic societies.

[103] Manning, *op. cit.,* p. 4.

[104] "A Farmer," *Virginia Gazette and General Advertiser,* May 22, 1793.

[105] "The Green Mountain Boy," *Vermont Gazette,* April 18, 1794; this writer

rect tax on real property, the election of "plain farmers" to the councils of government, and the opening of the Mississippi and the St. Lawrence River routes.[106] Since these planks are found repeatedly in the platforms of the various popular organizations, it seems reasonable to conclude that the poor farmers were giving their support to the societies. Add to this the fact that David Bradford, vice president of the Washington, Pennsylvania, club and spokesman for the agrarians, could not be caught after the Whiskey Insurrection, because the "majority was for him" and protected their leader from arrest.[107] The Republican Society of Lancaster relied upon the common sense "of our plain and industrious farmers . . . that respectable class of people," to keep Americans from being misled.[108] Now and then an untutored farmer became president of a society, as in the case of James McCullough, of Newcastle, Delaware.[109] The following "Advice to Country Politicians" can be understood if seen against the background of the insurgency of the yeomen:

> Go weed your corn, and plow your land,
> And by Columbia's interest stand,
> Cast prejudice away;
> To able heads leave state affairs,
> Give railing o'er and say your prayers,
> For stores of corn and hay.

adds that the democratic societies may be expected to stop favors to the rich and "reduce people more to a state of level."

[106] Harry Innes, letter, Aug. 27, 1791 (copy), in the Kentucky Historical Society, also describes the peasantry in Kentucky as "perfectly mad" against lawyers and "men of fortune." Also *Pittsburgh Gazette*, Sept. 27, 1794; and [Thomas Paine?] *Cautionary Hints to Congress Respecting the Sale of the Western Lands,* a pamphlet written to oppose letting speculators garner huge tracts of land, and to favor government control in guaranteeing small tracts that the settler could buy and improve.

[107] *Philadelphia Gazette,* Dec. 13, 1794. Samuel Duncan, a humble pack-horse master, was arrested for protecting Bradford; Craig Letterbook, Dec., 1794, Carnegie Library, Pittsburgh, Pa. Thomas McKean believed "the lower class" to be the most intractable during the Whiskey Revolt, as against "the upper class"; McKean to J Ingersoll, Aug. 29, 1794, Emmet Collection, New York Public Library.

[108] *American Daily Advertiser,* Jan. 26, 1795.

[109] "The Administration of the Estate of James McCullough," Newcastle County, 1829; Hall of Records, Dover, Del. This item shows McCullough to have been a reader of *Aurora,* a patient of Dr. Tilton, and a poor man whose estate, after debts were paid, amounted to $229.

With politics ne'r break your sleep,
But ring your hogs and shear your sheep,
And rear your lambs and calves;
And Washington will take due care
That Britons never more shall dare
Attempt to make you slaves.[110]

The statistical analysis presented at the beginning of this chapter indicates, rather conclusively, that workmen and mechanics outnumbered all other classes in the popular societies. While they were not a class-conscious proletarian group in any modern sense of that phrase, they had drawn a distinction between the interests of an "aristocratic junto" and their own. In 1785 the New York mechanics petitioned the legislature for incorporation. The request passed the house, but received stubborn resistance in the senate, where Aaron Burr argued that the bill would give this class "too much political importance." In commenting upon Burr's position, Charles Tillinghast, a mechanic, wrote to his friend, Hugh Hughes, saying that Whigs and Tories always coalesce when their interests are threatened and adding that

Such sentiments convince me of the absolute necessity for a firm union of that class of honest and virtuous citizens, for when opinions like that of the Colonel's are thus openly avowed, it is surely high time to watch with an attentive eye the conduct of such haughty and ambitious characters.[111]

By 1794 the mechanics were on the alert, as evidenced by the existence of Mechanical Societies in all the principal cities. Important, here, is the fact that the Mechanics and Coopers Societies usually coöperated and worked closely with the democratic-republican clubs.[112] The personnel and leadership of the two overlapped, as

[110] Callender, *History of the United States* . . . , p. 37.
[111] The Lamb Papers, March 7, 1785. In 1794 Hughes and Tillinghast were critical of Hamilton and the administration in power; see same collection, Aug. 10, 1794.
[112] *Annals of the General Society of Mechanics and Tradesmen of the City of New York from 1785 to 1820*, ed. by Earle and Congdon, p. 32; Warner, *Means for the Preservation of Public Liberty*, an oration delivered July 4, 1797, at a joint celebration by the Democratic, Tammany, and Mechanic Societies; Scharf, *The Chronicles of Baltimore*, p. 267.

did also their political principles.[113] The aphorism "a man is known by the enemies he makes" is applicable to social groups as well as to individuals. The enemies of the societies give us many clues as to the personnel of their membership. William Woolsey, of New York, writing to Oliver Wolcott, Jr., March 6, 1794, says of a Democratic Society meeting that it was attended by "the lowest order of mechanics, laborers, and draymen." [114] The New England conservatives looked with fear and trembling upon "modern democracy" creeping into their midst, and Timothy Dwight wrote that its leaders, "like the devil of old, takes up a tenement in a herd of swine." [115] Thomas Dwight expressed his feeling that the societies were composed of people with no respectability.[116] And Hammond, the English minister, said that Genet, through "his" Jacobin clubs, was directing attention principally to the mechanics and the lower classes of the people.[117]

— Although the various popular societies contradicted almost everything else the Federalists said about them, the clubs did not deny the fact that they appealed to the farmers and the mechanics. On the contrary, they proudly insisted that "It must be the mechanics and farmers, or the poorer class of people (as they are generally called) that must support the freedom of America." [118] Or, as the Ulster democratic society stated it, the societies everywhere must be "on their guard against designing men in office and affluent cir-

[113] Wm. Rouse was active in both organizations in Charleston, S.C. (*City Gazette*, April 1, 1795), and Peter R. Maverick and White Matlack were equally so in New York City (Earle and Congdon, *op. cit.*, p. 23). For comparative purposes, see the principles of the two organizations in the *Pittsburgh Gazette*, Feb. 16 and Aug. 10, 1793.

[114] The Wolcott Manuscripts, Vol. XIII, No. 30, Connecticut Historical Society.

[115] *Ibid.*, Dwight to Wolcott, June 3, 1794.

[116] To Theodore Sedgewick, Dec. 13, 1794, Sedgewick Papers, Massachusetts Historical Society.

[117] Hammond to Grenville, March 19, 1794, F.O.5, Vol. I, No. 16.

[118] *Newark Gazette*, March 19, 1794. One hesitates to disagree with the historian, Charles Beard, in his *Economic Origins*, p. 246, n., where he says "One striking feature of this partisan conflict [1790's] was the absence of any considerable appeal to the working classes or 'mechanics' in the towns." He adds that neither Federalists nor Republicans made an attempt to win the vote of the mechanics. It is the belief of the present writer that the very success of the Republicans rested upon their popular appeal to the common man. The membership structure of the societies of protest would seem to bear this out.

cumstances who are ever combining against the rights of all but themselves." [119]

The sailors, and the men connected with maritime life such as ship-carpenters, sail-cloth makers and sea-captains, what may be said of them? International events were working against their interests; they were being subjected to impressment and their ships to seizure. In all the seaboard ports, the sailors were meeting, passing resolutions, calling upon the people or Congress for action concerning the hazards they suffered on the brine.[120] Consequently, many were unemployed and insisted upon remaining so, even after Madison's embargo was lifted, because of the risks on the sea.[121] Philadelphia feared trouble with the idle seamen in the spring of 1794, and the governor sent a militia unit to guarantee order.[122] The Federalists, especially, looked askance at restless and dissatisfied tars, and talked of the trouble they might cause.

The democrats came to the defense of "our honest seamen," mentioning that the sailors, too, disliked England, "who had robbed them." [123] The spirit of Liberty, Equality, and Fraternity was wooing the sailor; Britishers were deserting ships of their nation in 1794, and hundreds of American seamen were applying to Genet to serve for France.[124] In fact, Genet and his country both were popular among the seagoing people. The Society of Master Sailmakers in New York was ultra-democratic in its position, toasted the Fourth of July, a free press, freedom for African slaves, and, most noteworthy of all, "To the societies of America as nurseries of

[119] *New York Journal,* Feb. 5, 1794.

[120] Fauchet, the French minister, kept records of these meetings in Baltimore, Wilmington, Philadelphia, and New York. See Affaires Étrangères, Vol. XL, Part 6.

[121] Alexander Martin to Richard D. Spaight, May 23, 1794, Spaight Letterbook 1792–95, North Carolina Historical Commission Library.

[122] For evidence of unemployed seamen, see Genet to Jefferson, July 9, 1793, Genet Papers; Mifflin Documents, Vol. XXVIII, No. 34, in the State Library of Pennsylvania; *Independent Chronicle,* Sept. 25, 1794.

[123] *Ibid.,* Legarenne to Noah Webster, Aug. 7, 1793, N. Webster Papers, New York Public Library. The artistically illustrated "Sea Journal of Captain Benjamin Carpenter," covering the years 1790–94, in the Essex Institute, reveals a pro-French bias on the part of the sailors.

[124] The desertion of British seamen was causing international complications. See Misc. Letters, Feb. 16, 1794, Department of State, National Archives. For sailors applying for service with France, see Genet Papers, May 17, 1793.

Republicanism." [125] The Kensington district of Philadelphia was predominantly an area devoted to naval establishments. Thence came the ship-carpenters, ropemakers, and others who took part in the "riot" against John Jay and his treaty in 1795.[126] The Massachusetts Constitutional Society made special provisions in its constitution to excuse absent members who were "at sea." [127]

They were not a polished lot, these sailors, and would not be counted among the cultured and refined classes of their day. The mariner's humor is intriguingly represented in the *Feast of Merriment*, printed and distributed by the democratic Henry Kammerer. It heroized sailors in pornographic anecdote, and the upper classes bore the brunt of its salacious jibes. Comparable to it is the bawdy frontier poetry of Johnson's *Kentucky Miscellany*, printed by the equally democratic John Bradford and making speculators, lawyers, and preachers the butt of its ribaldry.[128] One could expect that William Willcocks, "columnist" for Hamilton and enemy of the popular societies, might receive a note signed "A Sailor," and reading:

If your name continues in the papers, under such damned dirty pieces, you will soon be a corpse. By the immortal God that made me I will sacrifice you the first convenient opportunity.[129]

With the farmers and settlers, the mechanics and coopers were the maritime workmen,—all commoners to whom William Manning wished to address his appeal for the organization of an international "Labouring Society." They formed the soil for a regenerated democracy.[130]

[125] *New York Journal*, Nov. 14, 1795.

[126] Saint-Mery, *Voyage aux États-Unis de l'Amerique, 1793–1798*, ed. by Mims, p. 107; Wood's *Newark Gazette*, July 15, 1795. Promoters of a patriotic festival in Boston in 1794 were asked to keep the cost low so that unemployed tradesmen and sailors could attend. (*Independent Chronicle*, March 20, 1794.)

[127] *Boston Gazette*, Jan. 20, 1794.

[128] "Feast of Merriment by Well-Fed Domine Double Chin, Esq." Johnson, *Kentucky Miscellany*. These rare examples of the humor of the masses are to be found in the Library of Congress and the University of Chicago Library.

[129] *Massachusetts Spy*, Nov. 28, 1793. The devout Bishop Asbury writes in his journal for July 22, 1794, at Boston, "I took up my cross and preached in a large room, which was full enough and warm enough; I stood over the street, the boys and Jack-tars made a noise, but mine was loudest." (*Journal of the Reverend Francis Asbury*, II, 198.

[130] For further statements of the workingman and farmer support of the re-

But these common folk were not on the bottom rung of the ladder of fortune. Below them were the indentured servants and the Negro slaves. Even though many of the bondmen were German and Irish or other white stock, they fared as badly or worse than the blacks in matters of flogging and mistreatment. When freed, they were often considered "lower" than the Negroes.[131] They were bought and sold just as were the black men [132] and were as tightly bound to their masters during the period of indenture. The story of Negro slavery is well known and recognized. In that "age of reason" a Negro in Charleston was hanged, after being convicted of witchcraft.[133] And Timothy Ford, of the Revolution Society of that city, was advancing, as early as 1794, a "mud-sill theory" of slavery. He said that the presence of slaves caused free men to strive to preserve their rights and liberties, that they might keep above the servant level. Therefore, slavery insures freedom! [134] The great paradox of that time, of human bondage combined with high talk of liberty, equality, and fraternity still gives one pause.

This bottom-most class of *les misérables* was not represented in the membership of the popular societies. However, out of sight was not out of mind. Trouble was brewing. Some indentured slaves were running away to join the French navy, and others were gaining freedom by the direct work of French consuls. As inflammatory ideas seeped into the ranks of the Negro slaves, underground rumblings were heard, portending the shattering of democratic society inconsistencies and of the greater paradox between practice and precept of a republican people.[135]

publican cause, see Wansey, *An Excursion to the United States,* p. 23; Luetscher, *Early Political Machinery in the United States,* p. 60; and Robinson, *op. cit.,* p. 99.

[131] "Diary of Hezekiah Prince," *New England Magazine,* IX, 733.

[132] See "Two German Servants to Be Sold," a baker and a cooper with two and three years respectively to serve, in the *Columbian Mirror,* Sept. 27, 1796. Miller ("The Effects of the American Revolution on Indentured Servitude," *Pennsylvania History,* VII [1940], 1) points out that the Revolution made no perceptible alteration in the institution of slavery of whites.

[133] *Carlisle Gazette,* Dec. 4, 1793.

[134] From the article by "Americanus" [Timothy Ford], in *City Gazette,* Oct. 27, 1794.

[135] Jefferson to Genet, July 11, 1793, Genet Papers; M. A. B. Mangourit *Mémoire de Mangourit,* p. 31. The subject of the danger of slave insurrections will be discussed more fully in chap. viii.

The number of young men that one seems to find as members of the democratic societies is an additional point of interest concerning the membership. John Hinckley Mitchell and Thomas Lee, of Charleston, were twenty-two and twenty-four respectively; Peter S. Duponceau and Benjamin F. Bache were thirty-two and twenty-four years of age. In Kentucky all the most prominent leaders were under forty-five, including Bradford, Breckinridge, the Todds, and the Browns. Seamen, as a whole, were youthful, according to Samuel E. Morison,[136] and St. Julien Ravenel has written that in general the Federalists were older gentlemen, while the republicans were young men.[137] Moreover, there was a Juvenile Republican Society, about which we know little, organized in New York in 1795.[138] Perhaps the aberrations of idealistic youth troubled the sleep of fathers as much in that decade as they have in others. The devotion of youth to the contemporary radicals doubtless gave rise to the pamphlet entitled *The Rights of Youth*, which counseled all lads to be dutiful and to attend to their superiors.[139]

A second point of emphasis regarding the membership of the republican clubs is the great number of former Sons of Liberty, members of Committees of Safety, and Revolutionary War leaders which one finds. Every society had its honored members who had served in the war for freedom, and usually they were elevated to positions of leadership. In Ulster, New York, there was Arthur Parks, a major of the minutemen, and John Nicholson who took part in the assault on Quebec.[140] In Columbia County, of the same state, was club president Philip Frisbie.[141] President of the Newark Republican Club was William S. Pennington, whose war diary is preserved in the New Jersey Historical Society. Boston had William Cooper, friend of Samuel Adams, as president of its Constitutional Society,[142] together with Perez Morton, Charles Jarvis, and Ben-

---

[136] *The Maritime History of Massachusetts, 1783 to 1860*, p. 109.
[137] *Charleston, the Place and the People*, p. 379.
[138] *American Daily Advertiser*, July 10, 1795.
[139] Bradley, *The Rights of Youth*, in Bradley Papers, Box 1, Library of Congress.
[140] Clearwater, ed., *The History of Ulster County*, p. 109.
[141] Ellis, *The History of Columbia County, New York*, p. 325.
[142] Tuckerman, *William Cooper*. Cooper served as a clerk of some of the

jamin Austin, who served in the Revolution and became outstanding leaders. Among those in Vermont were Isaac Clarke, better known from his war days as "Old Rifle." [143] The president of the Norfolk society was Thomas Newton and a well-known member was Josiah Parker, both of whom served on Committees of Safety in 1775.[144] In Charleston, Stephen Drayton, president of the Republican Society, had performed his part, too, in the struggle for independence.[145]

So one might go on endlessly, pointing out the heroes of the war. But there is other evidence to support the statement that many society members were old patriots. Consider the barb hurled at the Boston democrats by Joseph Dennie, when he wrote,

I always had a high admiration of your "old whigs of 1775," but the measure of their folly was never completely filled till they gave Tarts and Tailors a civic feast and taught the rabble that they were all viceroys.[146]

This admission, by a conservative, would seem to indicate a balance of "old whigs" with the democratic movement. On the other hand, the Democratic Society of Chittenden County, Vermont, baited the more aristocratic elements by daring them to come forward and reveal their service stripes. "Where are your scars?" they queried.[147] New York society members called upon their enemies to step up and show their records of 1775.[148] It is doubtful whether the citizens of the popular associations would have thrown this gauntlet had they not been sure of their own superior Revolutionary War record.

---

famous "Tea Meetings" in 1773. See *Massachusetts Historical Society Proceedings*, XX, 10.

[143] Hemenway, *op. cit.* I, 907. Isaac Clark was a brother-in-law of Matthew Lyon.

[144] *The Virginia Magazine of History and Biography*, XXX, 86, 307; *ibid.*, VI, 421–24.

[145] Drayton to Horatio Gates, March 14, 1792, Gates Papers, New York Public Library.

[146] Dennie to his parents, April 25, 1793, Dennie Papers.

[147] *Vermont Journal*, Feb. 9, 1795.

[148] *Gazette of the United States*, June 17, 1794.

Chapter Five

THE SOCIAL PHILOSOPHY OF
THE DEMOCRATIC CLUBS

An exclusive right to form or alter a government is annexed to society in every moment of its existence.

JOHN TAYLOR, of Caroline

Tyrants have trembled at the restless activity and the speculative curiosity of the human mind.

JOHN I. JOHNSON, of the New York Democratic Society

THE ANCIENT PROBLEM of permanence and change has been no less disturbing to political thinkers than it has been to the physicist or to the metaphysician. From Greek times on scientists and sages have pondered over the quest for certainty, now finding it in this absolute principle and now in that one. In chasing this elusive will-o'-the-wisp of permanence, from era to era men have built their thinking and life security around certain utilitarian social concepts. These ideas have reflected the absolute principle of changelessness, and have been rationalized into a universal scheme of things accepted as eternally true. At certain historical moments it was theocracy and its dogmatic tenets that prevailed; at other times it was monarchy, oligarchy, and even democracy that set up finalities which were to be changeless and God-ordained. However, new social and economic conditions, or new "truths" discovered by the physical scientist have upset the best laid plans of mice and men. In spite of all efforts, change has persisted and has rolled relentlessly on, and final truths have turned out to be at their best but "relative absolutes."

The eighteenth century certainly would appear to be an age in which change struck telling blows at rigid governmental institutions. Social thought was just beginning to react seriously to the implications of Copernican heliocentrism and Newtonian physics. Men were subjecting their social institutions to scientific as against supernatural tests. A political or social proposition was valid if it proved to be useful in human experience, that is, if it worked out in actual life situations. The proposition was unscientific if it had to be justified by principles of otherworldliness, that is, by assertions that it was true not in human experience but in the world to come. Feudalism rested upon the latter concept. The hard-shelled absolutes of feudalistic society were being cracked and broken by those who applied the new scientific outlook to man and his government.

In particular the divine right of kings was one of these absolutes to be tested by scientific procedure. The contract principle of the day demanded that this institution, too, be criticized by human experience. Politics had to become a science. To men of feudal thinking, this was tantamount to creating disorder and chaos. This new scientific frame of reference, which pointed to the increase of man's knowledge and control, stirred the complacent stability of a society that found security in a personal deity and his personal earthly vicegerent.

Filmer, Hobbes, Locke, and Rousseau were among those who sought to restore permanency in this seething world of change inaugurated by science. While Hobbes and Filmer built a rationale to bolster kingly government, Locke and Rousseau formed fresh principles incorporating the world-view of science and still offering stability to social life. The new absolutes posited by the latter were natural law and its corollary for government, the sovereignty of the people. The eighteenth century was divided in varying degrees of acceptance or rejection, by those who upheld the old or proclaimed the new.

After the Revolution of 1688, when John Locke wrote to justify that violation of the hoary rights of kings, an increasing body of thinkers rallied around the concept of limited sovereignty. These Whigs believed with Locke that government rested upon the consent of the governed, that the people possessed the natural right to choose their monarch, and that once having chosen, all should proceed smoothly, without popular discord. The power of consent, argued the Lockians, would actually prevent social uprisings, which they disdained as much as the followers of Hobbes did.[1] The supreme power of the people to alter their government was to be used only when their rights were violated. and when a majority joined in dissolving the government.[2] In the interim between mandates from the people, the chosen ruler or rulers were the supreme authority, as arbitrary in power as a king. Therefore, Locke theoretically had two sovereigns; the people and the people's trustees. Because the people were sovereign only in choosing their rulers, the chosen could reign with the scepter's sway. This philosopher left but little room for popular democracy to assert itself. It became a system too permanent, therefore, to allow for increasing change. It stood, however, to justify the American Declaration of Independence, but received its first serious challenge in French Revolution days.

The philosopher of the Jacobins was Jean Jacques Rousseau.[3] His major significance for us here was that he refused to accept Locke's vacillation between two sovereigns—the people and their chosen rulers. Rousseau's liberty was to be achieved by law, and law was a product of the *volonté général*. The will of the people was to be the single sovereign, the supreme authority, the absolute or universal for this thinker.[4] Ernest H. Wright says of Rousseau that he had "little hope of the representative system so popular with the Parisian Anglophiles of his day." [5] Why did he lack faith in

[1] Lamprecht, *The Moral and Political Philosophy of John Locke*, pp. 146–50.

[2] Locke, *Two Treatises on Civil Government*, chap. xi; Scherger, *The Evolution of Modern Liberty*, p. 148.

[3] Brinton, "Political Ideas in the Jacobin Clubs," *Political Science Quarterly*, XLIII (1928), 249.

[4] Mead (*Movements of Thought in the Nineteenth Century*, pp. 13–24) says that Rousseau was against arbitrary authority because men were beginning to see society as rationally as they saw the law-abiding physical world.

[5] *The Meaning of Rousseau*, p. 85.

the Lockean concepts as practiced in England? The answer appears in *The Social Contract:*

The deputies of the people are not their representatives; they are but agents, and may not conclude anything definitely. Every law is void which the people do not ratify in person, and is no law. The English believe themselves to be free. They deceive themselves. They are free only during the time they elect members of Parliment. When these are elected they are slaves; they are nothing.[6]

In other words, the general will cannot be alienated; a man cannot delegate his will; he cannot transfer his sovereignty from himself to another. Instead, the will must be active at every moment in history if a government of free men is to exist.

The great issue of the hour in the 1790's was not between those advocating monarchy and those forwarding republicanism. Rather the crucial issue grew out of a disparity in the ranks of the followers of "the great Mr. Locke." One group believed in representative government and looked upon any popular criticism of the duly elected rulers as factious and discordant, leading to anarchy and mob rule. Another group, equally devoted to Locke's right of consent, followed Rousseau in maintaining that the people's will must at all times be expressed through representative agents, and that therefore free speech, press, and assembly, and a frequent rotation of officers, were essential to keep a constant check upon government. Men like Edmund Burke, in England, and Hamilton and Adams, in America, were in the first group of Lockeans; while men like Paine and to some extent Jefferson supported the deviation from Locke. It may well be that Jefferson was referring to the inadequacy for social change in Locke's system when he declared, "Locke's little book on Government is perfect as far as it goes."[7] Jefferson and the popular societies wished to go further. "Hence it was," as Merle Curti has written, "that divergent interests appealed to contradictory doctrines and implications in Locke's political thought."[8]

[6] Rousseau, *The Social Contract,* III, 15.
[7] Curti, "The Great Mr. Locke, America's Philosopher, 1783–1861," *The Huntington Library Bulletin,* No. 11 (April, 1937).
[8] *Ibid.,* p. 136. The following is a contemporary illustration of the division

Among the deviators from Locke who followed Rousseau, none was greater in influence in the 1790's than that zealot for democracy, Thomas Paine. In his *Rights of Man* he refers again and again to Rousseau.[9] In the *Dissertation on First Principles* he attacks concepts of permanency in government, saying that England in 1688 was foolish to pledge itself "to William and Mary, their heirs and posterities forever."[10] Rather, for a changing world, he would agree with Rousseau that to make a state durable, we must not dream of making it eternal.[11] Paine stated it this way: "A nation, though continually existing, is continually in a state of renewal and succession."[12] Because of his devotion to democratic ideals in Europe and America, Walter P. Hall has said that Thomas Paine was the best known international figure of his day and that his *Rights of Man* "had a wider circulation and a more profound influence than any book issued in the radical cause."[13] Popular societies in France, England, and America sang his praises, toasted his name, and distributed his *Rights* with missionary ardor.[14] If we should grant, for the moment, that an individual may make significant history alone, then it was not Genet but the internationalist Thomas Paine who deserves the credit for fathering the democratic societies.

These three philosophers, Locke, Rousseau, and Paine, all in-

among those who appealed to Locke for their authority: Knox (*Essays on the Political Circumstances of Ireland. . . . With an Appendix Containing Thoughts on the Will of the People*, p. 221) upheld Edmund Burke and attacks *The Social Contract* for stating that the general will is the only source of law and the essence of sovereignty. The Constitutional Society of Sheffield, on the other hand, criticized Burke as a "Knight Errant of Feudality," in a pamphlet entitled *The Spirit of John Locke on Civil Government.*

[9] Harry H. Clark, "Thomas Paine's Relation to Voltaire and Rousseau," *Revue Anglo-Americaine*, IX (April and June, 1932). See also, Clark's "Toward a Reinterpretation of Thomas Paine" (*American Literature*, V [1933], 133–45), where it is pointed out that Newtonian science also influenced the more flexible governmental theories of Paine.

[10] Paine, *Dissertation on First Principles of Government*, p. 16.

[11] Wright, *op. cit.*, p. 85.   [12] Paine, *op. cit.*, p. 11.

[13] W. P. Hall, *British Radicalism, 1791–1797*, pp. 85, 95.

[14] Thomson, ed., *A Tribute to the Swinish Multitude, Being a Choice Collection of Patriotic Songs*; Conway, *Writings of Thomas Paine*. In the introduction Conway states that Paine gave the proceeds from his *Rights of Man* to the Constitutional Societies of England; Conway, *The Life of Thomas Paine*, pp. 308 ff., discusses Paine's founding of the first Republican Society in France in 1791; *City Gazette*, July 20, 1791.

fluenced, directly or indirectly, the social thinking of post-Revolutionary America. In the backcountry, where books were scarce,
children sometimes learned to read and spell from the *Essay Concerning Human Understanding*.[15] Men like Bache and Freneau
acknowledged their indebtedness to Rousseau and Condorcet.[16] The
Federalists, by means of certain cartoons of the day, heaped ridicule
upon Rousseau because they thought his writings championed dangerous ochlocracy.[17] In the writings of the democratic societies and
their members, evidence is overwhelming that Locke's theory of
consent was accepted. But they insisted, however, with Rousseau
and Paine, that a free government must be maintained by the con-
tinuous expression of the public will.

The constituency of the democratic societies caught even the more
profound scientific basis upon which these political thinkers built
their democratic philosophy. The leaders of the Baltimore Republican Club wrote that politics is a science and that it must always be
studied, just as one studies astronomy or mathematics, "and if from
the latter we may learn to trace the wanderings of a planet, so
from the former may we know the certain effect of certain laws
and government to a people." [18] The Baltimore club incorporated
into its constitution the statement that freedom was "a moving principle through every class of society" and that as a natural right it
must be guarded "with incessant watchfulness." [19]

Locke's theory of consent was not enough for this group. In their
opinion a changing world demanded that government, too, change
and adapt itself constantly to the omnipotent general will. Furthermore, the general will could not delegate itself to a body of repre-

[15] Moore, *Reminiscences of York*, p. 29.
[16] Forman, "The Political Activities of Philip Freneau," *Johns Hopkins Studies in History and Political Science*, Series XX, pp. 9–103.
[17] Broadside collection for 1798 in the Pennsylvania Historical Society. For Rousseau, Godwin, and Montesquieu in William and Mary College, see Jos. C. Cabell to David Watson, March 4, 1798, Minor-Watson Papers, Library of Congress.
[18] *New York Journal*, Dec. 20, 1794. This remarkably modern point of view, which refuses to treat social laws as though they were in a separate category from physical laws, is also implied in the writing of another democratic society member, viz., James P. Puglia, *The Federal Politian*.
[19] *Baltimore Daily Intelligencer*, May 24, 1794.

sentatives who might be expected to give it faithful expression. A few think this can be done, wrote the Patriotic Society of Newcastle, Delaware, but, it added, "we cannot be jockeyed out of our liberties by such sort of logick." If the people have certain inalienable rights, the society continued, they must not be accused if they practice them and censure the conduct of their elected officials.[20] The Republican Society of Newark, New Jersey, believed "that the different members of the government, are nothing more than the agents of the people, and as such, have no right to prevent their employers from inspecting into their conduct, as it regards the management of public affairs."[21] The Massachusetts Constitutional Society expressed it in this way:

That the people, upon having formed a government, are implicitly to resign themselves to the agents and delegates appointed by them, without any kind of attention to their own liberty and safety, is a doctrine calculated to undermine the foundation of freedom, and to erect on her ruins the fabric of despotism.[22]

Inherent in these statements is the right of revolution, the right to alter or abolish the existing form of government whenever the general will of the people demands such action. The Portland, Maine, Republican Society and the Democratic Society of Norfolk, Virginia, among others, directly stated these rights in their pronouncements.[23]

If public opinion was to reign supreme, it must have a vehicle through which it could continuously find expression. The democrats, being admirers of the pristine democracy of the classical world and

[20] Patriotic Society of Newcastle, Delaware, *Circular*, copy in the Delaware Historical Society.
[21] Wood's *Newark Gazette*, Dec. 31, 1794.   [22] *Boston Gazette*, Jan. 20, 1794.
[23] *Gazette of Maine*, Aug. 23, 1794; *South Carolina State Gazette*, July 25, 1794. Haswell, Vermont democrat, in his *Oration Delivered at Bennington, Vermont, August 16, 1799*, well states the philosophic position of the popular societies. He says, in part, "The necessity of government, in civilized society, has in all ages, and forever will, induce men to form social compacts, and depute certain powers to individuals or public bodies, constituted as actors in behalf of the sovereign people. But *when the people have deputed they are not defunct;* the sovereignty is not annihilated; and however constitutions may point out no way for the sovereign to make its will known, yet the power exists, its dreadful voice is heard at solemn intervals, and at its awful voice tyrants are wont to tremble." Italics ours.

of the system used by the Genevan Republic, turned to these for a precedent.[24] Here they found government being operated through meetings of the freemen in their various localities.[25] History, then, would seem to indicate to the men of the eighteenth century that democracy functioned best through small governmental units. Rousseau advocated the right of the people to assemble as need arose and based his advocacy of this system upon the precedent of the ancient states. According to Wright, Rousseau believed in the small state, where all the people could be active, federated with other small states for purposes of protection.[26] Godwin, whose writings were influential in America,[27] had the same idea in his principle of the "parish federation." [28] Likewise did Helvetius, says H. N. Brailsford, believe in a number of commonwealths, each so small that public opinion could act powerfully within them.[29]

The popular societies followed this philosophy, fostering, wherever they could, the town meeting, the county association, and a state federation of these units. That is why the Democratic Society of Pinckney District, for example, felt itself to be "one indivisible community" with all the people of South Carolina,[30] and also why the "mother society" of Philadelphia wrote in its constitution that it would be "co-extensive with the state, but for the conveniency of the members, there shall be a separate meeting in the city of Philadelphia and one in each county, which shall choose to adopt this Constitution." [31]

[24] Pseudonyms below newspaper articles of the day were nearly always taken directly from classical heroes, or they were "Latinized." See also Logan, *Five Letters Addressed to the Yeomanry of the United States*, in which Dr. Logan argues from classical-world precedent. Both Federalists and Republicans read and quoted from classical precedents; see Mullett "Classical Influences on the American Revolution," *Classical Journal*, XXXV (1939), 92–104.

[25] Swiss democracy, which is said to be the purest form ever to have existed, arose out of communal land ownership—the *landsgemeinden*—when the people convened to plan the use of their land; see McCracken, "The Real Origin of the Swiss Republic," *American Historical Association, Reports*, 1898, pp. 357–62.

[26] Rousseau, *op. cit.*, p. 85.

[27] Edward Livingston to Albert Gallatin, May 6, 1798, Gallatin Papers, Vol. V; Sheffy, *Speech of the Honorable Daniel Sheffey.*

[28] H. H. Clark, *Toward a Reinterpretation of Thomas Paine.*

[29] *Shelley, Godwin and Their Circle*, p. 120.   [30] *City Gazette*, Nov. 5, 1793.

[31] The state, in contradistinction to the national government, was thought of as a basic governmental unit (Mudge, *The Social Philosophy of John Taylor of Caro-*

The hierarchy built up by the great majority of the popular societies, starting with the town meeting and by a representative system forming county and state bodies, has already been traced. That which warrants emphasis here is, first, that this was a democratic process in which each group chose its members for the higher body by an election [32] and, secondly, that political information traveled from national group to the local units and vice versa. This helps to account for the courthouse meetings of the societies and for the fact that county clerks, sheriffs, or both, were almost always active club members. News of Congress was sent to these local officials for distribution and publicity.[33] State legislative information was often spread in the same manner.[34] These men served as *liaison* agents for news to and from the individual popular organization. With the county and state organizations united by committees of correspondence and in contact with the national government, it is not difficult to see a form of political machinery shaping itself, a machinery which, as we shall note later, was to aid in displacing the Federalists in 1800.[35]

In principle, and to some degree in actual practice, the societies expressed a concern for an international democracy which would extend their heirarchy from town meeting to a world democratic

---

line, pp. 74–75). Lerner, "John Marshall and the Campaign of History," *Columbia Law Review*, XXXIX (1939), 410, suggests that the Federalists feared the state legislatures because they had always opposed the moneyed classes, and had responded to the plights of the common man, and had upheld farm as against city interests.

[32] See Canaan, N.Y. Democratic Society, *New York Journal*, March 8, 1794; Patriotic Society of Newcastle, Del., announcement of plan to organize a hundred meetings, *Delaware Gazette*, Nov. 20, 1795; for the organization of townships in Western Pennsylvania, see *Pittsburgh Gazette*, Sept. 7, 1793; for Kentucky see *Kentucky Gazette*, March 8, 1794. Cf. Robinson, *Jeffersonian Democracy in New England*, p. 63.

[33] Thomas P. Carnes Papers, May 6, 1794, Duke University Library; *State Gazette of North Carolina*, Jan. 14, 1796. County officials were accorded much more honor at that time in our history. For the importance of the sheriff's office, see Julian P. Boyd, "The Sheriff in Colonial North Carolina," *North Carolina Historical Review*, V (1928), 151.

[34] The famous resolutions on the Alien and Sedition Laws passed from the Virginia legislature to the various county courts, to be read and discussed by the people; *Virginia Argus*, Oct. 11, 1799.

[35] Woodfin ("Citizen Genet and His Mission," p. 494) states that the purpose of the societies was to set up political machinery of a permanent nature.

society. Their lodestar, Thomas Paine, believed that the new system of government must pervade the entire earth. North Carolina democrats, in 1796, were toasting *The Rights of Man* and the Tree of Liberty, adding for the latter, "may its roots be cherished in this its mother land, until its branches shall extend themselves over the remotest corner of the earth." [36] The two clubs in Philadelphia, meeting together on May 1, 1794, drank the following toasts:

The Great Family of Mankind—May the distinction of nation and language be lost in the association of freedom and friendship, till the inhabitants of the various sections of the globe shall be distinguished only by their virtues and talents.

The Democratic and Republican Societies of the United States— May they preserve and disseminate their principles, undaunted by the frowns of power, uncontaminated by the luxury of aristocracy, until the Rights of Man shall become the supreme law of every land, and their separate fraternities be absorbed in one great democratic society comprehending the human race.[37]

Often toasts were proposed "To the Democratic Societies throughout the world" and to those who were persecuted in Europe because of their political faith.[38] Had America been geographically nearer to Europe, doubtless the societies would have been more closely affiliated with French and English groups.

As it was, they made efforts to practice their precept of cosmopolitanism. In Charleston the democrats worked closely with Mangourit, the French consul. He gave them a stone from the Bastille, upon which they intended to engrave the cap of liberty. Two months later they voted to send an address of friendship to the French National Convention.[39] The New York society welcomed Joseph

---

[36] *North Carolina Gazette*, July 16, 1796.

[37] *American Daily Advertiser*, May 5, 1794.

[38] *Goshen Repository*, Oct. 28, 1794; *City Gazette*, March 6, 1794; Wood's *Newark Gazette*, July 16, 1794.

[39] Stephen Drayton to Mangourit, Feb. 15, April 14, 1794, in "Correspondence of the Republican Society of Charleston." The Baltimore society sent an American Flag to the French governing body by the naval hero, Commodore Joshua Barney, who joined the French navy (Wm. F. Adams, ed., *Commodore Joshua Barney*, p. 212). The Philadelphia club was prevented from addressing a greeting to the National Convention by the actions of moderates in its membership; see the minutes of the society.

Priestley as a representative of a mutual cause and invited him to join its membership.[40] The same club also invited the "Republican Natives of Great Britain and Ireland," as well as the German democrats of the city, to join with it in building fortifications on Governor's Island.[41] In the more distant district of Maine, the Portland Republican Society resolved "That this Cociety [sic] be disposed to assist and releave [sic] all distressed Republicans of what nation so-ever to the utmost of their abilities." [42] Some glimmer of international coöperation evidenced itself, and the societies knew themselves to be loosely coördinated parts of a world-wide movement.

The ideal of the affiliated clubs was to keep their membership closely unified and constantly informed, that they might give the people "the truth" and bring the weight of combined opinion to bear upon governmental decisions.

A constant circulation of useful information, and a liberal communication of republican sentiments, were thought to be the best antidotes to any political poison, with which the vital principles of civil liberty might be attacked.[43]

Established societies urged the formation of others, so that through correspondence many could be brought into their orbit. James Tilton, Caesar Rodney, and Robert Coram were appointed a committee by the Delaware Patriotic Society to draft an address to all societies in "sister states," requesting their fellowship and exchange of "political knowledge." [44] Canaan, New York, citizens, hoped that other towns in Columbia County would form clubs to preserve democracy, "which is untenable without social union and communication." [45] To all these, close association, as used by the

---

[40] *American Daily Advertiser,* June 10, 1794; Wansey, *An Excursion to the United States,* p. 73. According to Wansey, Priestley declined the invitation, stating that he had come here to study, to be with his family, and to avoid politics.

[41] *Diary* (New York), June 7, 11, 1794; *New York Daily Gazette,* June 2, 1794.

[42] Resolutions passed July 17, 1794; rough draft in the Portland Republican Society Papers. Manning (*The Key of Libberty*) doubtless was inspired by the popular societies, rather than the Cincinnati, when he proposed an international "Labouring Society" which he hoped would abolish war.

[43] See chap. i, *supra.*

[44] *Delaware and Eastern Shore Advertiser,* Dec. 20, 1794.

[45] *Western Star,* May 6, 1794.

Revolutionary committees, had led to victory in the past and was now increasingly important in order to maintain and perpetuate the earlier gains.

However, the committee of correspondence was not the sole means of maintaining federation. The system of intervisitation by the members of the various clubs was widely put to use. The New Yorkers felt that the influence of the popular associations would be increased if they were to admit visitors from other organizations to their membership. It would, they said, "strengthen our intercourse," keep them aware of others' opinions, aid them toward unified action, and help them find friends when they visited in other states. In order to prove membership, they suggested the issuing of a certificate which the member would carry for purposes of identification.[46] Whether or not New York was the first to adopt this scheme is not known; that Philadelphia and Baltimore both made use of it is proved by the records.[47]

Another characteristic of the democratic societies, consistent with their general social philosophy, was the insistence upon frequent elections of club officers. The Revolutionary militia companies al-

[46] *Circular of the Democratic Society of New York*, copy in the New York Historical Society. This particular circular is addressed in ink to the Philadelphia Democratic Society and bears the original signatures of Melancton Smith, William Allum, Thomas Gilbert, and Tunis Wortman.

[47] The membershp certificate of Benjamin F. Bache is owned by Mr. Franklin Bache, to whom the writer is indebted for his hospitality and generous help. A picture of the certificate is in Faÿ's *The Two Franklins*, facing p. 166. The original seal and certificate, belonging to Capt. Joshua Barney of the Baltimore Republican Society, cannot be located. It is mentioned in *Harper's Encyclopedia of United States History*, III, 79–80. Lossing, *The Pictorial Field-Book of the War of 1812*, p. 88, n., gives a picture of the seal and a copy of the reading on the certificate: "To all other Societies established on principles of Liberty and Equality, Union, Patriotic Virtue and Perseverance.

"We, the members of the Republican Society of Baltimore, certify and declare to all Republicans or Democratic Societies, and to all Republicans individually, that Citizen Joshua Barney hath been admitted and now is a member of our Society, and that, from his known zeal to promote Republican principles and the rights of humanity, we have granted him this our certificate (which he hath signed in the margin) and do recommend him to all Republicans, that they may receive him with fraternity, which we offer to all those who come to us with similar credentials.

(Signed) Alexander M'Kim,"
President"

"In testimony where of, etc.
George Sears, secretary."

ways had elected democratically their superior officers at frequent intervals, lest one man threaten freedom by holding office too long. So, too, the societies practiced a regular rotation of their elected officials at least once each year. Dr. Michael Leib, member of all three of the popular associations which existed in Philadelphia from 1790 to 1800, urged frequent elections in a speech he made to the house of representatives of Pennsylvania, February 24, 1796. With numerous references to Godwin, he said:

Now as the expression of the people's will can only be fairly and substantially given at the election of their Representatives, and as this will ought at all times to be consulted, the more frequent the elections, the more frequent the opportunity of consulting it. If elections are not frequent, the will of the Representatives, instead of the will of the people, becomes the Supreme Law.[48]

Lieb and others of his ilk in the societies thought six years too long a time for senators to hold office. The distrust of men who seem important because of "family, estate and Machiavellian art" is indicated by the Canaan, New York, society:

Members of this cast will generally coalleace [sic] and bear great weight in almost every legislature, and when once elected are likely to be elected again, if their first service does not make sufficient provision for them.[49]

The only protection against "this cast" was to adopt the habit of changing officials often in the general government, as well as in the small society. The Portland republicans, organized by militiamen who had seen action in the Revolutionary War, decided to elect a chairman and a committee of correspondence every month, and a treasurer and a clerk annually.[50] Newark, New Jersey, chose a president, a secretary, and a treasurer twice each year.[51] Pinckneyville, South Carolina, like most of the others, chose their officers annually.[52] Seldom did a person hold office for more than a year, even though he proved to be a most conscientious leader.

[48] Lieb, *Dr. Lieb's Patriotic Speech.*   [49] *Columbian Mercury,* Oct. 1, 1794.
[50] *Gazette of Maine,* Aug. 23, 1794.
[51] Wood's *Newark Gazette,* Mar. 19, 1794.   [52] *City Gazette,* Nov. 5, 1793.

One of the strongest virtues of the popular associations, and one which makes them of interest to educators as well as to the political scientist, was their championship of free speech and their discussion of the lively issues of the day. They believed with Rousseau, Condorcet, Richard Price, and a host of others that ignorance was the irreconcilable enemy of liberty, and that, if public opinion was to be trusted, it must also be informed. They frowned upon any deliberate intention to convey "facts," as untrustworthy. Instead, truth for them was derived from hearing and weighing the arguments on both sides. They sensed that their enemies wished to present only one side and to crush societies and meetings of the people.[53] The mother society in Philadelphia spoke for all her offspring when she wrote:

Let us then exercise the right of peaceably meeting for the purpose of considering public affairs. Let us combat with Herculean strength the fashionable tenet of some among us, that the people have no right to be informed of the actions and proceedings of government. Nothing, surely, presents a stronger barrier against the encroachments of tyranny than a free public discussion. By this means the attention is aroused, the sources of intelligence are multiplied, and truth is developed.[54]

In 1798, after the Philadelphia Democratic Club had disappeared, the Republican Society of Norwalk, Connecticut, continued to foster the educative principles of its predecessor. Its constitution read to the effect that the people must always be active and vigilant and that

to exercise the right of speech, and freedom of debate, recognized by the Constitution; to perpetuate the equal rights of man, to propagate political knowledge, and to revive the republican spirit of '76, are the great objects of this institution.[55]

One may well believe that the societies were sincere in wishing for a truly "free public discussion," for they invited the opposition to come forward and state its case. The Democratic Society of

[53] *Address to the Republican Citizens of the United States*, May 28, 1794, in American Antiquarian Society collection of broadsides.
[54] *Philadelphia Gazette*, Dec. 23, 1794.
[55] *New London Bee*, April 4, 1798. Tunis Wortman, *A Treatise Concerning Political Enquiry and the Freedom of the Press*. This is an excellent brief, written by a society member, for freedom of speech, press, and assembly.

Canaan, New York, favored not only other groups like their own, but also "Aristocratical Societies," or "Tory Societies," for "we prefer societies (as a way of investigation and communication), because in them every grade of capacity can furnish something to the general stock of improvement, and because they tend to fraternity, consistence and due order." [56] This is an especially fine statement of democratic procedure, for it recognizes that in decision-making, all who are affected by the decision have an indispensable part to play.[57] The New Jersey farmers, members of The Political Society at Mt. Prospect, wrote in their simple, clumsily worded constitution,

Are several of you disposed to advocate an aristocratical or monarchical government? Where there is real opposition of sentiment, in a well regulated discussion, the righteous cause will probably shine with an additional lustre. Come forward, then, with your arguments; we are more generous than cowardly; liberty is yours, as well as ours; come on and vindicate your cause in the open field of reason; but we fear their characters will exclude most men of your opinion.[58]

Whether on subjects announced previously for debate, or on resolutions to be submitted to the press, the meetings of the clubs were, for the most part, forums for consideration of public affairs. Unusual though this may seem in a period when many talked of throttling free speech and passing seditious legislation, it is true, nevertheless, and to the credit of these popular organizations.

The devotion of the clubs and their members to the free play of intelligence and reason stemmed from another concept of change in the social thinking of the era. Feudal and theological attitudes toward human nature were being challenged. Instead of the old absolutes that man was sinful and depraved, many shared Crevecoeur's view:

Men are like plants the goodness and flavour of the fruit proceed from the peculiar soil and exposition in which they grow. We are nothing but what we derive from the air we breathe, the climate we inhabit,

---

[56] *Columbian Mercury*, Oct. 1, 1794. Italics ours.

[57] Kilpatrick, "Democracy and Respect for Personality," *Progressive Education*, XVI (Feb., 1939), says: "And in every human association, all concerned with the results of any policy shall share as far as humanly feasible, in making the policy."

[58] Wood's *Newark Gazette*, March 26, 1794.

the government we obey, the system of religion we possess, and the nature of our employment.[59]

This freeing and malleable approach to human nature led to an overoptimism in thinkers like Condorcet; but it also gave men a more firm basis for seeking human betterment and faith in natural progress. This spirit is illustrated in the following poem:

> May ignorance be banished hence!
> The right of man and common sense,
> With friendship and benevolence,
> Combine to civilize:
> No tyrant then shall ever reign;
> But Justice rule the wide domain,
> The Golden Age return again,
> A Heaven beneath the Skies.[60]

Leading American democrats like Bache, Wortman, and Duane followed the new school of thinking. Duane wrote that the doctrine of the innate depravity of man had caused untold miseries, degraded and enslaved mankind.[61] Once it was recognized that the nature of man was not fixed, but like Thomas Paine's idea of a nation, continually subject to "renewal and succession," democratic education could become a *modus vivendi*; free speech and the dissemination of information would become requisite necessities.

Federalist propaganda repeated so frequently the charge that the popular clubs were secret that the notion has prevailed down to the present day.[62] With a few exceptions the reverse was true.[63]

[59] Crèvecœur, *Letters from an American Farmer*, p. 48.

[60] *Vermont Journal*, May 27, 1793.

[61] For Bache following Condorcet, see B. F. Bache to Richard Bache, Jan. 10, 1793, Bache Papers. For Wortman see his *"An Oration on the Influence of Social Institution upon Human Morals and Happiness.* For Duane see Duane, (Jasper Dwight, pseud.), *A Letter to George Washington.*

[62] For cases of Federalist propaganda, see *The Works of Fisher Ames*, ed. by Seth Ames, p. 150; "The Demos in Council," *The Magazine of History*, (extra numbers) XXVII, 464; *Eastern Herald*, Nov. 17, 1794, where Christopher Gore (Manlius) says that the clubs meet at night under the shade of darkness; *Harper's Encyclopedia*, III, 79; Stauffer, *New England and the Bavarian Illuminati*, pp. 271, 309, n., for Federalist charges that the societies were secret and related to the Illuminati. For a more recent statement charging secrecy, see Childs, *French Refugee Life in the United States, 1790–1800*, p. 21.

[63] The societies' requirements for membership differed a little from place to

Tactics of secrecy would have violated the philosophy of general education and enlightenment which they all professed. The societies declared they were open "to all with democratic sentiments." By this, they meant any citizen who shared their point of view was eligible for membership. He could apply and be voted upon at the next regular session of the club. Even though rejected, it did not always preclude his attending as a spectator and taking part in the discussions of current problems.[64] Sometimes townspeople were invited to join in forums sponsored by the societies.[65] The falsehoods spread by those who had little or no faith in the ability of the rank and file to carry on orderly government have tended to obliterate the true nature of these precursors of adult educational programs. No longer may we dismiss them as secret, seditious, "dens of iniquity," which had their little hour of political Bacchanalia before sober Americanism was restored. On the contrary, a careful study

---

place. The standard procedure was to have the support of two or three persons who were already members, to pay a small amount for dues, twenty-five or fifty cents, and to sign the principles as set forth in the constitution. Because of the opposition, some societies were forced to make their membership status more rigid. In Newark the Federalists came to the first meeting of the Republican Society in such numbers as to put through a vote to the effect that such a society was unnecessary and should not organize; (Wood's *Newark Gazette*, March 12, 1794). In New York the self-styled "Friends of Good Order" set about to frustrate a meeting of democrats; see the Federalists' admission of such an attempt in Webb, *Correspondence and Journals of Samuel B. Webb*, pp. 197–98. It is hardly accurate to call the societies secret because they found it necessary to exclude enemies who sought to "bore from within." The Portland Republican Society, in the rough draft of its "Republican Articles," asks that no member reveal transactions that go on within the society. The final draft, however, which the members signed, did not contain this article (Portland Republican Society Papers). Washington's Neutrality Proclamation of 1793 made those societies which were concerned with Genet's projects in the Southwest more secretive about actions related to those plans. When by fiat the President outlawed their plans, they, too, were forced to carry on certain phases of their program secretly.

[64] For the Newark club inviting townsmen to take part in the discussions, see Wood's *Newark Gazette*, Feb. 4, 1795.

[65] Examples of societies stating that their doors are always open and publishing welcomes to spectators, "providing they do not interrupt the society," are to be found in the following: Wood's *Newark Gazette*, March 19, 1794; *Aurora*, April 11, 1795 (Essex County Democratic Society); *American Daily Advertiser*, Jan. 31, 1795 (Democratic Society of Washington, Pa.); *Delaware Gazette*, Aug. 27, 1794 (Patriotic Society of Newcastle); and the same society again, *New Jersey Journal*, Jan. 28, 1795; *Federal Intelligencer*, Jan. 27, 1795 (New York Democratic Society).

of the constitutions and principles of the forty societies reveals their ideal to be a firmly democratic one, germinating in the American Revolution, flowering in the culture of a world democratic sentiment, and sowing the tiny mustard seed for the strong Tree of Liberty.

Before leaving the subject of the social philosophy of the popular societies, there are one or two additional factors which must be presented. In the first place, the student of these clubs is interested in their attitude toward property and property rights. What was true of the popular organizations of Europe, in this regard, is equally true of their American counterparts. The French Jacobins did not attack the idea of private property, but on the contrary consistently defended it. True, they attacked the policy of the rich hoarding land and favored a degree of redistribution which would encourage an agrarian society of small proprietors.[66] In England the distinction was drawn between "equality of wealth and possessions" and "equality of rights." God and Nature, the "Friends of Reform" believed, were opposed to "perpetual equality" because it would destroy "all motives to exertion." Therefore, it was added, America, France, and The Constitutional Society have never advocated it, in spite of charges made by the opposition that the reform movement was made up of Levelers.[67] The Society of United Irishmen wrote:

By liberty we never understood unlimited freedom, nor by equality, the levelling of property or the destruction of subordination.[68]

Federalists and Republicans in America were in agreement on this question of private property. Both followed Montesquieu's

---

[66] Brinton, *The Jacobins: An Essay in the New History*, pp. 160, 169. What Brinton says on page 183 would apply to the American "Jacobins" as well:

"We may say that our mythical 'average' Jacobin would have accepted as a statement of his aims something like this: An independent nation-state, a republican form of government, universal manhood suffrage, separation of church and state; equal civil rights for all, and the abolition of hereditary distinctions and social privileges; a competitive industrial and agricultural society, with private ownership of property, but without great fortunes and without dire poverty; a virtuous, hardworking society, without luxuries and without vices, where the individual freely conforms to standards of middle-class decency."

See also Gottschalk, "Communism during the French Revolution, 1789–1793," *Political Science Quarterly*, XL (1925), 438–50.

[67] *Independent Chronicle*, Feb. 10, 1794.   [68] *Guardian* (N.J.), May 15, 1793.

Spirit of Laws in believing that too much inequality leads to aristocracy and too much equality leads to despotic power.[69] The only difference was that the republicans censured the few rich men, who sought to dominate government and perpetuate monarchical forms.[70] In other words, the schism, as far as property attitudes were concerned, was largely a matter of emphasis. Alexander Smyth, of the Democratic Society of Wytheville, Virginia, said:

> Republican principles do not point out *precisely* the quantum of property a representative may without danger possess, yet I think republicans will agree that the property of a representative ought not to be equal to the property of *one hundred* of his constituents, taken on an average. It is ascertained by experience that a Legislature composed of men of large property, will favor themselves in modes of taxation, by adopting such as do not fall on the citizen in proportion to his property, but in proportion to his consumption of articles necessary to his support and comfort.[71]

Joel Barlow, American democrat and at one time a member of the London Constitutional Society,[72] explained it in this manner:

> It is the *person*, not the property, that exercises the will, and is capable of enjoying happiness; it is therefore the person, for whom government is instituted and by whom its functions are performed.[73]

This statement with regard to property would have met the approval of the great majority of the democratic society leaders. They did not challenge fundamental economic relationships, but rather upheld a wider distribution of private property than the feudalistic systems had permitted.

Nor did the democrats always think of property rights in terms of land ownership. All were not advancing agrarian philosophy, like many of the French thinkers and John Taylor in Virginia. There is significance in the fact that men like Benjamin Franklin and Richard Price heard and criticized the rough draft of Adam Smith's

[69] *Mercury* (Boston), July 25, 1794; also "Americanus" (Timothy Ford), in *City Gazette*, Oct. 24, 1794.
[70] *Ibid.*, Aug. 22, 1793.
[71] Alexander Smyth, *A Letter from Alexander Smyth to Francis Preston.*
[72] W. P. Hall, *op. cit.*, p. 124.
[73] Barlow, *A Letter to the National Convention of France.*

Wealth of Nations.[74] They endorsed its appeal to the spirit of freedom of action not only with regard to land policy, but also with
regard to commerce and "useful manufactures." Likewise Thomas
Paine, as Harry Hayden Clark has indicated, was not a pure agrarian,
for he also believed in banking and manufacturing.[75] Dr. George
Logan, ardent democratic society member of Philadelphia, followed
Smith and Paine in upholding the industrial as well as the land
entrepreneur.[76] In the preceding chapter we cited other illustrations
of popular society members defending the growth of manufacturing. Therefore the issue was not between the propertied and the
propertyless, nor between industrial and farm interests, but rather
it turned upon the question of giving dominant financial power to
"the few," on the one hand, or, on the other, of giving freedom to
"the many" in both business and agriculture. The democratic societies defended the right of the many to private property.

As to the religious theory of the societies, it is not accurate to
make a blanket statement that the clubs were "atheistic" or even
dominantly deistic.[77] Rather, republicanism and equalitarianism appealed to many who were firm bulwarks of one or another of the
various denominations, such as the Scotch-Irish Presbyterians in the
West and the Southwest.[78] These and others were conservatives in
religion and radicals in politics. True, the intellectual leadership of
the clubs was more consistent and, in general, it saw the relationship between superstition in religion and gullibility in political life.
Tunis Wortman, of the New York Democratic Society, expressed
the viewpoint in these words:

Why should we read history without profiting by it? Ambition and
tyranny have always been fond of assuming the masque of religion and
making instruments of judges and divines.[79]

---

[74] Deborah N. Logan, "Biographical Sketches of the Life and Character of Dr.
George Logan," MS in the Logan Papers, Pennsylvania Historical Society.

[75] "Toward a Reinterpretation of Thomas Paine"; also Dorfman, "The Economic Philosophy of Thomas Paine," *Political Science Quarterly*, LIII (1938), 372.

[76] "A Farmer," Logan, *op. cit.*

[77] Ludlum, *Social Ferment in Vermont*, p. 29. Also Riley, *American Philosophy*,
p. 305.

[78] Morais, *Deism in Eighteenth Century America*, p. 22.

[79] Timoleon [Tunis Wortman], *A Solemn Address to Christians and Patriots.*

Superstition in religious creeds, and Despotism in civil institutions, bear a relation to each other. . . . The same principle which supports the one, tends to strengthen and invigorate the other.[80]

Elihu Palmer attacked supernaturalism in his *Principles of Nature* and also joined the Democratic Society of New York. But all the society members by no means went along with their deist colleagues such as Palmer, David Denniston, and John Sidell, when these formed a Deistical Society.[81] The same was true in Philadelphia, where certain democratic society members favored and others opposed the formation of a deistical club.[82]

Because the temper of the times was not conducive to otherworldliness in religion and because men were concerned with the here and now, with their new scientific outlook, and with the possibilities of building a better world, the religious conservatives bemoaned departures from customary ways and felt as did the old lady in Vermont when she wrote in 1796:

Thair seams to Be no fear of God or but very littel, in the place Religion is much oute of fashion. Sabbath Days are visiting or working Days with the biggest part of the peopel.[83]

Charles Nisbet, Pennsylvania conservative, could not understand the disrespect toward religion in America, and he was horrified that ministers had to work with their hands because subscriptions from their congregations would not support them.[84] Others were even more horrified to read in the newspaper that a £25 reward was offered for information concerning the "bedaubing" of the Rev. Mr. Krug's house with "the most filthy excrement." [85] A visitor to Ken-

---

[80] Democratic Society of New York, *Circular*, copy in the New York Historical Society. Internal evidence would indicate that this circular was probably written by Wortman.

[81] Wood, *A Full Exposition of the Clintonian Faction;* Morais, *op. cit.,* p. 131. Dr. Phineas Hedges was a devoted deist. See also Koch, *Republican Religion,* p. 122.

[82] Morais, *op. cit.,* p. 132.

[83] Anna H. Weeks to Holland Weeks, Oct. 20, 1796, Sheldon Museum, Middlebury, Vt.

[84] Nisbet to Charles Wallace, Sept. 21, 1790, Nisbet Letters, New York Public Library.

[85] *Maryland Gazette and Frederick-Town Weekly Advertiser,* Aug. 8, 1793.

tucky in 1795 wrote in his journal that among the denominations
in that country the strongest were "the Deists, nothingarians, and
anythingarians." [86]

Readers of Voltaire, Godwin, and Condorcet, and devotees of
Palmer and Paine in this country were not atheists and antireligious.
Instead they were anticlerical and saw no reason for sanctifying the
clergy or allowing the church to return to its control over political
and social life.[87] Such being the case, the members of the democratic societies could oppose clerical power and credalism and still
remain loyal to the more democratic denominations. Presbyterians
in Pendleton, South Carolina, called the officers of their Franklin
Society "moderator" and "vice-moderator." [88] Popular societies in
Vermont habitually attended church in a body on the Fourth of
July to hear a "patriotic sermon." [89] And every year the Democratic Society of New York joined with the Mechanic and Cooper
Societies in celebrating American Independence by a parade and a
service in one of the churches in the city.[90]

We could go on to mention individual members of the societies,
like John Swanwick, of Philadelphia, who gave a generous dona-
tion to the rebuilding of the German Lutheran Church,[91] where the
German Republican Society often met; or like Israel Israel, who
helped Elihu Palmer financially but would not permit him to join
his church—the Universalist Church—because Palmer "did not be-

[86] The Rev. David Barrows, "Journal," p. 181, Wisconsin Historical Society.

[87] *Kentucky Gazette*, for example, carried many poems and anecdotes which
ridiculed creeds and a sanctimonious clergy, but it did not print atheistic materials;
see, viz., the issue for Sept. 26, 1798. Elihu Palmer, in his Fourth of July Oration,
for July 4, 1793, said, "Indeed, had it not been that the clergy gained complete
ascendancy over the minds of men, the civil oppressions of the world would long
since have tumbled into ruin. But living on the spoils of the people, it was easy for
these imposters to preach up the beauty and excellency of humiliating poverty that
they themselves might riot on the luxuries of the earth." H. H. Brackenridge,
Political Miscellany, p. 24. Cf. Koch, *op. cit.*, p. 78.

[88] *City Gazette*, Oct. 28, 1795.

[89] *Rutland Herald*, July 13, 1795.

[90] *New York Journal*, July 1, 1796. One of these delivered by John M'Knight
on the Fourth of July, 1794, was especially pious in spirit. M'Knight declared
that God was the author of promotion—that this world was transitory and that
we would all enter the ocean of eternity, where the most obscure might aspire and
reach permanent promotion. *God the Author of Promotion*.

[91] Callender, *American Annual Register*, p. 42.

lieve in the divinity of Christ";[92] or Robert Patterson, who was instrumental in organizing the first Presbyterian Church in Lexington, Kentucky;[93] or Joel Linsley, of Cornwall, Vermont, who agreed with his friend Thomas Tolman in politics, but not in deism.[94] All these men favored separation of church and state, but they were not infidels. Freedom of action in religion, as well as in government, expresses the social ideas of the democrats toward the church.

Finally it is worthy of attention that the popular clubs of the last decade of the eighteenth century were sounding the first notes of the cacophonic American two-party system. As we have mentioned before, it was the hope of the followers of Locke and even Rousseau that popular government would be relatively calm and peaceful. "Faction" was an odious word to both Federalist and republican. To them, it smacked of "ambitious innovation"; the attempt of a minority to subvert the will of the people. As early as 1784 patriots such as John Breckinridge, James Madison, John Taylor, and James Monroe had formed a society called "The Society for the Preservation of Liberty," the principal object of which was to prevent the rise of faction in America.[95] Ten years later these republicans held the same idea. So also did the Federalists, and each accused the other of being the factious party. Said a Federalist,

In these United States where the people form one Republican society all constituted associations for promoting political views are useless, at least, if not dangerous, and should be discouraged.[96]

In other words, the prevailing conception was that two right political parties were impossible, for one was either the "friend to order" or

[92] E. Hazard to Jedidiah Morse, Philadelphia, April 20, 1795, Morse Family Collection, Yale University Library.

[93] Conover, *Concerning the Forefathers*, p. 265; Patterson Manuscripts, III, 44. Draper Collection.

[94] Smith, *Addison County, Vermont*, p. 436; Thompson, *History of Vermont*. William Boyd, society member from New York, was active in the New York Society for Promoting Christian Knowledge and Piety. Its object was to assist missionaries and to buy Bibles and distribute them among the poor on the frontier. See *The Constitution of the New York Society for Promoting Christian Knowledge and Piety*.

[95] *The American Historical Review*, XXXII, 550–52.

[96] *Baltimore Daily Advertiser*, March 31, 1794.

its foe. The Committees of Safety and Correspondence, argued the Rev. David Tappan, were satisfactory in a day when all America was combined in overthrowing tyranny; but, when a free government of the people's choice had once been established, such associations were needless and dangerous.[97] William Willcocks, mouthpiece of Hamilton, insisted with true Lockean logic that "the representatives are the people." [98] Once they were chosen, orderly government must follow.

Equally adamant for destroying party dissension were some of the leading democrats. Dr. George Logan wrote:

If men of every party would endeavor to understand the principles of genuine liberty and the just rights of our country, it would dissolve the spirit of party, heal our divisions and unite us all in one common cause —the promoting the prosperity and happiness of ye United States.[99]

As democrats and their societies saw it, the national government had been captured by a faction that did not believe in "genuine liberty." There could be no calm until the Sons of Liberty were restored to power.

The significant thing that came out of this impasse, with both sides demanding order and both deprecating the "spirit of party," was the first recognition that party alignments were valid. The popular societies of Philadelphia led in this, when they decided in 1794, that

Whether they be town or township meetings called to echo the preeminent virtues of administration, or whether they are associations of another kind, that approve or condemn as their judgment directs, *they are alike legal.*[100]

Followers of Locke, Montesquieu, and Rousseau all believed with their teachers that unity and freedom from party strife could be gained in a republican government. Some expected order after the adoption of the Constitution, others after the election of Washington. "The idea of the legitimacy of parties in a democracy was not

---

[97] *Christian Thankfulness Explained and Enforced.*
[98] *Catskill Packet,* Sept. 3, 1793.
[99] Logan Papers (Misc. MSS), Pennsylvania Historical Society.
[100] *Philadelphia Gazette,* Dec. 29, 1796. Italics ours.

then familiar to most Americans." [101] But the coveted calm did not appear. Men began to reconcile themselves to the "tempestuous sea of liberty" and the democratic societies were the first to recognize the validity of this long American tradition.

But of all the pioneering virtues of the popular organizations mentioned in this chapter, one stands forth as the basis of all the others. It is this: The recognition that men are men when they are masters of their own destinies. The societies sought to translate the classical doctrine of Rousseau's popular sovereignty into actual political life. New media of communication were imperative, to gain wider public participation. Through interrelated town meetings and associated committees of correspondence, the clubs hoped to make the general will realistic and active. This they accomplished to a large degree. Their sociopolitical organization was, then, their major contribution to eighteenth-century democratic thinking. The direction of democratic progress indicated by the societies was in line with the ceaseless creating and recreating of institutions to enable an ever-widening participation of the citizenry in public policy-making. This was their faith and this their immortality for all devotees of democracy.

[101] Faÿ, *Early Party Machinery*. Cf. Robinson, *op. cit.*, p. 53.

Chapter Six

THE PROGRAM AND ACTIVITIES
OF THE CLUBS

Laziness in politics is like laziness in agriculture; it exposes the soil to noxious weeds.
JOHN MILLER, Secretary of the Franklin Society, Pendleton, South Carolina

---

IN ONE WAY or another the popular societies were involved in every important issue in post-Revolutionary America. Any attempt to present an orderly picture of their numerous activities seems at first to be completely bewildering. Their membership, with men of opposite economic interest, their geographical location, with the attendant section issues, and their philosophy, with its appeal to a conservative and a revolutionary John Locke, creates a first impression of impossible gallimaufry. Nevertheless, the student can trace certain main threads running through their activities, east, west, north, and south. Neither the individual actions of a club, nor the distinct characteristics of a group of the clubs will be omitted. In all cases, an attempt will be made to delineate the activities of the popular societies and to give sufficient background for the reader to appreciate these activities.

As previously stated, the democrats were in sympathy with the French Revolution. In fact, the quality of one's republicanism was tested by one's attitude toward France and toward its ambassador, Genet. These touchstones were used to judge the sincerity of American democrats.[1] Caesar A. Rodney, of the Delaware Patriotic So-

---

[1] "Alcohol," writing in the *Columbian Mirror and Alexandria Gazette*, Oct. 5, 1793, gives seven tests for a true republican (alcohol) as against tainted monarchists (one, two, or three-proof "low wine"). Note in his tests that three of the

ciety, expressed the typical opinion of democrats when he said Britain warred with France because English rulers opposed the principles of liberty and that if England succeeded she would turn upon America, the "country that gave birth to the French Revolution." [2] The members of the Republican Society of Charleston made their case even more explicit when they declared,

If the present eventful European contest should terminate in the dissolution of the French Republic, we have no doubt but that the craving appetite of despotism will be satisfied with nothing less than American vassalage, in some form or other. The interest of absolute power requires that the voice of liberty should be heard no more, and in the event of the overthrow of the French Republic, the United States, then without an ally, may be forced to yield to European confederacy. And in as much as an aristocratic ambition has already manifested itself in the conduct, even of some Americans, and has lately been more strongly marked by its whispers of dissatisfaction to the cause of France, and of mankind, we do therefore intend our signatures to be an avowal of different political sentiments. And we do hereby declare, pledging ourselves to each other, and to the world, that we and each of us, will contribute to the utmost of our ability towards the support of equal liberty and national justice, as well in respect to the French Republic, as of the United States against tyranny and iniquitous rule, in whatever form they may be presented by any character or body of men, appearing in these United States. [3]

seven refer to France: (1) Was I more concerned for the death of Louis than I should have been for that of any other person, not inferior to him in moral qualities? (2) When I call myself a Friend of Liberty do I limit the idea of it to myself and my friends, whom I think entitled to a greater proportion of it than the people at large? In short, do I not consider the doctrine of equal liberty and equal rights as preposterous and subversive of those distinctions in society without which no government can exist? (3) Should I not be vexed to see, in a competition for a place of honor or profit, a man of *no family* preferred to one well born? (4) Am I not influenced in my estimation of a man by the amount of money he possesses, giving respect because of wealth? (5) Am I secretly pleased at the alleged misconduct of Genet? Do I exaggerate any indiscretions of which he may have been guilty? (6) Do I dwell more on the excesses of France, rather than affirm their basic principles? (7) Do I shun virtue in rags? Do I pay court to a knave in embroidery?

[2] MS address by Rodney, July 12, 1797, Rodney Papers in the Delaware Historical Society.

[3] *Baltimore Daily Repository*, Sept. 18, 1793; also "Correspondence of the Republican Society of Charleston," Item 11.

Every popular society wrote into its constitution a clause similar to that of the Charleston body—a clause upholding France and its Revolution.

The democrats had great disappointment in store for them. On the basis of the enthusiastic reception of Edmund Charles Genet, they anticipated the full coöperation of the American government.[4] Washington, however, and even Jefferson stood aloof. Despite the fact that France, in February, 1793, opened all her colonial ports to America, and in May of the same year removed all restrictions on American vessels, the Federalist administration was adamant.[5] It was expected that Hamilton would do everything in his power to prevent aid to France. One could hardly have supposed, however, that Jefferson would have advised Washington against advancing payments on our debt to France, thereby preventing Genet from purchasing indispensable supplies in this country.[6] Yet that is what happened. Genet and his consuls reminded the administration in America of the fact that France had supported the American Revolution and that the treaty of 1778 accorded the French certain privileges in our ports, which they now needed and expected.[7] Repeated protests from the consuls and the Francophiles,

---

[4] The mixed motives in the affection between French and American democrats should always be kept in mind. The following extract from a letter written by John Stewart of Richmond, Va., to Genet, May 10, 1793 (Genet Papers), is an excellent example: "In the existing commotions of Europe, when the nation you here represent is conflicting with tyrants leagued for the subversion of its liberty and government, opportunities for enterprise peculiar to the junction are discernible; opportunities which combine the most powerful springs of action, by uniting to exertion in the Cause of Freedom, the prospect of accumulating wealth."

[5] French Legation Letters, Department of State, Feb. and May, 1793, in the National Archives. Washington admitted in his message to Congress in 1793 that France had favored our trade, while England had preyed upon it. See *A Message of the President of the United States.*

[6] Misc. Letters, Department of State, June 6, 1793, in the National Archives. Jefferson asked, in this letter, that his opinion on the matter be kept secret. It was at this time that Aedanus Burke, of South Carolina, dubbed Jefferson "that half-way democrat."

[7] Hauterive to the governor of New York, June 9, 1793, Letters from State Governors, Department of State, National Archives; Justin Winsor (*Narrative and Critical History*, VII, 463) says that the United States, by the treaty of 1778, did extend special favors to France, among them being the right to receive its prizes in American ports, the right to forbid privateers of the enemies of France

addressed to Washington and Jefferson, did little good, and the Federalists continued to hamper direct aid to France in every possible way.[8] The popular societies took up the cause of Genet and France, to attack England and the monarchical powers of Europe and, indirectly, the Washington administration at home.

In upholding the Franco-American alliance of 1778 and in befriending Genet, who based his actions upon the rights granted to France in that treaty, the societies from Maine to Georgia, one after another, published resolutions insisting that America remain true to its treaty agreements.[9] As the Republican Humain [sic] Society of Portland wrote,

That treaties solemnly made with nations who act with sincere friendship and preserve zealously their faith towards us, ought to be inviolably adhered to and guarded from infractions at every risk; that the cause of France is our own, that our Interest, Liberty and public happiness are involved in her fate, that we are bound to support her by every type of principle and gratitude as well as principle of self preservation. That for any man or set of men either in private or public, and particularly those to whom the welfare of our community are intrusted to advocate doctrines and principles derogatory to the cause of France or her commerce with America, or in support of the base measures of the combined despots of Europe, particularly that Piratical Nest of British is a convincing manifestation of sentiments treacherous and hostile to the interest of the United States and well deserves the severest censure from all true Republican Citizens of America.[10]

The Rutland, Vermont, society opposed any disregard of the treaty duties with France; [11] and Boston reminded the American patriots

from fitting out in our ports, and the right of French consuls to claim a jurisdiction regarding their prizes.

[8] Genet objected to the heavy tonnage duties which were levied upon French ships. He said this was not in accord with the sentiments of the American people for friendly coöperation with France. See Hauterive to Genet, July [?], 1793, and Genet to Jefferson, Oct. 29, 1793, in Genet Papers. The consuls also disapproved, as a violation of treaty agreement, of local courts taking under jurisdiction the question of legal prizes. See Genet to Jefferson, June 25, 1793, Genet Papers.

[9] Genet to Jefferson, May 28, 1793, Genet Papers.

[10] Portland Republican Society Papers, in the Maine Historical Society.

[11] Farmer's Library, May 27, 1794.

of the aid France had given to them in their hour of distress.[12] The societies in Philadelphia repeatedly toasted "the alliance between the sister republics," and the New York democrats, as late as 1797, invited Genet to attend the feast to celebrate the anniversary of the famous alliance.[13]

So dominant was this note of resolute adherence to a treaty that many of the popular clubs openly advocated war in behalf of their ally. The Republican Society of Portland, Maine, in 1794 asked each member to equip himself with arms and ammunition "agreeable to the laws of the United States, and be prepared to defend the Rights of Man." [14] The Committee of Correspondence of Fayetteville, North Carolina, resigned itself to war, even though it preferred peace.[15] Charleston and Pinckneyville, South Carolina, prepared themselves for what they deemed the inevitable, for although "war is a calamity," it was better than "dishonourable submission." [16]

Therefore, one may well imagine how the societies felt toward Washington's Proclamation of Neutrality. Though some hesitated to criticize the President, others spoke out in "painful necessity" to the effect that "only a Washington surrounded with popular favor would so violate Republican government." [17] The societies were not alone in their criticism of Washington, for both Madison and Jefferson joined them.[18] And even the Federalist, Rufus King, recognized that Washington's Proclamation was without precedent. But, he added, although America cannot avoid its treaties, it can,

---

[12] *Boston Gazette*, Jan. 20, 1794.

[13] *American Daily Advertiser*, May 5, 1794; *City Gazette*, March 6, 1794, and Feb. 6, 1795; the Genet Papers, Feb. 4, 1797.

[14] Portland Republican Society Papers. It is to be noted in passing that the decision to arm never appeared in the published resolutions of the society. It is another illustration of the difference between what the societies actually did and their printed addresses and resolutions.

[15] Affaires Étrangères, Vol. XL, Part 6, April 18, 1794.

[16] *City Gazette*, March 17, 1794; *South Carolina State Gazette*, April 29, 1794.

[17] *American Daily Advertiser*, July 29, 1794. Here the Washington Democratic Society says the proclamation sounds like a decision made by Congress, but Congress was overlooked. In the *City Gazette*, March 17, 1794, the Charleston club points out that proclamations are for the purpose of informing people of the laws already enacted. This proclamation, it adds, is a person's own will and is therefore unconstitutional and despotic.

[18] *The Writings of James Madison*, ed. by Hunt, VI, 131; Jefferson, *Writings*, ed. by Ford, VI, 259.

with due caution, avert its commitments.[19] The Neutrality Proclamation, originated by Hamilton and advanced by Washington, was hailed by many of the large and prosperous commercial interests of the day. The chambers of commerce were flattered over the recognition their organizations had received from the Federal government.[20] The democratic interests began to talk of the importance of a thoroughgoing change of men and measures in the central government. In the interim, the societies, especially those of Kentucky and Vermont, as will be seen later in this chapter, adopted the position of "neutrality," which called for all aid to France short of war.

The fire of criticism leveled at George Washington became more intense when the popular clubs heard of the appointment of John Jay as special envoy to Great Britain. Jay, to the democratic-minded, was an aristocrat, who had a score of unpopular counts against him.[21] For Washington to elevate him to the position of special negotiator with the country's greatest enemy, at the same time that the President refused to consider a treaty with France, because Congress was not in session, seemed strange indeed. Furthermore, as Caesar A. Rodney, of Wilmington, indicated, Washington's act was unconstitutional, for he had violated the separation of powers by appointing the Chief Justice as an ambassador. One man was holding two offices and merging the executive and judicial functions! [22] Enlarging upon the dangerous implications of such an appointment,

[19] Charles King, *The Life and Correspondence of Rufus King*, ed. by Charles King, I, 439.

[20] See the address of the merchants and traders of Baltimore in the *Federal Gazette*, June 5, 1793; Hamilton, *Works*, ed. by Lodge, IV, 272. Cf. Bowers, *Hamilton and Jefferson*, p. 140, where the author says "The various Chambers of Commerce were Federalist Clubs that could be summoned to action on a day's notice."

[21] A number of these are mentioned in a broadside entitled "Plain Facts" (New York, 1798) in the Harvard Library. The following words from Jay, uttered at the New York Constitutional Convention, are pertinent here: "Why suffer the people of Europe to mingle with you? What can they bring you but vicious habits, depraved morals, and corrupt politics? What can you receive from Ireland but Roman Catholics? What from Scotland but Presbyterians? What from England but the dregs of workhouses, and the scourings of prisons?" The democratic societies also reminded the people that Jay had defended the right of England to hold the western posts; *Philadelphia Gazette*, Nov. 29, 1794.

[22] Rodney to Joseph Miller, June 26, 1795, Rodney Papers in the Delaware Historical Society.

the Pennsylvania Democratic Society said that the judiciary cannot fairly judge treaties if it has had a part in making them; that for the president to bestow offices of honor and profit upon a judicial officer tends to make judges subservient and biased; and that in case of impeachment of the Executive, the Chief Justice would be prejudiced, and the court would no longer be the "inflexible guardian of the constitution and laws." [23] All the other societies debated and passed resolutions condemning the appointment. The Madison Society, of Greenville, South Carolina, felt that the offices of government should be divided among citizens according to ability and that for a few to monopolize the important offices was a "dangerous thrust of power." [24] The Washington, Pennsylvania, club wrote this democratic opinion:

The Revolution in France has sufficiently proved that generals may be taken from the ranks, and ministers of state from the obscurity of the most remote village. Is there not fire still remaining in the rock, and billows in the oceans?

Therefore, the society concluded, Washington was centralizing the government in the hands of a few individuals. This was aristocracy.[25] Among others, the Prince William County Society, meeting at Dumfries, Virginia, reëmphasized the words of the "mother" society concerning the fact that a chief justice presides at impeachment of the president.[26]

When the bold democrat, George Mason, read the Jay Treaty, he violated the efforts of the administration to keep it secret by sending it to Benjamin Bache, who at once gave it publication. The fat was in the fire, and from one end of the country to the other emotions were enflamed and protestations heard. Bache, while visiting in Boston, wrote his wife of the orderly, serious meeting of protest which was held there and persided over by Dr. Jarvis. One thousand, five hundred people heard the treaty read and explained, and the gathering opposed it unanimously. Bache was impressed by Jarvis's fairness and his patience in getting every one to understand

[23] *City Gazette*, May 28, 1794.   [24] *American Daily Advertiser*, Sept. 4, 1794.
[25] *Ibid.*, July 29, 1794.   [26] Innes Papers, Vol. XIX, No. 124.

exactly what he was voting for or against. He hoped that Philadelphia might have such a meeting.[27] And Philadelphia did, with "that ignorant, turbulent blockhead and president of the Democratic Society, Blair McClenachan," leading out.[28] John Beckley, however, describes the meeting as dignified and orderly and attended by about 5,000 citizens. In this letter he urges his correspondent, De Witt Clinton, to keep all the republicans in line against the treaty, and to coöperate in all things *pro bono publico*.[29] Evidently Clinton did his bit, for George Clinton, Jr., of the Ulster County Republican Society, wrote that public action was imminent against the Jay Treaty in his county. Petitions were to be circulated and articles for the press were to appear.[30]

The South as well as the North was not quiescent about accepting Jay's negotiations. John Miller, at Pendleton, South Carolina, called the treaty "Washington's Treaty," before the Franklin Society. It was read to that society and to the militia companies of the district. All spurned it as an machination to enslave America. Long

[27] July 15, 1795, Bache Papers.
[28] Timothy Pickering to Stephen Higginson, July 27, 1795, Pickering Papers, Vol. VI in the Massachusetts Historical Society. The Philadelphia Society voted to republish the resolutions made against the appointment of Jay; *American Daily Advertiser*, July 21, 1795.
[29] Beckley to D. Clinton, July 24, 1795, and April 11, 21, 1796, in Clinton Papers, Columbia University Library. Beckley, a loyal agent of Jefferson, was virtually the chairman of the Democratic-Republican National Committee of his day. His widely scattered letters, full of political wisdom, are addressed to Madison, Monroe, Jefferson, Clinton, *et al.* From his post as clerk of the House in Philadelphia, he kept Jefferson and his colleagues carefully informed on all political details. Jefferson, without a doubt and even though he claimed to be retiring from politics, kept his fingers on the pulse of America after he left Washington's cabinet. He caught the trend of events from his own wide correspondence and from the invaluable information from Beckley. Typical of Beckley's fascinating and important letters is one addressed to Monroe, Dec. 14, 1795, in the Monroe Papers, New York Public Library. Here he introduces to Monroe, who is in Paris, "my friend James Smith," whom he hopes the ambassador can help. Secret code in this same letter reveals that "James Smith" is none other than Theobald Wolfe Tone, the leader of the United Irishmen, who wishes to talk with Monroe about sending a French expedition to aid in Irish freedom. Hamilton Rowan was also in America at this time and appeared before the Philadelphia Democratic Society on July 27, 1795. Wm. T. W. Tone, *Memoirs of Theobald Wolfe Tone*, p. 197; *Courier of New Hampshire*, Aug. 8, 1795.
[30] George Clinton, Jr. to D. Clinton, Oct. 19, 1795, Clinton Papers.

and heated resolutions were passed against it by the Franklin Club and, although the members decided not to take time to burn Jay in effigy, they added, "if the original were here—!" [31] The Kentuckians had ceased calling their popular meetings by the name Democratic Society, but they were none the less alert.[32] Meetings in both Scott and Fayette Counties deprecated the treaty, and assigned it to the same place that the remonstrances on the navigation of the Mississippi River had evidently gone.[33]

During these lively debates on the treaty, the first toasts favoring Jefferson as the national leader began to appear. One read,

May the patriots of '76 step forward with Jefferson their head and cleanse the country of degeneracy and corruption.[34]

The Canaan, New York, society blasted at the "British Treaty" and added that Jefferson, for "he is incorruptible," warned them to preserve their Revolutionary heritage.[35] Jefferson let it be known that he thought the Jay Treaty "an execrable thing." [36] By July, 1796, some were saying that Washington would have real difficulty being elected for a third term, should he be choose to run. Kentucky, for one state, was now supporting Jefferson.[37] Had the Federalists stopped to listen then, they could have heard the faint toll of their death knell.

Another phase of the activities of the democratic societies was their involvement in certain border projects which coincided with French interests of the time. Just as there were popular societies existing before the arrival of Genet, so also before his coming there were certain projects on foot in the West which encroached upon the terri-

[31] *City Gazette,* Oct. 28, 1795; *South Carolina State Gazette,* Nov. 26, 1795.

[32] John Bradford testified in 1808 that the people of Kentucky were afraid, in the summer of 1794, that the government would send troops among them. Leaders urged the people to take care, lest the Executive would be upon them as he was in Western Pennsylvania; Innes Papers, Oct. 30, 1808, Vol. XIX, No. 220.

[33] "Diary of Samuel Shepard" (1787–1796), in the Massachusetts Historical Society. See entry for Aug. 25, 1795. Also *City Gazette,* Oct. 19, 1795.

[34] Breckinridge Papers, Vol. XII, No. 2071.

[35] *New York Journal,* Oct. 14, 1795.

[36] Jefferson, *Writings,* ed. by Ford, VII, 40.

[37] H. Taylor to Madison, July 18, 1796, Madison Papers, Vol. XIX, No. 7.

tory of neighbors. These have usually been called "Genet projects," [38] but they long antedate the footfall of the republican ambassador at Charleston. They might better be regarded as projects of land-hungry citizens, frontiersmen, and avaricious American traders who resented Spanish and English trade monopolies with the Indians.

Six years before the arrival of Genet, the Political Club of Danville, Kentucky, framed a circular letter demanding the right to navigation down the Mississippi.[39] In 1779, eight years before the Kentuckians became active, the inhabitants of Louisiana made secret overtures to the French and to the Americans, asking for the restoration of the province to France.[40] Alexander Smyth, president of the Wytheville, Virginia, Democratic Society, admitted a plan to invade the Spanish country in 1787 and set up a "Republican colony." [41] In 1791 La Fayette advised the United States to wrest the Mississippi territory from Spain and to wait no longer for negotiations.[42]

Of course Genet knew before he left France of this widespread sentiment for expanding American borders. He heard of it from the lips of Joel Barlow and Thomas Paine.[43] Paine was a close friend of Dr. James O'Fallon, George Rogers Clark's brother-in-law. O'Fallon had asked Paine to present Clark's plans against the Spanish country to the French Executive Council. On February 17, 1793, Paine wrote O'Fallon that he had presented the matter to the Provisional Executive Council and that, if Spain joined the war against France, Clark could be sure of France complying with his wishes.[44] In this same letter Paine added that Genet, "my sincere friend," was coming to America and that he knew all about O'Fal-

[38] See for example, "The Mangourit Correspondence in Respect to Genet's Projected Attack upon the Floridas, 1793–1794," ed. by Turner, *American Historical Association, Annual Report,* 1897, Introduction.

[39] Brown, *Political Beginnings of Kentucky,* pp. 79–80.

[40] Lyon, *Louisiana in French Diplomacy, 1759–1804,* pp. 66–67.

[41] Smyth, *The Third and Last Letter from Alexander Smyth to Francis Preston,* p. 32.

[42] Bemis, *Pinckney's Treaty,* p. 176.

[43] Lyon, *op. cit.,* p. 71. This author says Barlow was active in France in the plans to attack Louisiana.

[44] Clark Manuscripts, Vol. XII, p. 60; Vol. XXXIV, pp. 75–76, in the Draper Collection, Wisconsin Historical Society.

lon and Clark. "This is the great hour for Liberty, doctor," said Paine in his closing sentence.

It would appear that the so-called "Genet Projects" were really initiated by Americans, who turned to France for aid. French and American economic interests coincided sufficiently in the New World so that the aid was forthcoming. Consequently, a more accurate appellation might be "Gallo-American projects." The democratic-republican clubs figure prominently in the three main projects— the Carolinians' plan to attack the Floridas, the Kentuckians' plan to gain an outlet down the Mississippi, and the Vermonters' designs upon Canada, with the St. Lawrence River as the prize. A brief résumé of the activities of the clubs with regard to these various plots follows.

Whether or not the specific details to march against the neighboring provinces were worked out by the popular societies is conjectural.[45] In all cases, however, the societies seemed to be lending their support to a preconceived plan, by supplying leadership, provisions, and organized encouragement. The two moving spirits, cooperating with the French consuls in the plot upon the Floridas, were Stephen Drayton, president of the Charleston Republican Society, and William Tate, secretary. Drayton, whose extant correspondence indicates him to be an honorable, conscientious man, resigned from his state office to assist in the Florida project. He firmly believed that he was aiding the cause of universal liberty, in which all America should join.[46] The Tates maneuvered in the hinterlands of the Carolinas, William at Pendleton and Robert at Pinckneyville.[47] These and others were supplied with commissions in the French army by Genet, and they went through the countryside

[45] The plans for the Florida project were matured at the French consulate in Charleston, where Mangourit presided. See "The Mangourit Correspondence," p. 631.

[46] Drayton to Genet, Dec. 9, 1793, Genet Papers; and Drayton to Mangourit, Feb. 15, 1794, in Correspondence of the Republican Society of Charleston, Boston Public Library. Link, "The Democratic Societies of the Carolinas," *North Carolina Historical Review*, XVIII (1941), 259.

[47] Misc. Letters, Department of State, Dec. 6, 1793, National Archives. The pay offered to the recruits was twenty-five cents a day for the privates, and a division of the land spoils. The recruiting extended up as far as Fayetteville, N.C.; see Hugh Williamson to Randolph, Jan. 20, 1794, Misc. Letters, Department of State.

recruiting a "Republican Army" to carry out their filibuster.[48] Although the Charleston Republican Society made solemn promises to aid the venture, it actually gave little support. The shipowners and captains of privateers in the society saw in the undertaking a chance to use the seaports of a "free" eastern Florida for lucrative prize-selling. Drayton, Mangourit, and C. F. Bert, the Savannah French consul, expected the society to furnish a ship for a sea attack on St. Augustine, while the forces recruited by Tate moved southward on land.[49] According to Mangourit, only a few society members showed a vital interest in a project that did not guarantee a money reward, and the ship never materialized.

When Drayton, Tate, John Hamilton, and other democrats were arrested and hailed before the state legislature of South Carolina for their recruiting activities, the popular societies spoke out in their defense. The defense argument was, in the first place, that these men had violated no existing law. A citizen, according to a widely prevalent conception of the time, was a free agent, who had the full right to expatriate himself and to join the forces of another nation, especially if that nation were a liberty-loving one, like France.[50]

[48] Turner, "The Policy of France toward the Mississippi Valley," *The American Historical Review*, X (1905), 31. A copy of Tate's commission to serve in the Republican Army may be found in Affaires Étrangères, Supplement, Vol. V; also, *American State Papers* (Washington, 1832), Class I, I, 310–11.

[49] "The Mangourit Correspondence," pp. 664–65. Also Bert to Mangourit, Dec. 13, 1793; Hammond to Mangourit (n.d.), in the Boston Public Library. "Correspondence of the Republican Society of Charleston." A part of these letters are in code and employ the use of secret signs.

[50] In the letter of John Stewart to Genet (*op. cit.*), the following paragraph is pertinent to contemporary attitudes on expatriation: "It is time to supersede the prejudices and errors of local jurisprudence when they militate the diminution of Natural Right, and the prolongation of slavery and oppression. Liberty is the gift of God to mankind and wheresoever a violation is attempted, it is the bounden duty of man, as a Citizen of the World, and a member of the Society of Man, to resist it. The universality of its importance is not to be estimated by the example of past ages nor the number of its advocates to be restricted by the dogmas of municiple regulations." Charles Pinckney and James Monroe wrote in the same vein; the first in his *On the Right of Expatriation*, the second to Jefferson in *The Writings of James Monroe*, ed. by S. M. Hamilton, I, 263. The Palmetto Society of Charleston in 1794 among other democratic toasts lifted the cup to "The right of expatriation to all those who wish to quit our country," *City Gazette*, June 30, 1794.

"Man is born free," wrote the Franklin Society of Pendleton, South Carolina, and "may remove out of the limits of these United States" at will.[51] In the second place, both the Pendleton and Charleston Societies condemned the state legislature for acting illegally and exceeding its legislative powers by assuming executive and judicial powers.[52] The popular societies must have been in the right, for Drayton, Tate, Alexander Moultrie, and their colleagues admitted that they had recruited, but they were never convicted of crime.

As in the Carolinas, so in Kentucky the plots were fostered by prominent Americans who were determined to act and to defy the unresponsive Federalists. If the plans of the westerners and their French collaborators had matured—that is, the sea attack upon the Florida ports, the march under the leadership of William Tate into Spanish country, and George Rogers Clark's movement down the Mississippi—the efforts were to have been coördinated, and the invading forces would have met in the lower Mississippi country.[53] Both Governor Moultrie and Governor Shelby knew of the intentions of their friends and either favored them or at least refused to discourage invasion attempts.[54] Clark's old Revolutionary friends in his famous Illinois regiment volunteered to join him and to bring others. Two of these "influential old Buffalo Hunters" were John Montgomery and Benjamin Logan, both members of democratic societies and both willing to accept French commissions bearing the slogan "To break the chains of an oppressed people."[55] There were the Todds, all of whom, like the Tates in South Carolina, were involved in the projected attack. Robert, Levi, and

---

[51] *Ibid.*

[52] *Ibid.*, June 25, 1794. For actions of the South Carolina legislature, see "The Journals of the Senate of South Carolina," Dec. 7, 1793, in the Historical Commission Library, Columbia, S.C.

[53] "The Mangourit Correspondence," pp. 677–78.

[54] *American Historical Association, Report,* 1896, pp. 952, 1010, 1018, 1023; Shelby to Jefferson, Jan. 13, 1794, Letters from State Governors (1790–1812), Department of State, National Archives. Here Governor Shelby states that he knows of no law to prohibit citizens expatriating themselves and joining the French army.

[55] J. Brown to [?], Feb. 26, 1794, Misc. Letters, Department of State, National Archives.

Thomas Todd were active in the Lexington Democratic Society.[56]

French agents were active also. Genet was represented by Andre Michaux, the botanist, who came to Kentucky with a letter of introduction from Jefferson to Governor Shelby, and from James Brown, the Kentucky senator, to George Rogers Clark and to "some merchants of Lexington." [57] Michaux informed Clark that Genet would support his expedition and would send commissions for those who wished to serve in "The Revolutionary and Independent Legion of the Mississippi." [58] However, the French agents, Lachaise and De Pauw, came into closer contact with the Kentucky popular societies. De Pauw helped to circulate a broadside which was written by Genet and called upon the French in Louisiana to rise and overthrow the Spanish despots, promising them the aid of their free neighbors.[59] He asked John Bradford, Secretary of the Democratic Society, to insert this broadside in his *Kentucky Gazette*. Bradford agreed, but insisted on deleting a sentence which read "That the Republicans of the Western Country are ready [?] the Ohio and Mississippi" because it would stir the opposition of the government.[60] Lachaise went even further in embroiling the western democrats by suggesting to the Democratic Society that it align itself with the National Convention of France, but the society firmly rejected this offer, stating that it would remain a part of the American Union. The letter rejecting the suggestion of Lachaise did, however, speak in enthusiastic praise of the French Republic and pledged the society to aid France in every way.[61]

[56] Robert Todd to I. Shelby, Sept. 17, 1793, Shelby Papers, Historical Society of Kentucky. "Record of the family of Judge Daniel Breck," in J. Clark Todd's Papers, Filson Club Library.

[57] *American Historical Association, Report*, 1896, p. 933; the Clark MSS, Vol. LV, Nos. 3, 5, and 8, Wisconsin Historical Society.

[58] Genet's commission and instructions to Michaux are in the Genet Papers, July 5, 12, 1793. A commission signed by Genet and issued by Clark to Henry Lindsay, Jan. 11, 1794, is in the Durrett Collection, University of Chicago Library (Clark MSS, Vol. XII, p. 68).

[59] This broadside to "Les Français Libres à leurs frères de la Louisiane" may be seen in the Thomas Jefferson Papers, Vol. IX, No. 16,543, or in the Genet Papers (n.d.), box dated 1794.

[60] Bradford to De Pauw, Dec. 19, 1793, *American Historical Association, Report*, 1896, p. 1023.

[61] Harry Innes Papers, Vol. XIX, Nos. 85 and 122. In the latter Lachaise says

All the western societies affirmed and in some way endorsed the designs to gain the navigation of the Mississippi. The Kentuckians said that they were thinking and acting as "they did in 1776 in the Atlantic states" and that they were just as right as they were in the Revolutionary days.[62] The Lexington popular association passed strong resolutions for the free navigation of the Mississippi, which included the wish that "a bold, decent and determined" remonstrance be sent to the President and to Congress and that the blocking of the Mississippi by Spain be put to a test by sending an "American bottom" down the river.[63] John Breckinridge, president of the Democratic Society, wrote the remonstrance to Washington and to Congress, and at its next meeting the society accepted it exactly as their leader had written it in rough draft.[64] About the same time, the society sent out a circular "To the Inhabitants of the United States west of the Allegheny and Appalachian Mountains," urging them to form democratic societies and to unite to bring pressure upon the central government.[65] Still another circular was addressed directly to the popular societies west of the Allegheny mountains, demanding the right to navigation of the Mississippi.[66]

These appeals from Lexington brought responses from surrounding societies. Wytheville, Virginia, was a frontier settlement, situated on a fork in the Wilderness Road into Kentucky, and was the home of John Montgomery. The society there resolved to appoint a committee of correspondence, to keep in touch with others who

he intends to work among the leaders in the maritime towns and their patriotic societies, in an effort to elicit their support for freeing Louisiana. The Democratic Societies were never a part of any western scheme to separate from the Union, such as was sponsored, for example, by Wilkinson. They made it clear that they were demanding Mississippi navigation, repeal of the excise, and so forth, and had no intention of allying with Britain, Spain, or France. See Coulter, "The Efforts of the Democratic Societies of the West to Open the Navigation of the Mississippi," *Mississippi Valley Historical Review*, XI (1924), 376 ff. As late as 1808, Dr. Frederick Ridgely, who was doubtless a member of a Kentucky patriotic society, testified before Judge Harry Innes that the societies never talked of separating from the Union, much less passing such resolutions. Innes Papers, Vol. XIX, No. 218.

[62] *Albany Register*, Dec. 24, 1798.
[63] *American Daily Advertiser*, Dec. 21, 1793.
[64] Breckinridge Papers, Vol. X, Nos. 1–23 (Dec., 1793), Library of Congress.
[65] *Ibid.*, No. 1583 (Dec. 13, 1793).
[66] Innes Papers, Vol. XIX, No. 105.

were attempting to gain the free use of the great river.[67] Robert Johnson, Richard Henderson, and Bartlett Collins, of the committee of correspondence for Scott County, Kentucky, answered the Lexington club's remonstrance and favored all but the sending of a boat down the river.[68] The Bourbon County society, meeting at Paris, Kentucky, heard the resolutions of Lexington as read by James Smith [69] and proceeded unanimously to approve them.[70] The Democratic Society of Washington, Pennsylvania, weighed the Kentucky remonstrance. Some in the meeting opposed it as inapplicable to Western Pennsylvania. Out of a feeling of oneness with all westerners (doubtless induced by the common opposition to the Federalist excise), the society signed the Kentucky resolutions and sent them to President Washington and to William Irvine at Philadelphia.[71]

But the Lexington society, together with its satellites at Paris and Georgetown, Kentucky, did more than arouse the western country on the Mississippi question. The Clark expedition needed food, military supplies, and transport boats, and these the clubs undertook to provide. Lachaise wrote to Peley in 1794 that

La société Démocratique de l'Exington sur le cautionnement de Général Clark nous avoit fourni les provisions de bouche et de guerre, et les batteaux de transport nécessaires.[72]

George Rogers Clark reported to Genet that all the project needed was money; that the Democratic Society had advanced ammunition "and given all the encouragement in their power." [73] In the list

[67] *Ibid.*, No. 128. From the "Journal de André Michaux," *Proceedings of the American Philosophical Society*, XXVI (1889), 99, we know that this Frenchman traveled the Wilderness Road and stopped for a time at Wythe Courthouse on Nov. 24, 1793.

[68] Innes Papers, Vol. XIX, No. 104.

[69] James Smith is the hero of the historical novel by Neil H. Swanson, entitled *The First Rebel* (New York, 1937). A recent cinema version of Smith's Western Pennsylvania exploits was called "Allegheny Uprising."

[70] *American Daily Advertiser*, Aug. 11, 1794.

[71] Innes Papers, Vol. XIX, No. 103; *Pittsburgh Gazette*, April 5, 1794.

[72] *American Historical Review*, III (1897), 514; Lachaise to Committee of Public Safety (n.d.), Affaires Étrangères, Vol. XLIII, Part 3; cf. Marshall, *History of Kentucky*, p. 109.

[73] April 28, 1794, Genet Papers.

of subscribers to the Clark expedition are the names of Levi Todd, Robert Patterson, John Bradford, Thomas Todd, John Cock, and others. Doubtless all of the subscribers were members of the Democratic Society.[74] Since they were cashless westerners, they were able to raise almost four times as much in contributions of ammunition as in money. All their efforts ended in disappointment when Lachaise informed the society in a letter of May 14, 1794, that "unforeseen events had stopped the march" and that Genet's successor had canceled all aid to the project.[75]

Plans for attacking Canada and gaining control of the St. Lawrence River as a waterway had been rife since Revolutionary War days. Frontiersmen, as we have said, were certain that England was stimulating the Indians to impede any American expansion; land disputes between Canadians and Americans were numerous; trade rivalries with the Indians were keen; and, finally, England had refused to give up the forts at Niagara and Detroit. Both Jefferson and his Vermont friend, Joseph Fay, were concerned with land developments impinging upon Canadian territory. Early in 1793, before Genet arrived, Fay sent Jefferson copies of the Canadian newspapers, in exchange for the *National Gazette*. He wrote with joy that the "spirit of liberty begins to kindle in Canada."[76]

Genet was well aware of this friction and set about to coöperate with the dissatisfied elements in the Northwest, as he was doing in the South and Southwest. As elsewhere, both on the American frontier and in French-inhabited cities, such as Montreal and Quebec, in Canada, Genet knew in advance who the leaders of the restless groups were.[77] He instructed his consul, Hauterive, in New York, to keep informed concerning developments in Vermont and Canada. Like Mangourit in Charleston, South Carolina, Hauterive was to encourage the Americans to assert their old War of Independence spirit.[78] The field agent for Genet was a handsome young

---

[74] *Amer. Hist. Ass'n, Report* (1896), p. 1073; Innes Papers, Vol. XIX, No. 53.
[75] Clark MSS, Vol. XII, pp. 67–75, Draper Collection.
[76] Fay to Jefferson, Feb. 13, March 12, 1793, in Jefferson Papers, Mass. Hist. Soc.
[77] Affaires Étrangères, Section on Canada, Supplement, July 16, 1794.
[78] Genet to Hauterive, June 4, 1793, Genet Papers. No one knew that Hauterive's

man, of good address and an excellent speaker, by the name of Henri Mezières, a French Canadian. This dashing democrat set out, under Genet's instructions, to spread the philosophy of the "Rights of Man" along the Vermont frontier and in Canada.[79] Armed with copies of American newspapers telling of French victories, English and French editions of *The Rights of Man,* some patriotic songs, copies of a Fourth of July sermon by an American Presbyterian clergyman—"which should affect a numerous group of this faith at Montreal"—and 350 copies of an address to Canadians written by Genet,[80] Mezière went forth to "employer tous les moyens possibles pour faire germer en Canada les principes sacrés des droits de l'homme." [81]

In 1794, the year that the democratic societies of Vermont were the most active, revolts broke out in Montreal and its vicinity. Popular clubs were discovered to be in existence, and Canada was on the verge of revolutionary change.[82] Lord Dorchester firmly believed that citizens of the United States in general, and of Vermont in particular, had a hand in the trouble and were pushing for an immediate conquest of Canada.[83] The President of the United States was said to have received a petition signed by 100 "of the most influential characters" in Vermont, asking permission to march

heart was not in the machinations of Genet. The New York consul confided only to his diary that he opposed the plans against Louisiana and Canada and that he considered Genet rash and impudent. The historically interesting "Alexandre Hauterive Diary" (1793), throwing light upon American and French characters of the period, is in manuscript in the New York Historical Society. It might be added that even Mangourit, Genet's most trusted aid, thought the ambassador impractical to plan and promise so much, with so little financial resource to implement his schemes. See Mangourit, *Mémoire,* p. 15.

[79] Genet to Meziere, July 8, 1793, Affaires Étrangères, Supplement, Canada; Sulte, "Les Projects de 1793 à 1810," *Proceedings and Transactions of the Royal Society of Canada,* V (1911), 30.

[80] A MS copy of this address is in the Genet Papers, 1793; a photostat of the printed address is in Affaires Étrangères, Vol. XXXIX, Part 2. It raises the famous Rousseau paradox, viz., "Man is born free, by what fatality has he become subject to his own species?"

[81] Mezière to Genet, Affaires Étrangères, Vol. XXXVIII, Part 2; Woodfin, "Citizen Genet and His Mission." Chap. xii is especially helpful on these projects.

[82] Sulte, *op. cit.,* pp. 35–36.

[83] Dorchester to Dundas, April 26, 1794, Canadian Colonial Correspondence Vol. LXVII, British State Papers; *ibid.,* June 7, 1794, Vol. LXIX.

20,000 men against Montreal and Quebec.[84] Because of this tense situation, Lord Dorchester uttered his provocative speech of February, 1794, in which he called upon the Indian tribes to prepare themselves for attack. This speech stirred the American frontier and made Vermont warmly indignant, as reflected in the resolutions of the popular societies there.[85]

Strong circumstantial evidence tends to implicate the Vermont societies and their leaders in the activities for an attack on Canada.[86] The procedure was directed from New York City. Colonel Udney Hay, member of the New York Democratic Society as well as the society in Burlington, Vermont, was one of Genet's principal collaborators.[87] During the Revolution, Hay was state agent of New York for supplies and worked with Melancton Smith, his assistant, both men becoming anti-Federalists and warm democrats.[88] Like so many of the leaders of the popular groups, Hay was interested in the buying and selling of land and in 1794 was the New York City agent to sell Vermont lands belonging to Ira Allen.[89] Hay and his friends, William Coit and Stephen Pearl, officers of the Chittenden County Democratic Society, were concerned about land which

[84] *Connecticut Gazette*, April 3, 1794.

[85] Affaires Étrangères, Vol. XL, Part 6.

[86] The investigator could find no original records of the Vermont societies other than those in the newspapers. Since the clubs in other parts of the country never published their intentions to aid the French-American projects, these intentions had to be uncovered in manuscript sources. In the case of Vermont, the lack of source materials on this subject forces one to resort to inference and opens one to possible error. At least twice Hauterive forwarded Mezière money which the consul had collected in New York. Mezière also received money from a "Mr. Hale," an Albany merchant; Mezière to Genet, Affaires Étrangères, Vol. XXXVIII (Sept., 1793). Hauterive speaks in his "Diary" (*op. cit.*) of visiting barracks near New York, where the French had a magazine, a military hospital, sentinels, and an arsenal: "c'est comme dit M. Jefferson, une puissance dans une puissance." Woodfin (*op. cit.*, p. 431) says recruiting was going on in New York for an attack upon Canada and that the recruiters succeeded in gathering a band of "Irishmen and malcontents."

[87] Affaires Étrangères, Vol. XXXIX, Part 2, Aug. 26, 1793.

[88] M. Smith to Hay, Sept. 7, 1780, Emmet Collection, No. 736, New York Public Library. The William Heath collection in the Massachusetts Historical Society contains much about Hay's revolutionary activities. See Hemenway, *The Vermont Historical Gazeteer*, 942–43, for a sketch of Hay.

[89] Hay to Allen, Sept. [?], 1794, Ira Allen Papers, Fleming Museum, University of Vermont.

both they and the Canadians claimed.[90] Thus French revolutionary zeal and a strong personal interest combined again to stimulate the actions of the democrats. Udney Hay wrote the constitution of the Chittenden County Society, which other clubs in Vermont copied almost verbatim. He recommended to Genet that a certain Jacques Rous, a Canadian who had lived in the United States since 1777, aid Mezière in Canada. Furthermore, he was suspected of encouraging frontier leaders such as Isaac Clarke, Matthew Lyon (Clarke's brother-in-law), John A. Graham, and Anthony Haswell to accept French commissions and to support the projected "freeing" of Canada.[91] Both Clarke and Graham were members of Vermont societies, but as for Lyon's affiliations, we are not sure. He doubtless did, however, assist Genet.[92] His *Farmer's Library*, August 19, 1794, welcomed the reports of a rising revolutionary spirit in Canada. After Dorchester's speech to the Indians, only a hair kept the war sword from falling in the midst of these people. The Democratic Society at Burlington then issued the statement that the Vermonters wished to live at peace with the Canadians, but if the latter continued to be misled by the English, dire trouble would ensue.[93]

Before proceeding to some other activities of the democratic-republican clubs, it may be said, in summary of their work in cooperation with France, that although the societies did not initiate these various projects, they did encourage the efforts and did give them direct aid. It has been written, and erroneously, that Genet organized the clubs as vehicles to carry out the so-called "Genet projects." On the contrary, it is evident that several of the clubs antedate Genet, and that they were formed by Americans to gain long-standing ends which the Federalists ignored and opposed.

[90] *Records of the Governor and Council of the State of Vermont*, pp. 115–16, 149.

[91] Sulte, *op. cit.*, pp. 38, 61; Affaires Étrangères, Vol. XXXVIII (Sept., 1793); Isaac Tichenor to Noah Webster, Dec. 14, 1795, Webster Papers, New York Public Library.

[92] *Canadian Archives, Report*, 1891, p. 63. John Stevens wrote to Genet Nov. 10, 1793, that the people of Vermont were excited about the French Revolution and were favorable toward freeing the people of Canada; Affaires Étrangères, Canada, Supplement.

[93] Affaires Étrangères, Vol. XL, Part 5, dated March 17, 1794.

Because of mutual economic interest, combined with Francophile idealism, the republicans were willing to incorporate into their programs collaboration with France and all aid to the French Revolution.[94]

There were three active popular societies in Western Pennsylvania when the Whiskey Insurrection broke out. One, and the best known, was the Democratic Society of Washington, a wing of the Philadelphia club. Another, the Society of United Freemen, met at Mingo Creek and has usually been known as the Mingo Creek Society. A third was called the Republican Society of the Yough.[95] In various degrees, all three were implicated in the anti-excise outbreak.

The Washington club was sponsored by the leading men in the community, landowners and lawyers of wealth and prestige, who, although they opposed the excise, were not willing to take radical action, as the poorer farmers around Mingo Creek were doing.[96]

[94] Faÿ, *Revolutionary Spirit in France and America*, pp. 326–30. This author is right in saying that the French consulates were bureaus of propaganda and publicity, but nowhere in Genet's instructions to his consuls is there a statement that patriotic societies should be formed. Genet's agent in Boston, by name Lequoy, wrote to him, Nov. 25, 1793 (Genet Papers), to say that a patriotic society had been organized there and that "it was the work of our friends," meaning Austin, Jarvis, and Morton. Genet repeatedly urged the consuls to stir enthusiasm for France, expose its enemies, and gain the friendship of influential Americans, without violating the laws of a free people. See Genet to Moissonier, undated, in 1793, Genet Papers; also in same collection, Genet to Hauterive, June 4, 1793; Genet to Dannery, June 7, 1793. Hammond, the British ambassador, wrote to Grenville, Aug 10, 1793, that instead of Genet prompting the democratic societies, the direct opposite was true—the democratic societies advised Genet. In this same letter Hammond says that Genet, upon arrival, "found a party already formed with whom a common interest naturally and instantaneously arose." See British Archives, F.O.5, Vol. I, No. 17. In western Pennsylvania the sentiment was strong for striking at England by invading Canada. No less a personage than Hugh Brackenridge favored such action; *The Standard of Liberty* (Philadelphia, 1802), p. 52. See also an account of a meeting of the election districts of Allegheny County, where those present wished to block English boats at Presque Isle from carrying weapons to the Indians. Affaires Étrangères, Vol. XL. Part 6.

[95] Chap. i, *supra*. Hugh Brackenridge, together with Thomas Morton and W. H. Beaumont, virtually had a democratic society organized at Pittsburgh in April, 1794, to consider an address from the Kentucky societies. The Pittsburghers affirmed the demand for an outlet down the Mississippi and favored invasion, if necessary. There was no formal organization set up, and there are no records of subsequent meetings. *Pittsburgh Gazette*, April 5, 26, May 17, 1794.

[96] McFarland, *Twentieth Century History of the City of Washington and Wash-*

Even so, the Washington society admitted that seven of its members took a direct part in the revolt.[97] One of these was James Marshel, the president of the club, who must have had some support from the popular organization he led. At the Parkinson Ferry meeting of August 14, 1794, Marshel called for the formation of a Committee of Public Safety, to be composed of representatives from each county.[98] He knew the value of unity and communication. Assisting Marshel was David Bradford, another officer of the society, and John Hamilton, the honored sheriff of the county, and John Canon, both society members.[99] On the eve of the trouble, September 22, 1794, the whole society went on record as unanimously opposed to the excise law, and individual members made objections to Governor Mifflin against the "type and character" of excise collectors sent into the community.[100] If the Washington club was unwilling to endorse the direct actions of certain of its more radical leaders and members, it was at least involved in some "indiscreet" measures, which led David Redick to resign and to suggest that the organization be disbanded.[101] Here again the historian is hampered by having only the published resolutions of this society, to aid in determining its program and activities. These are deceptive, as indicated, for there is an important divergency in what the societies actually did and the resolutions they published.

The task of appraising the program of the Yough Republican Society and that of the United Freemen at Mingo Creek is much easier. These two societies were integrally related, the first growing

---

ington County, Pennsylvania, p. 107; H. H. Brackenridge, Incidents of the Insurrection in the Western Parts of Pennsylvania, III, 26.

[97] Pittsburgh Gazette, Jan. 24, 1795.

[98] The Gallatin Papers, Vol. IV, in the New York Historical Society.

[99] Pittsburgh Gazette, Oct. 19, 1793. A summons for colonels of battalions to rendezvous at Braddock's Field on Aug. 1, 1794, is in James Marshel's handwriting and is signed by him, J. Canon, B. Parkinson, D. Bradford, and others. The summons states that further words are useless and that now action is needed on the excise question. Yeates Papers, July 28, 1794, in the Historical Society of Pennsylvania.

[100] For letters objecting to excise collectors, see Misc. Letters, Department of State, April 18, May 27, 1794, National Archives; Pittsburgh Gazette, Jan. 24, 1795.

[101] Philadelphia Gazette, Jan. 23, 1795, article signed by Redick.

out of the second. The idea was to organize the four counties of Western Pennsylvania into a republican society, with representatives elected from each colonel's district in the respective counties.[102] Colonel Hamilton's district was already organized into the Mingo Creek Society of United Freemen. It was formed in February, 1794, and was the first popular society in that part of the country. In truth, as Hugh Brackenridge wrote, this society was "the cradle of the insurrection," for all of its known members were active in the trouble. On February 19, 1794, the society resolved that excisemen who seize whisky must be prosecuted. This led to the attempt to drive the hated collector Neville out of the country.[103] During this attempt James McFarland, the first chairman of the Society of United Freemen, was killed, shot while attempting a truce under a white flag.[104] After his death, Benjamin Parkinson was elected leader of the society and he worked closely with Bradford and Marshel in the insurrection.

Societies in other parts of the country, especially along the Atlantic seaboard, deprecated the use of direct action in the West. While they opposed the excise, they also insisted that change should be brought about through constitutional measures.[105] Nevertheless, there was a strong sentiment against marching an army to suppress the westerners,[106] and disagreement as to the degree to which they should be censured caused a mortal split in the mother body at Philadelphia. Thirty members favored caustic words and twenty-

[102] *Pittsburgh Gazette*, April 26, 1794.
[103] "Insurrection in Western Pennsylvania," Vol. I, Rawle Papers; Brackenridge, *Incidents*, II, 18; Alexander Hamilton to Thomas Fitzsimmons, Nov. 27, 1794, in *The Works of Alexander Hamilton*, ed. by Lodge, VIII, 329.
[104] In the graveyard at Mingo Creek meetinghouse Capt. James McFarland is buried: "He served during the war with undaunted courage, in defense of American Independence against the lawless and despotic encroachments of Great Britain. He fell at last by the hands of an unprincipled villain, in support of what he supposed to be the rights of his country, much lamented by a numerous and respectable circle of acquaintances." Creigh, *History of Washington County, Pennsylvania*, p. 68, n.
[105] *Philadelphia Gazette*, Aug. 7, 1794.
[106] Fee, *The Transition from Aristocracy to Democracy in New Jersey, 1789–1829*, pp. 50–57; *New York Journal*, Sept. 20, 1794. Alexander Smyth, president of the Wytheville Society, wrote that he would not lead an army against the Whiskey Boys, but would, on the contrary, join them; Smyth, *op. cit.*, p. 34.

nine left the hall with Blair McClenachan, favoring merely a mild reprimand. After President McClenachan left his chair, Benjamin Bache took his place *pro tempore* and the society voted not to criticize the insurrectionists unduly. Instead they published an approval of the mild and prudent action of the President of the United States and the governor of Pennsylvania, in their nonmilitary attempts to pacify the western counties.[107] The Ulster County, New York, society passed resolutions voicing the same feeling. While critical of the West's resorting to force, this society held that the democratic societies were not to blame, but that the true cause of the insurrection was the Secretary of the Treasury and his odious policies! [108]

Two of the western societies, who were so bold as to be involved in the Whiskey Insurrection, were also determined to defy the expensive system of courts. The Republican Society of the Yough stated in section ten of its constitution:

All matters in variance and dispute shall be laid before the society and all citizens in the district, before suing before a justice of the peace, shall first apply to the society for redress.[109]

The members at Mingo Creek not only formed their own court for settling disputes among themselves, but they also took up a collection from time to time to remunerate those who had suffered loss at the hands of the exciseman.[110] The farmers were doing all that was possible, through individual and group effort, to present a united front against their enemies across the mountains. In one other case the records reveal a society arranging to settle difficulties out of court. The Republican Society of Portland had an arbitration

---

[107] Minutes of the Democratic Society of Pennsylvania, Sept. 11, 1794, in the Historical Society of Pennsylvania. *Philadelphia Gazette*, Sept. 13, 1794.

[108] *Gazette of the United States*, Nov. 5, 1794; Miller, "The Democratic Societies and the Whiskey Insurrection," *The Pennsylvania Magazine of History and Biography*, LXII (July, 1938), 324–49. Miller rightly holds that by and large the societies had little or nothing to do with the insurrection, but that they were blamed with it for political reasons. As for the societies of Western Pennsylvania, however, Miller does not give sufficient weight to the activity of the Republican and United Freemen societies.

[109] *Pittsburgh Gazette*, April 26, June 28, 1794.

[110] Rawle Papers, Vol. I.

board of seven, to hear and make decisions on disputes among its membership.

Although the frontier societies were bold in their program and activity, the seaboard organizations did more than merely talk and propagandize. The Constitutional Society of Boston upheld the vice-consul Anthony Du Plaine, when he refused to allow a United States marshal to take over a French prize vessel in the harbor, in violation, as the society saw it, of treaty agreements with France.[111] The New York society aided in fort-building; the societies at Baltimore, Norfolk, and Charleston watched with eagle eye to see that no English ship violated Washington's none-too-popular Neutrality Proclamation. The Charleston republicans were forced to go, with a militia unit as a guard, to disarm a British vessel in their harbor. After repeated requests, the captain of the English sloop refused to cease stocking his ship with war instruments. With the aid of friendly militia, the Republican Society took action.[112] It was determined in its conclusion that if American democrats could not aid France, neither could Federalists abet England.

All the societies, without exception, were early American pressure groups that doled out their blessings or their curses on the representatives in Congress who affirmed or defied their interest. It was becoming more and more evident to the popular associations that if they were to gain their ends they would need to displace men now in office, to center their attention upon nominating better men, to diffuse truthful information about candidates for public office, and to see that fair elections were held. All this early became a part of their activities. The Baltimore society, for example, met with the Carpenter and Mechanical Societies on October 4, 1794, to nominate delegates for the state general assembly.[113]

Electioneering was a common practice. It included the making public of antidemocratic statements by the various candidates, watching

---

[111] *The Life and Letters of Harrison Gray Otis*, ed. by Morison, I, 50.

[112] *American Daily Advertiser*, Aug. 27, 1793. For the English side of the story, see Hammond to Grenville, Sept. 17, 1793, British Archives, F.O.5, Vol. I, No. 19.

[113] *Baltimore Daily Intelligencer*, Oct. 16, 1794. The Republican Society of Lancaster, Penn., aided in forming a ticket for the elections in 1795. *Lancaster Journal*, Sept. 9, 1795.

at the polls to counteract the Federalist tactics, and publicizing the principles for which a candidate stood both before and after election.[114] The Wytheville group prevailed upon the voters not to support men who moved contrary to the wishes of the people. "To trust yourself to speculators, what is it, but to commit the lamb to the wolf to be devoured?" [115] Therefore, they were advised to give their vote and their congratulatory resolutions to true republicans and to do all in their power to defeat the enemies of the people. The Charleston society pledged its support to "Citizen James Madison" in 1794, for his helping America to "preserve her faith in her allies." [116] The Addison County society in Vermont complimented "the patriotic representatives" from that state for their actions in Congress and distributed a circular throughout the county bearing a statement of the compliment.[117] There are hundreds of like instances in which the societies, individually and collectively, brought pressure to bear in the legislative halls. Doubtless during their regular meetings the question of the actions of elected representatives was the most time-consuming as well as the paramount issue, in most of the clubs.

The Fourth of July might have been forgotten or twisted into a vapid nationalistic rite if the Federalists had had their way and the democratic-republican clubs had never appeared. Hamilton made every effort to emasculate the day by advancing the idea that the American Revolution was a special one. "Grave," "decorous," "orderly," and "dignified" were the words he used. The French

[114] Innes Papers, Vol. XIX, No. 124, tells of the political activity of the Prince William County, Va., society. The constitution of the Pinckneyville, S.C., club (*City Gazette*, Nov. 6, 1793) inveighs against corrupt election practices. An article by David Reddick in the *Philadelphia Gazette*, Jan. 23, 1795, tells of the use of electioneering by the Democratic Society of Washington, Penn. A fine study of the influence of the New York Democratic Society on the election of 1794 has been written by Miller, "First Fruits of Republican Organization," *The Pennsylvania Magazine of History and Biography*, LXIII (1939), 118–43.

[115] *American Daily Advertiser*, Aug. 2, 1794.

[116] Republican Society to James Madison, March 12, 1794, Madison Papers, Vol. XVII, No. 36, Library of Congress.

[117] *Farmer's Library*, Oct. 28, 1794. See also Democratic-Republican Society of Washington, N.C., to Thomas Blount, *Virginia Chronicle*, July 28, 1794; Democratic Society of Northumberland County, Penn., in *Aurora*, March 23, 1795; and Chittenden County, Vt., society in the *American Daily Advertiser*, Feb. 28, 1795.

Revolution, said the Secretary, was the opposite—rabble-controlled and wicked.[118] Fisher Ames, for example, confessed to Christopher Gore what seemed to be a rather common attitude of the Federalists, namely, that he opposed the celebration of the Fourth of July.[119] Joseph Dennie called it the "unlucky day." [120] When one compares any democratic newspaper of the 1790's with one of the Federalist press, one can note the added space and emphasis given by the republican printer to Independence Day. It is no wonder the *status quo* gentlemen disliked the occasion, for it gave the Rutland, Vermont, society a chance to come forward with a toast like this: "May the plebeians of the eastern states awake." And the Baltimore Republican Society offered this one: "The Fourth of July, may it ever prove a memento to the oppressed to rise and assert their rights." [121]

The day also provided a special time each year when all the "mobocratic" societies met and hailed the spirit of '76. With the mechanics, the carpenters, the coopers, and the cordwainers in their various societies, the popular clubs joined to make "the glorious Fourth" a common man's remembrance of a common man's struggle for freedom. The New York Democratic Society, for instance, met each year, up to 1799, to celebrate the Fourth with the working-man's organizations. So long as Genet lived on his Long Island farm, he was always invited to join the festivities.[122] Each society assigned a member some part on the program of the celebration. In 1795 the Democratic Society appointed Edward Livingston to read the Declaration of Independence, and in 1799 Samuel L. Mitchell, the scientist, was requested to deliver the patriotic oration.[123] Wherever popular clubs existed, they always made the most of the birthday of American freedom.

[118] Alexander Hamilton Papers, XXI, 2903.
[119] Dec. 3, 1796, in Seth Ames, *op. cit.*, p. 205.
[120] Dennie to his mother, May 20, 1800. Dennie Papers, Harvard.
[121] *Farmers Library*, July 8, 1794. *Baltimore Telegraphe*, July 6, 1796. This democratic paper, sponsored by Paul Bentalou, printed all the toasts given at the celebration, while the other Baltimore papers briefly mentioned the occasion.
[122] Genet Papers, June 28, 1794; July 6, 1796.
[123] "Minutes of the Society of Mechanics and Tradesmen of New York," June 24, 1795, and June 5, 1799, in Mechanics and Tradesmen Library, New York City.

Some activities were but indirectly related to the mounting struggle between the Washington administration and its antithesis. For instance, out of the social philosophy of the Enlightenment, proclaimed by the patriotic societies, grew a revolutionary attitude toward crime and the criminal. Tunis Wortman, of the New York society, has stated this philosophy in his *Oration on the Influence of Social Institution upon Human Morals and Happiness*.[124] Wortman and his contemporaries were giving up the idea that man was born with base instincts, for the newer precept that education and social institutions mold men for good or for evil. Following this viewpoint, another democrat, Joel Barlow, wrote:

There is a manifest difference between *punishment* and *correction;* the latter among rational beings may always be performed by instruction, or at most by some gentle species of restraint. But punishment, on the part of the public arises from no other source but a jealousy of power.[125]

Not all democratic society members shared this new view of crime and punishment, for William Slade, the sheriff of Addison County, Vermont, believed in "whipping criminals 'til blood ran." [126] But others, individually and through their popular associations, were attempting to eliminate imprisonment for debt, "sanguinary, cruel and unjust" criminal laws, and capital punishment. The New Jersey legislature received a petition from "A Freeman" in 1793, asking it to change the penal laws of the state, as Pennsylvania had done. Imprisonment for debt, added "A Freeman," has too great an "affinity to a Bastille" for a free country.[127] In Kentucky, the Lexington Democratic Society sent a memorial to the state general assembly, asking it to give attention to the reform of the criminal code. It was too harsh, according to the memorial, with inferior crimes capitally punished, and offenders destroyed who "might be reformed and restored good members to society." The club members wanted "a radical change" and the institution of a "new system" of

[124] Published in New York in 1796.
[125] *A Letter to the National Convention of France,* 55.
[126] Matthews, *The History of the Town of Cornwall, Vermont,* pp. 68–69.
[127] Wood's *Newark Gazette,* Nov. 5, 13, 20, 27, 1793.

criminal procedure.[128] William Keteltas and Edward Livingston of the New York society, throughout their lives, spoke up for the poor man caught in crime. Because of the spirited opposition of Keteltas to imprisonment for debt, unfair punishments, and corrupt politics, he was a popular hero whom the crowds followed, shouting "The Spirit of '76." [129] On the Fourth of July the democratic societies of New York and Philadelphia practiced the habit of visiting prisoners and making donations to the more worthy of them who were incarcerated for debt or minor offenses.[130] The humanitarian movements of the day were, of course, buttressed by much wider support than just that of the popular societies. Federalists and republicans quite often joined in nonpolitical societies to advance such reforms as the abolition of slavery and imprisonment for debt.

One might well ask whether or not these societies of the Enlightenment supported or were related to the abolitionist societies of the period. In answer, we cannot give a categorical yes or no. While there is no record of a society ever pasing a resolution against slavery, one may be sure that the subject was debated in free-for-all sessions. Any decision, in the nature of a resolution would have ruined what unity the societies had attained, for both slaveholders and abolitionists were on the membership rolls. This, however, may be said, that many slaveholders in the republican societies were manumitting their servants [131] and that among the antislave people were some of the societies' most brilliant leaders. Alexander McKim, president of the Baltimore Republican Society, was also vice president of the Maryland Society for the Abolition of Slavery.[132] In the same society were the Buchanans, relentless opponents of the

[128] *American Daily Advertiser*, Dec. 21, 1793; Breckinridge Papers, Vol. X, Nos. 1571, 1572, Library of Congress.

[129] *American Gazette*, March 25, 1796; Pomerantz, *New York, An American City*, pp. 266–67, 326–27.

[130] *New York Journal*, July 7, 1798; *New London Bee*, July 11, 1798; *American Daily Advertiser*, May 5, 1794.

[131] The "Chattel Record" for 1794 in the basement of the courthouse at Baltimore shows that Dr. Edward Johnson and John Steele purchased slaves in that year, but that John McKim, John Stricker, Thomas McCreery, and Thomas McElderry freed the slaves they owned. All these men were members of the local Republican Society.

[132] Scharf, *Chronicles, op. cit.*, p. 258.

slave system.[133] Democrats on the rolls of the Pennsylvania Society for Promoting Abolition of Slavery included George Logan, Peter S. Du Ponceau, Dr. James Hutchinson, and Absalom Baird. In Delaware was Robert Coram, in Virginia, Josiah Parker, and in New York, James Nicholson, another society president, Tunis Wortman, Samuel L. Mitchell, Melancton Smith, and Philip Freneau.[134] So we may conclude that while certain outstanding individuals in the popular clubs gave unstinting effort to the freeing of slaves, the clubs themselves avoided definite action on the emotion-charged question.

Others of the numerous activities of the popular societies, some anti-Federalist in character and some not, are of interest and worthy of mention here. The Committee of Correspondence of Carlisle, Pennsylvania, gathered flour to send to France for relief purposes. Two doctors, Gustine and M'Coskrey, sponsored this effort.[135] The Baltimore club raised money to pay the ransom of a group of Americans held by the Algerines,[136] and the Charlestonians collected funds to pay the passage of the famed Scotch democrat, William Muir, to America.[137] The Kentucky society worked for a convention to change the constitution of that state. It resolved:

Let us unite in a remonstrance to the Assembly, stating our dissatisfaction with their former refusal to comply with our desire, and declaring our determination to obtain a new Convention; and if they still persist in refusing to comply, we know our last resource.[138]

The civic devotion of one such club is revealed by the following resolve of the Portland republicans: "That this society will as soon as Convenant fix themselves for extinguishing fires, being determined to exercise Friendship and Humanity." [139] Finally, the frontier societies must have been used for meeting friends, talking over

[133] Mary S. Locke, *Anti-Slavery in America* . . . , pp. 93–104.
[134] Logan Papers, Misc. MSS in Historical Society of Pennsylvania; "Minutes of the Society for the Manumission of Slaves," 1785–97, in the New York Historical Society; Poole, *Anti-Slavery Opinions before the Year 1800*, p. 76.
[135] Broadside dated July 26, 1793, in the Gilpin Library, Historical Society of Pennsylvania.
[136] *Baltimore Daily Intelligencer*, July 21, 1794.
[137] *City Gazette*, Feb. 19, 1794.   [138] *Kentucky Gazette*, April 12, 1794.
[139] "Republican Articles" in papers of the Portland Republican Society.

the current news, and having a social good time. The Pinckneyville Society, in western South Carolina, after completing its business, gave over the remainder of the evening to "social intercourse, and a mutual exchange of patriotic sentiments." [140]

The diverse character of the activities of the societies was due to the local and sectional problems with which each was confronted. Features common to all came as a reaction to steps taken by the national government, with which they disagreed. As the culture of the time was influenced by the Enlightenment, the clubs, too, reflected the rationalist rays. The members of the societies, as a whole, were constitutionalists and had no intention of overthrowing the government, as the Sons of Liberty had done. Rather, they were concerned with defending and preserving the Revolution and liberty. An enlightened public was an essential for democracy. The clubs' activities in behalf of education is the subject of the next chapter.

[140] *South Carolina State Gazette*, April 29, 1794.

Chapter Seven

SCHOOLS OF POLITICAL KNOWLEDGE

The collision of opposite opinions produces the spark which lights the torch of truth.
Patriotic Society of Newcastle, Delaware

"THE moral principle of revolutions is to instruct, not to destroy." So wrote Thomas Paine,[1] and his words were substantiated by both the American and the French Revolutions. These deep social alterations released education from narrow confines and made it the *sine qua non* of liberty and democratic government. Knowledge and science were toasted not only before the learned societies of the day, but also repeatedly before the popular councils in France, England, and America. This ubiquitous yearning for information and instruction stemmed from two ideas in the social philosophy of the era. These we have mentioned in a previous chapter, but they are so important as to deserve reiteration at this point. In the first place, the philosophy of the Enlightenment held that progress was possible and that all men could take part in it. The implications for education in this position would seem to be apparent, and the subject has been enlarged upon by other writers.[2] The second idea is more subtle, but equally important, even though it

[1] *Dissertation on First Principles of Government*, p. 31.
[2] Hansen, *Liberalism and American Education in the Eighteenth Century*, chap. i; Mordecai Grossman, *The Philosophy of Helvetius*, pp. 51, 146–48; Van Duzer, *Contributions of the Ideologues to French Revolutionary Thought*, chap. iii.

has not received the emphasis of the first. It was this: namely, that government by a small unit, one which the people could constantly control, such as the Greek city-state for example, was much to be preferred to a centralized superstructure, remote from popular checks. How could a nation, composed of a number of states, gain unity and at the same time preserve the people's ever-active participation in government? The answer to this vital question—How can democracy survive in a republican nation?—was given by the popular societies in both word and deed. Their answer was intercommunication and the diffusion of useful information. With the use of these techniques they were potent educational forces.

Education and democracy were so closely allied, in the outlook of the societies and their leaders, that any attempt to separate the two would have ended in the destruction of both. Dr. George Logan wrote:

There can be no liberty where knowledge and science do not flourish. The more these are diffused the more does the haughtiness of power lose its oppressing force.[3]

And from the pen of Tunis Wortman came this pithy sentence:

If ignorance furnishes an apology for despotism; despotism, grateful for the favor it receives, perpetuates ignorance.[4]

The New York Democratic Society believed that "Ignorance is the irreconcilable enemy of liberty" and that the informed voice of the people must be expressed through democratic societies whose members "are composed of and mingle with every class of citizens" and who give a certain portion of their time to good citizenship.[5] The German Republican Society, the first society to organize in the 1790's, wrote cogent educational beliefs into its call to organization.[6]

[3] Logan Papers, Misc. MSS, Historical Society of Pennsylvania.
[4] A Treatise Concerning Political Enquiry, p. 131.
[5] New York Journal, May 31, 1794. A broadside of this statement is in the 1794 collection in the American Antiquarian Society.
[6] See chap. i, supra. The Essex County, N.J., society wrote that it was necessary to erect institutions "peculiarly devoted to political instruction." Ibid., April 11, 1795. And the Charleston society stated that "as we were willing to risk life and fortune to establish freedom, we are now willing to do the same to defend it." Genet Papers (Broadside), Aug. 20, 1793.

Watchfulness, active participation, and united effort in government were its keynotes. These were to be implemented by informed and virtuous men.

Thus the societies everywhere called upon the citizens to defend the liberties they had gained in the Revolution. Pre-Revolutionary popular societies had made freedom a reality by their combined action; the post-Revolutionary societies must preserve that freedom by relentless educational effort.

As between the "few" and the "many," as William Manning would distinguish them, it was the latter—the poor frontier farmer, the mechanic, and the craftsman—who threw their united support behind the broader concepts of universal education.[7] Farmer Manning wrote that a cheaper mode of conveying knowledge than the expensive newspaper was necessary. The common people, he said, lacked information, which if they had, would make them as intelligent as anyone.

For their is not one fift part of the common farmers and labourers that are the most interested in the measures of the times that git any information from them for they cannot beat the Expence of the time and Money they Cost.

And even when these "most interested" people do get a newspaper,

A labouring man may as well hunt for pins in a hey-mow as to try to colect the knoledge necessary for him to have from such promiscous piles of controdiction.[8]

The New York Mechanics, from their inception as a society in 1785, always upheld popular education; and when the Democratic Societies arose, the two organizations coöperated, in New York, in Charlestown, and elsewhere, in promoting educational projects.[9]

[7] *Address of a Convention of Delegates from Twenty Towns and Five Plantations, etc.* This address states that the Maine farmers are too poor to provide adequate education. "Every town containing fifty families ought to have a schoolmaster teaching reading, writing, English language, arithmetic, orthography and decent behavior." For, "it is by education only that liberty can be understood, defended and preserved."

[8] To Thomas Adams, Manning Papers, Harvard University Library.

[9] Hugh Hughes to Chas. Tillinghast, March 7, 1785, Lamb Papers; *Annals of the General Society of Mechanics and Tradesmen of the City of New York . . . ,* ed by Earle and Congdon; *City Gazette,* Oct. 16, 18, 1794.

So we may say that strong impetus for popular education in the
post-Revolutionary period came from the so-called "lower order"
of men" and was of, by, and for the "many."

The "few," on the other hand, generally spoke for the education
of the well-born, for the "subject matter necessities" of the time,
for the indoctrination of "fundamentals" without raising doubts
or questions, and for the suppression of contrary ideas. Garritt Minor
wrote Joseph C. Cabell about Princeton, at the end of the century.
He complained that a "tyrannick despotism prevails there," that
there was "no discussion of any subject connected with the lectures,"
and that it was all "dumb and obedient silence." Furthermore, according to Minor, "No liberal modes of independent thinking and
acting are encouraged" and the students were expected to use the
language of the textbooks, rather than their own words. There
were no courses in philosophy, no investigation of the rights of man,
and no attempt to explain the nature of our institutions and government. Such education, he added, endangered the Constitution, and
one could rejoice that at William and Mary College, where the
democratic spirit was strong, it was quite different.[10]

Fisher Ames, arch-Federalist, believed that his brand of "Americanism" should be indoctrinated and that the un-Americanism
around Boston in 1798 must be due to the failure of the schools
and academies. As far as adult education was concerned, the Sedition
Act was Ames's idea of "good" procedure. He favored the Sedition
Bill and called his brother, Dr. Nathaniel Ames, "a political Quix-
ote" because the doctor spoke out against the infamous legislation as
a "gag act." [11] While the democratic societies were seeking to extend information and education by inviting the opposition to come
forward and present its arguments, the Federalists called the writ-

[10] July 8, 1800, Cabell Collection, University of Virginia Library.
[11] Fisher Ames to Thomas Dwight, Nov. 12, 1798, Ames Papers. A sharp contrast can be seen between the educational point of view of Fisher Ames and that of
Dr. Richard Price, whose *Observations on the Importance of the American Revolution* was widely read. Ames in his essay on "School Books" (*Works,* pp. 405–6)
holds that instead of children's books about a rich boy and a poor boy, the Bible
should be used as a text. "The reverence for the sacred book that is thus early impressed lasts long, and probably, if not impressed in infancy, never takes firm hold
of the mind."

ings of Benjamin Bache and his friends criminal. Using the familiar distinction between liberty and license, certain Federalists argued that Bache's use of free speech and free press was license and must therefore be stopped.[12] Freedom of thought, a prerequisite of sound education, was not always championed by the aristocracy.

This clash, between "the many" and "the few," over the function and the purpose of education caused the democratic societies to realize the importance of continually educating themselves and their fellow citizens. In fact, this is the great heritage we have from these clubs. Even though the Federalists disrupted the meetings of the New York Debating Society, intimidated republican writers, and shouted for the passage of the Alien and Sedition Acts, the democrats continued to work "with caution" to counteract efforts to deprive the people of necessary information.[13] The societies, from their inception, had advocated no secrecy in government, no Senate sitting behind closed doors. When this latter point was gained in 1794, the societies then suggested a gallery in the Senate chamber, where citizens might hear the debates.[14] Not only did they hold discussions in their own meetings, as has been indicated in an earlier chapter, but they also sponsored debating societies and awakened the search for information in the Tammany organizations, in which their membership often predominated.[15] Letters from abroad and from nearby and far-away states, together with newspaper items, were grist for the mills of these popular forums. Every channel of information was fully exploited. What Robert Birley has written about

[12] Will Heth to Washington, July 20, 1798, Heth Collection, University of Virginia.

[13] *New York Journal*, May 5, 1798. Tunis Wortman, with the aid of James Nicholson and his son-in-law, Gallatin, stated he was preparing an expose of Federalist "intrigue and artifice," from the Constitutional Convention of 1787 to date (1798); Wortman to Gallatin, Feb. 12, 1798, Gallatin Papers, Vol. V, New York Historical Society.

[14] *American Daily Advertiser*, July 7, 1794; *Independent Chronicle*, March 27, 1794.

[15] Wood's *Newark Gazette*, March 26, 1794; Matthew L. Davis to Gallatin, April 21, 1798, Gallatin Papers, Vol. V; *The Correspondence and Public Papers of John Jay*, ed. by Johnston, pp. 238, 240, n. Minutes of the New York Tammany Society, Oct. 24, 1791, to Feb. 23, 1795, New York Public Library. [William Pitt Smith] *Observations on Conventions*.

the English "Jacobin" clubs is equally true of the American, namely, that all looked upon education "as a universal talisman." [16]

Such being the case, the popular societies rose in defense of the right of free assembly, where free speech and inquiry might be followed without fear of molestation. Each insisted upon the uncontrolled freedom of inquiry and the unlimited expression of opinion. Article four of the Addison County, Vermont, society reads:

It shall be the objects of the business and pursuit of this society, to study the constitution, to avail ourselves of the journals, debates and laws of Congress, reports and correspondence of Secretaries, and such other publications as may be judged necessary to give information on the proceedings of Congress and the departments of government. . . . And on information, we will speak; and upon deliberation, we will write and publish our sentiments. [17]

The United Freemen of Mingo Creek made available for this use copies of the laws of the United States and "the minutes" of Congress and the Assembly of Pennsylvania, so that they could recommend capable persons to the legislative bodies. [18] Upon studying into the laws, the Canaan, New York, Society resolved against the "dark, intricate, antiquated formalities" and the "obsolete phraseology," which bewildered the people and prevented all but the lawyers from grasping the meaning of the laws. These democrats abhorred "the mystical solemnity of forms, impressed with a kind of magic awe." [19] The people must, if the "social state" was to survive, ever study into their government and its actions, find the truth, and then proceed to act upon their best thinking. Elias Buell, president of the Rutland County, Vermont, Democratic Society, in a Fourth of July oration in 1796, pleaded that the people must not be driven into decisions without thinking,

But let the people be led to the means of deliberate, unbiased investigation, and they will decide rightly—and every man of associated delib-

---

[16] *Ibid.*, p. 15.   [17] *Farmer's Library*, Sept. 9, 1794.
[18] "Insurrection in Western Pennsylvania," Rawle Papers, Vol. I, Historical Society of Pennsylvania.
[19] *New York Journal*, Oct. 4, 1794.

eration, must add useful improvement, or we derive no advantage from cultivating the virtues of our social nature. To suppose a freeman of the constitution hath an individual right, and yet that he may not exercise this right by associated improvement is a solicism [*sic*] in politics. We claim by the constitution of Nature, by the constitution of the United States, and of this state, as individual citizens, the right of speaking and publishing, with truth and decency, our sentiments respecting the men and measures of government; and we esteem it the palladium of our liberty. As social beings, formed for society and government, for mutual and social benefit, we claim this exercise of this right, associatedly, for mutual improvement.[20]

So many popular societies incorporated strikingly forthright statements in defense of the requisites of democracy—free speech and free assembly, with full diffusion of information—that it is impossible to mention all of them. But it should be said that even under the shadow of the reactionary Alien and Sedition Acts, the Republican Society of Norwalk, Connecticut, was, in 1798, stating as its purpose,

To exercise the right of speech and freedom of debate, recognized by the Constitution; to perpetuate the equal rights of man, to propagate political knowledge, and to revive the republican spirit of '76, are the great objects of this institution.[21]

With Tunis Wortman, all the popular societies heartily agreed that "wherever Freedom of Enquiry is established, Improvement is Inevitable." [22]

The practice of the democratic societies to check continuously on a representative to state or natural legislature, after having elected him to office, was an important educative procedure of the clubs. The Kentucky societies often called upon their representative in Congress, when he was at home, to appear at the next meeting and face queries.[23] At other times they drew up pointed ques-

---

[20] *Farmer's Library*, Aug. 8, 1796.
[21] *New London Bee*, April 4, 1798. The New York Society, with James Nicholson and Edward Livingston, and the Constitutional Society of Norfolk, Va., with Arthur Lee, are other examples of organized activity against the Sedition Act; see *New York Journal*, July 25, 1798; *Norfolk Herald*, March 16, 1799.
[22] Wortman, *op. cit.*, p. 128.   [23] Innes Papers, Vol. XIX, No. 127.

tions and sent them to the Congressman. The answers he gave were then read and discussed before the society.[24] The Newark, New-Jersey, club ridiculed the "slavish doctrine" that state affairs were so intricate that the common man could not be expected to understand them. Instead, it felt it must watch the government and know the positions taken by the various Congressmen.[25] The right of the people to instruct their legislative agents was granted. In towns and districts all over the country, popular meetings were called, to canvass opinion upon important issues and to forward instructions to the duly elected delegates.[26]

A general feeling among the democrats of this period was that the avenues of information were not open as they should be for the enlightenment of the people. The "few" directed affairs, and the majority of the printers did not escape this direction.[27] The self-imposed task of the patriotic societies was to break through the conspiracy of silence and censorship in every way possible. The newspapers of Maine, for example, were all Federalist in 1794, so that the Republican Society of Portland was at a loss for certain kinds of news. Samuel Hewes, secretary of the Constitutional Society in Boston, heard of Portland's plight and at once sent David Bradish "a bundle of southern and other papers," a sermon—"a '75 one"—and some late copies of the Boston *Chronicle*. Hewes promised that henceforward the republicans of Portland should have newspapers.[28] Democratic writers kept the columns of sympathetic sheets filled with their propaganda. And the societies inserted in the press whenever they could, information about themselves, such as their resolutions, which were thoroughly didactic; circular letters to and from other societies; patriotic speeches; addresses to the President, Congress, or "to the citizens of the United States"; and articles which made clear the distinction between the political points of view of the time.[29] The New York Democratic Society actually financed the

fed. papers

---

[24] Breckinridge Papers, Vol. XI, No. 1741.
[25] Wood's *Newark Gazette*, March 12, 1794.   [26] Weld, *Travels*, p. 99.
[27] *American Daily Advertiser*, March 28, 1795.
[28] Hewes to Bradish, March 2, 1795, Portland Republican Society Papers.
[29] *At a Meeting of the Democratic Society*, May 28, 1794, broadside in the New York Historical Society; Dannery to Genet, Feb. 3, 1794, Genet Papers; *Aurora*,

publication of a supplement, in Greenleaf's *New York Journal*, April 20, 1794, giving the full statement of the principles and constitution of the Associated Democratic Society of Chittenden, Vermont.

But the societies did not stop with using the press as a vehicle for the distribution of knowledge. The pamphlet and the broadside barrage was as important as the press cannonading. The societies were pleased when the Rev. Ebenezer Bradford called them "Schools of Political Knowledge" in a sermon, and they advised the minister to have his discourse published.[30] Again, the New Yorkers requested Samuel Miller, minister of the United Presbyterian Church, to have his Fourth of July sermon published by Thomas Greenleaf.[31] The reader will remember that this printed sermon was used by Mezière to fan the democratic embers in Canada. Many societies saw it as their mission to give wide distribution to treatises on republican government. The most popular of all was *The Rights of Man*, and it was not uncommon to find societies, like the one at Wytheville, Virginia, aiding in its distribution.[32] Clubs in Philadelphia, New York, and Newcastle, Delaware, had several hundred copies of their constitutions printed and given general circulation. The Republican Society of Ulster County, New York, and others often sponsored the printing and distribution of patriotic orations, given before the organization.[33] Poems written for or about the popular societies were released in newspapers and broadsides, to counteract the rhyming of those poets with Anglomania. Freneau, Mrs. Anne Julia Hatton, and St. George Tucker wrote

---

Sept. 23, 1793; *Delaware and Eastern Shore Advertiser*, Dec. 27, 1794; *Kentucky Gazette*, Aug. 31, 1793; *South Carolina State Gazette*, Oct. 10, 1794; *American Daily Advertiser*, June 14, 1794; *Catskill Packet*, April 11, 1795.

[30] Ebenezer Bradford, *The Nature of Humiliation, Fasting, and Prayer Explained.*

[31] Samuel Miller, *A Sermon.*

[32] *Virginia Gazette and General Advertiser*, July 23, 1794. The society took up a subscription for this purpose and raised $24.75.

[33] *Delaware and Eastern Shore Advertiser*, Dec. 17, 1794. Hedges, *An Oration Delivered before the Republican Society of Ulster County; Archibald Buchanan, An Oration Composed and Delivered at the Request of the Republican Society of Baltimore.*

verse about or dedicated to the democratic societies.[34] And as late as 1799 the Constitutional Society of Norfolk, Virginia, was raising money to print a thousand or more copies of an address against the Alien and Sedition Acts.[35] All this was done in the devotion to the ideal of diffusing information, for, again to quote Wortman, "knowledge is not a rare and uncommon gem, which a few are destined to monopolize; on the contrary, its treasures are susceptible of universal application."[36]

The numerous toasts given by the popular societies to "Education and Science" were not only implemented in the several ways that we have already mentioned, but also by the close association of the societies with and their support of educational developments.[37] It was common for the societies to meet in schoolhouses or "at the university." Robert Coram welcomed the Wilmington club to his schoolroom; Moses Combs, Newark teacher, did likewise; and quite often the Philadelphia club announced its meeting place to be "the university in Fourth Street."[38] "Our university—may our legislators be its nursing fathers," so toasted the Republican Society of New Haven, whose members were proud of their local institution, but favored government aid and, by implication, control.[39]

Public schools were brought to the attention of the people by these popular associations long before public education actually began. In 1795 the Philadelphians resolved that "the establishment

[34] Warner, *Means for the Preservation of Public Liberty;* "Ode on the Re-Taking of Toulon, Addressed to the Democratic Society of New York," by Mrs. Anne Julia Hatton, *The Providence Gazette,* March 29, 1794; [St. George Tucker], *The Probationary Odes of Jonathan Pindar.* This last volume contains poems dedicated to the Democratic Societies, critical of Knox, Hamilton, and Washington, and these leaders' policy of neutrality, which made America comparable to a "eunuch" or "hermaphrodite."

[35] *Norfolk Herald,* March 16, 1799.   [36] Wortman, *op. cit.,* p. 48.

[37] *Rutland Herald,* July 13, 1795; Dumfries, Va., drank a toast to "Public Seminaries. May the people be more and more impressed with the Great Truth that on the diffusion of knowledge depends all rational Liberty." See *The Republican Journal,* July 7, 1796.

[38] Wood's *Newark Gazette,* Feb. 11, 1795; *American Daily Advertiser,* Jan. 5, 1795.

[39] *Connecticut Journal,* Oct. 9, 1793. Samuel and Abraham Bishop undoubtedly had a hand in this New Haven Society. Their zeal is expressed in Abraham's *An Oration on the Extent and Power of Political Delusion.*

of public schools upon proper principles, will ensure the future of independence and republicanism." This society further agreed that the children of the poor must have equal opportunity for getting useful knowledge, if the nation was to be founded upon a broad and firm basis. Moreover, it urged the government to exert itself for the accomplishment of these ends.[40] "To encourage teachers of schools" was a main purpose written into the constitution of the frontier association, the Society of United Freemen.[41]

But of all the efforts made by the various societies to support education, that of the Patriotic Society of Newcastle, Delaware, was the most clear and explicit. At a meeting on August 30, 1794, Jesse Higgins made the following motion, seconded by Caesar A. Rodney:

Whereas by our declaration of principles, we have pledged ourselves, among other things, to promote the diffusion of knowledge among our fellow citizens;

Therefore resolved that this society do recommend to their fellow citizens the establishment of schools throughout the state of Delaware, under direction of the government, whereby the unfortunate children of indigence and neglect may be educated and enlightened among the children of opulence and vigilance, which is an essential means of preserving that equality so necessary to the preservation of a pure Republican government and that a committee of three be appointed to prepare a memorial to be laid before the legislature of this state, and report the same to our next meeting.

The committee appointed by the poor farmer-president of the society, James M'Cullough, included Robert Coram, educator, as chairman, Nicholas Vandyke, and Caesar A. Rodney. It was not until December 24, 1794, that the committee brought in its report for consideration by the members of the society. It read:

To the Legislature of the State of Delaware, the Memorial of the Subscribers, freemen of the county of Newcastle, in the said state, respectfully sheweth:

That your memorialists, deeply inpressed with the sense of the

---

[40] *Federal Gazette*, March 21, 1795.   [41] Rawle Papers, Vol. I.

inestimable benefits arising from a general and public system of education, calculated to extend to all the citizens of the State, are constrained to pray your attention to this important subject.

Your memorialists beg leave to suggest, that, although the necessity of some general system of instructing the people hath been long felt and universally acknowledged in most parts of Europe, as well as in the United States, although immense benefits have arisen from such institutions in Scotland and the New England states; although a constitutional provision for public instruction hath existed for some years in this state; although there is scarce a charge given to the Grand Inquests from the Courts of Justice of the United States which does not forcibly inculcate the necessity of public instruction; in short although the political horizon of the United States hath been long enlightened with so many luminous principles on this momentous subject which we would have thought must have darted into every mind, and expanded every heart; yet we are sorry to say, that those to whom the authority of making laws hath been hitherto delegated, have done nothing in the business; and there still remains in the minds of many, a torpor on this subject, as difficult to account for, as to excuse.

Far be it from us to presume to dictate to the Legislature, which at present we have the honor to address; yet we cannot help lamenting the fatal effects of such listless inattention to the first principles of society, which guarantees to every member of the community, the means of acquiring a knowledge of those duties, the performance of which is expected from them. By such inattention to fundamental principles, the bond of society becomes a rope of sand:—and the history of all nations abundantly testify, that no tears can wash away the fatal consequences, or the indelible reproach of such neglect.

As freemen, deeply interested in the happiness of our fellow citizens and anxious for the honor of our country we cannot avoid pressing the Legislature with our earnest solicitations, to take the premises into consideration, and to make some beginning in this important business: —being fully convinced that such government is happiest, and will be most durable, which is supported by citizens well instructed in all their social duties.

This memorial was unanimously adopted and not only sent to the state lawmaking body, but also to other individuals and groups in the state, urging them to send similar addresses to the government.[42]

Impressive, too, is the number of ways in which members of the democratic clubs were related to or active in some of the leading educational projects of the period. For example, Donald Fraser, the New York poet and teacher, was treasurer of the Society of Associated Teachers,[43] an organization thoroughly democratic in spirit that dared to welcome Priestley to America, when conservatives here and abroad were subjecting the doctor to scurrilous attacks.[44] Fraser also wrote books for the instruction of youth and brief biographies of Locke and Newton for general readers.[45]

In most places where libraries or library societies appeared, one may be sure that the democrats had their share in forwarding these enterprises. Matthew Lyon and his friends, Nathaniel Dickinson and John Brown, were instrumental in starting the Fairhaven Library Society.[46] Robert Coram and William Blamyer were both librarians, one in Wilmington and the other in Charleston. Coram located the library at his school, thus making the latter the community and cultural center of his town.[47] John Miller, the fiery democrat of the Franklin Society at Pendleton, started the first public and circulating library in Charleston when he was living there in 1783.[48] And one finds the names of Robert and Levi Todd, Benjamin Logan, Robert Johnson, and Robert Patterson as promoters of the first library in Lexington, Kentucky. By 1795 additional names of democrats were to be found, including those of Robert Barr, John Bradford, John Breckinridge, and James Brown.[49] Charter members of the library company of Baltimore were

---

[42] *Delaware and Eastern Shore Advertiser,* Dec. 27, 1794.

[43] New York City *Directory,* 1799, p. 130.

[44] Wood's *Newark Gazette,* June 25, 1794.

[45] Books by Donald Fraser are *The Columbian Monitor, The Mental Flower Garden,* and *A Collection of Select Biography.*

[46] *Farmers Library,* Aug. 19, 1794; Hemenway, *The Vermont Historical Gazeteer,* III, 699.

[47] Conrad, *History of the State of Delaware,* II, 409; Charleston *City Directory,* 1795.

[48] William L. King, *The Newspaper Press of Charleston, South Carolina,* p. 36.

[49] Conover, *Concerning the Forefathers,* p. 255 and *passim;* Peter, *History of Fayette County, Kentucky,* p. 384.

George Sears, James Buchanan, James McCulloch, William Mac-Creery, and Thomas Rutter, all active in the Baltimore Republican Society.[50] A writer in the *New York Journal* for February 26, 1794, indicated that republican societies should be formed in every state, county, and town, the first task of which would be to distribute tracts on government, and the second to promote schools and libraries. At the moment he was writing, this was actually happening.

With Thomas Paine writing that half the revenue of the country should be divided between funds to relieve the plight of the poor and to advance education, it is little wonder that those who toasted and admired him should be concerned in educational ventures.[51] Below is a list of a few of the academies and colleges from Vermont to South Carolina, which were begun by or aided by the members of the popular societies:

Vermont

Castleton Seminary. The first trustees were Dr. James Witherell and Isaac Clarke.[52]
University of Vermont. William Coit, president of the Chittenden Democratic Society, was a "zealous patron" of the university and "contributed liberally" to its support.[53]

New York

Montgomery Academy in Ulster County. Nearly all of the trustees were leaders in the popular society of that place, and the principal was Nathan White, also an active member.[54]

Pennsylvania

Franklin College. This college was started by and for the German citizenry in Lancaster. The Muhlenbergs were active here.[55]
University of Pennsylvania. Dallas, Du Ponceau, McClenachan,

---

[50] *The Maryland Historical Magazine,* IX (No. 3), 105.
[51] W. P. Hall, *British Radicalism, 1791–1797,* p. 91.
[52] A. N. Adams, *A History of the Town of Fairhaven, Vermont,* p. 122.
[53] Sanders, *A Discourse on Occasion of the Death of William Coit, Esq.*
[54] Headley, ed., *The History of Orange County,* p. 319.
[55] Richards, *German Pioneers in Pennsylvania,* p. 23.

Hutchinson, Rittenhouse, Sergeant, and others served as trustees or as faculty members.[56]

✓ *Washington Academy.* Books came from B. F. Bache's bookshop, "in preference to any other." David Bradford was secretary of the board of trustees from the beginning to 1794. Other trustees and "whiskey boys" were James Marshel, James Edgar, John M'Dowell, Absalom Baird, David Redick, and James Allison.[57]

Canonsburg Academy (Jefferson College). Three members of the Washington Democratic Society also started this educational institution. They were Col. John Canon, James Allison, and John M'Dowell.[58]

Maryland

The House of Industry (Maryland School for Boys). Dr. Edward Johnson was a founder of this school.[59]

Kentucky

Transylvania Seminary. At different times both John Bradford and John Breckinridge served as president of the board of trustees. The Todds, Robert Patterson, and other democratic society members contributed books and money to build up the library.[60]

Bourbon Academy. Among the first trustees were the democrats John Allen, Thomas Jones, James Brown, and James Kenny.[61]

Rittenhouse Academy. Trustees included Robert Johnson, Bartlett Collins, William Henry, John Payne, and Samuel Shepard.[62]

---

[56] Cheyney, *History of the University of Pennsylvania,* pp. 182–208, 435.

[57] Minutes and Proceedings of the Board of Trustees of Washington Academy. Manuscript volumes in the business office of Washington and Jefferson College, Washington, Penn. Benjamin Bache wrote to Charles Debrett, Dec. 3, 1796, that he was ready to publish anything on the subject of education or of an educational nature. Monroe and Bache collaborated in printing materials attacking the Adams administration. In these letters from Monroe to Bache, Oct. 9, 15, and Nov. 6, 1797, and March 26, 1798, the author warns the "radical" printer against errors, for a minor mistake will be magnified into grave criticism. These letters are in the Bache Collection. Wansey (*An Excursion,* p. 121) writes of the agreeable reception awaiting one upon a visit to Bache's bookshop.

[58] *Biographical and Historical Catalogue of Washington and Jefferson College,* p. 7; *Pittsburgh Gazette,* Jan. 19, 1793, tells how the students paid for their tuition in produce.

[59] Coyle, *The Mayors of Baltimore,* p. 92.

[60] Records of the Proceedings of the Board of Trustees for Transylvania Seminary, in Transylvania University Library; Sonne, *Liberal Kentucky,* contains much of interest to the student of early Kentucky life.

[61] Thos. D. Clark, *A History of Kentucky,* chap. xiii.   [62] *Ibid.*

Virginia

Wythe Academy. Alexander Smyth, Jesse Evans, Daniel Sheffy, and William Tate were trustees at its inception in 1792.[63]

South Carolina

Winnsborough Academy. First sponsored by the Mt. Scion Society, for "to promote knowledge is the firmest cement of the state." Its purpose was to maintain and educate poor orphans and indigent children. Revolutionary leaders and republican society members who lent their support included Robert Howard, Dr. James Lynah, Alexander Moultrie, Edward Lacey, William Moultrie, Jr., William Tate, Simeon Theus, Alexander Gillon, and James Kennedy.[64]

Eleemosynary institutions, such as orphanages and charity schools, found ready aid from the popular societies or certain of their more affluent members. On July 4 each year the New York Democratic Society took a collection, to be turned over for the aid of the local charity school. When Col. Henry Rutgers, a member, died, he had not only given support to the founding of Rutgers University, but he also asked that his funeral expenses be kept at a minimum, so that more money would go to the infant School Society.[65]

As for the education of women, the leading democrats were neither silent nor indolent, in a day when the children of the Enlightenment were reading and quoting Mary Wollstonecraft. William Boyd, of Boston, read his poem entitled *Woman* in the Harvard University Chapel on April 19, 1796. The poem praised Mary Wollstonecraft and endorsed her defense of women's rights.[66] Benjamin Bache believed that women "could add to the knowledge of the common fund" and was sorry that in the past they had been denied educational opportunity.[67] John Swanwick,

---

[63] French and Armstrong, *Notable Southern Families*, V, 564; *Tylers Quarterly Historical and Genealogical Magazine*, II, 282.

[64] Easterby, *A History of the College of Charleston*, p. 16; City of Charleston, *Yearbook* (1887).

[65] McMurray, *A Sermon Occasioned by the Death of Colonel Henry Rutgers.* The names of Robert Howard, Thomas Lehre, and James Gregorie will be found as supporters of the home for orphans in Charleston, *City Gazette*, Sept. 20, 1793.

[66] William Boyd, *Woman.*

[67] Bache to M. H. Markoe, Nov. 26, 1789, Bache Papers.

merchant, and poet by avocation, often made women the subject of his verse and was a benefactor of the Young Ladies Academy of Philadelphia.[68] Swanwick, however, was concerned with the promotion of all types of education. He advocated a system to bring learning to the poor throughout the state of Pennsylvania and spoke in the state house of representatives for grants to the university and to Dickinson College.[69] This, besides his encouragement to female education and his devotion to adult education as manifested by his activity in the local popular society, would classify him as one of the outstanding exponents of education in his state.

Even more interesting is the work of Dr. John Willard, in Middlebury, Vermont. Willard was firmly back of the movement to establish a college in his locality and used his influence to get important men to give the idea support.[70] Ida Strong was disappointed that the college did not admit women, so she started the Female Seminary. Unfortunately, this pioneer died in 1804. Then it was that the charming, twenty-year-old Emma Hart came into the frontier community, to continue the work of Miss Strong. The seminary was woefully in need of help, for one reads that because of lack of fuel Miss Hart and her students danced around in order to keep warm. After her marriage to Dr. John Willard, the course of the school was smoother. He gave enthusiastic assistance to his idealistic young wife, brought the school into his spacious and comfortable home, and helped Emma face all comers who made censorious remarks on the right of women to an education.[71] Willard was an officer of the Addison County Democratic Society in 1794, and both he and his wife were republicans, "friends of Mr. Jefferson."

Of the several plans offered in the decade of the 90's for a national system of education, two were written by outstanding mem-

[68] Swanwick, *Poems on Several Occasions* (Phil., 1797); *The Aurora*, May 19, 1794; Mary S. Benson, *Women in Eighteenth Century America* (N.Y., 1935), pp. 142, 162–63, 166.

[69] *Gazette of the United States*, Sept. 27, 1794.

[70] Willard to Asa Aldis, Sept. 9, 1810 in New York State Library.

[71] Swift, *History of the Town of Middlebury*, pp. 250–51; Lutz, *Emma Willard, Daughter of Democracy*, pp. 38–44.

bers of the democratic societies—Robert Coram and James Sullivan.[72] Benjamin Rush, who, as we have seen, may have been a member, also wrote out a plan.[73] All three of these plans recognized the organic relationship between democracy and education; all three were certain that a government must educate for democracy. Of all the plans, Coram's and Sullivan's were particularly clear on the need for constant reform and reconstruction in government and in education, if democratic progress was to be obtained. Education must not be devoted to old forms of social thinking, but, giving opportunity to all, it must promote progress and seek a continual revision of customs and institutions.[74]

So, not only as sponsors of forums, as disseminators of information and opponents of restrictive acts designed to suppress free speech, but also as champions of public schools, as benefactors of early colleges, and as pioneers in female education, the people's societies and their members made contributions. These clubs were powerful instruments both for and in behalf of public instruction.

While the Federalists imbibed toasts for "A speedy downfall to modern democracy" and for the most part defended special education for the few and charity schools for the many, the Republicans sought to underpin democracy with popular education. Even the revolutionary Negroes of Haiti, whom the southern slaveholders eyed with fear and trembling, wrote in their constitution that a plan should be set up for the establishment of public schools.[75] In our own country, men such as De Witt Clinton, Joel Barlow, and

[72] Coram, *Political Inquiries, to Which Is Added a Plan for the General Establishment of Schools throughout the United States;* James Sullivan, *Thoughts upon the Political Situation of the United States of America,* and also *Observations upon the Government of the United States of America.*

[73] *A Plan for the Establishment of Public Schools and the Diffusion of Knowledge in Pennsylvania; to Which Are Added, Thoughts upon the Mode of Education Proper in a Republic, Addressed to the Legislature and Citizens of the State.*

[74] Hansen, *op. cit.,* pp. 63, 78 and 88. This progressive and democratic ideal for education seems to be characteristic of the Jeffersonians. The Federalist tended not to object to religious control over education and to express a dread of too widely diffused public education. David Osgood, for instance, was sure that France's establishment of public schools was an attempt to destroy the altar of God: *Some Facts Evincive of the Atheistical, Anarchical and in Other Respects Immoral Principles of the French Republicans.*

[75] *American Daily Advertiser,* July 16, 1805.

James Monroe, all figures of national importance in the republican party, were writing and preaching that in order to survive, a democracy must provide for wide education and the diffusion of knowledge.[76] In this process the popular societies played a paramount role. By 1795, two years after the first clubs appeared, Americans as well as visitors from foreign shores were noting the "rage for politics" where "all ages and all conditions have become statesmen," and are "regulating the affairs of the world." [77] With the increase of interest in public affairs came an increase in voting and a new vigor at election time.[78] Consul Mangourit was right when he wrote of the political societies that "ces flambeaux de l'opinion publique éclairent chaque état." [79] The more liberal fathers of America believed that democracy could never die, if the free play of educational forces remained unhampered; that democracy is best defended by the advancement of education.

[76] For De Witt Clinton's work for education, see Edward A. Fitzpatrick, *The Educational Views and Influence of De Witt Clinton*. For Joel Barlow, see an interesting letter to Abraham Baldwin, Jan. 3, 1801, Barlow Papers, Box II. Here Barlow has some doubts about Jefferson's republicanism and he asks Baldwin if Jefferson will follow his predecessors, or will he boldly change conditions and build a great America? Will the new president be satisfied with the present system of education, or will he see its inadequacies and mold it for the betterment of mankind? For Monroe, see *Writings of James Monroe*, ed. by Hamilton, pp. 306–7.

[77] See the traveler, Chastellux, in the *Independent Chronicle*, March 9, 1795; also, "The Middler, No. II," *The Maryland Gazette*, Feb. 26, 1795.

[78] Robinson, *Jeffersonian Democracy in New England*, p. 10.

[79] Mangourit, *Mémoire*, p. 23.

Chapter Eight

THE ATTACK UPON DEMOCRACY

The rich have grate power and Influence over the poor, and that Selfe in the Best of Men is two much like an object that is plased before the Eye which hinders the site of anything beyond; and that touch a mans Interest or his Eydeayes thereof and eue may be sure to have him in opposition with his full strength; also that in all governments their is naturally two distinct Contending partyes and the grate Dividing Line is between those that Labour for a Living and those who git one without or as they are generally termed, the few and the Many.

From WILLIAM MANNING'S manuscript letter to the state legislature of Massachusetts, February 6, 1790, giving his reasons for opposing the funding system

---

THE following, just one of numerous examples, indicates the seething emotions in the bosom of a Virginia lady, who signs herself "Xantippe," when the Kentucky Democratic Society was mentioned to her. She wrote:

But in Kentucky you have a Democratic Society—that horrible sink of treason,—that hateful synagogue of anarchy,—that odious conclave of tumult,—that frightful cathedral of discord,—that poisonous garden of conspiracy,—that hellish school of rebellion and opposition to all regular and well-balanced authority.[1]

What gave rise to such emotional outbursts and acid attacks upon the progressives and their organizations? This is the first problem this chapter will face, after which the methods to discredit the popular clubs will be considered. And finally, an appraisal will be made of the success of the conservatives in their struggles to rout the Sons of Liberty.

[1] *Virginia Chronicle*, July 17, 1794. See also *The Rights of Asses; Springer's Weekly Oracle*, Aug. 6, 1798; *Connecticut Courant*, May 27, 1793, June 12, Dec. 8, 1794.

The anti-republicans, delineated by Jefferson as the "old refugees and tories," "British merchants," "American merchants trading in British capital," "Speculators," and "nervous persons," were afraid of anything, or anybody, which might unduly stir the masses of the people.[2] From pre-Revolutionary days down to the appearance of the democratic societies, the critical problem for the wealthy merchants and gentlemen of property was to keep the "irresponsible classes" down.[3] The ochlocratic tendencies in a revolutionary milieu, marked by the actions of the Regulators, the Sons of Liberty, the Shaysites, and by the implications in radical state constitutions such as that of Pennsylvania, could not be tolerated. They appeared to be a threat to property and order.

The rich and well-born, colleagues and followers of Alexander Hamilton, felt this threat keenly. In New England it was the Essex Junto, a body of prosperous merchants, who with Hamilton directed the financial and foreign policies of the Washington and Adams administrations.[4] "Gain is their God, and present gain is their polar star," wrote Horatio Gates of this clique of eastern traders.[5] When pamphlets like *An Emetic for Aristocrats* appeared, though few in number as compared with the deluge of propaganda from the presses of the sycophants, the house of "good order" was thrown into terror.[6] Stephen Higginson, an Essex merchant, wrote to Hamilton in 1793 of the dangers from the "seditious and desparate" in Boston. He added that through the organizing of the merchants, these dangerous elements had been combated and subdued.[7]

[2] Thomas Jefferson Papers, Vol. XCVIII, Item 16893, Library of Congress.

[3] Schlesinger, *The Colonial Merchants and the American Revolution*, pp. 240, 256, 285, 307. Also *The Works of Fisher Ames*, ed. by Seth Ames, p. 140.

[4] Morison, *Maritime History of Massachusetts*, pp. 166, 167; Thomas, *Reminiscences of the Last Sixty-Five Years*, I, 16; A. E. Morse (*The Federalist Party in Massachusetts to the Year 1800*, p. 16) says the Junto was organized to check democracy.

[5] To Madison, Madison Papers, Vol. XVII, No. 37. Library of Congress.

[6] *An Emetic for Aristocrats*, 1795. This anonymous pamphlet criticizing Washington, Jay, Hamilton, Higginson, and others, was given away to the "rabble" who opposed "old Tories."

[7] Higginson to Hamilton, July 26, 1793, Hamilton Papers, Vol. XX, No. 2750. Library of Congress.

In New York and southward through the principal seaports, Hamilton's friends constituted still other speculators and merchants who were dominated by British commercial influence or were heavy investors in American funds. It is little wonder that Hamilton and the British Minister, Hammond, were on intimate terms, for they both agreed that "all the dearest interests of society were involved" in the war between France and England.[8] If America did not remain neutral but were to take up the cause of France, British investments on this side of the ocean would be unsafe, and a sweeping change in government might ensue. Nor is it any wonder that besides Hamilton, who, it was said, held investments in English securities,[9] men like William L. Smith, Rufus King, Fisher Ames, Elias Boudinot, and Ralph Izard, who held the famous American six per-cents, were out to stop any movement which might alter the *status quo*.[10]

To augment the fears of the conservatives, the popular societies had succeeded in doing what their predecessors, the Sons of Liberty, had failed to do. They had united the urban dissent with that of the country "levelling" ideas, and both groups believed in the right to alter or to abolish bad government.[11] When the spirit of revolt against the excise spread throughout the West in 1794, when certain popular leaders openly endorsed or hesitated to censure the action, and when popular societies were implicated and assumed

[8] Hammond to Grenville, April 27, 1794, British Archives, F.O.5, Vol. IV, No. 15; also April 2, 1793, F.O.5, Vol. I, No. 11. Cf. Bemis, "Jay's Treaty and the Northwest Boundary Gap, *American Historical Review*, XXVII (1922), 473.

[9] John Beckley to Madison, May 25, 1795, Madison Papers, New York Public Library. This letter says that Commodore Nicholson, president of the New York Democratic Society, has proof that Hamilton has a heavy investment in English funds. Nicholson warns that if Hamilton ever attempts to run for office, he will publish the facts immediately.

[10] Fisher Ames to Andrew Craigie, Dec. 2, 8, 1791, MSS in the American Antiquarian Society; Pinckney Papers, July 14, 1790, Library of Congress; Fee, "The Effect of Hamilton's Financial Policy upon Public Opinion in New Jersey," *Proceedings of the New Jersey Historical Society*, L (1932), 33–34. For two letters that show the fears arising in the minds of men like Oliver Wolcott or Theodore Sedgewick at the thought of war against England, see Wolcott to Noah Webster, May 3, 1794, Webster Papers, New York Public Library; and Thomas Dwight to Sedgewick, March 6, 1794, Sedgewick Papers, Massachusetts Historical Society.

[11] Morais, in *The Era of the American Revolution*, ed. by Morris, pp. 279–80.

extralegal powers, it was to be expected that the propertied interests would be profoundly agitated. Even the big landowners, many of whom had become leaders in the societies because they favored restraining Indian, English, and Spanish competition for lands, turned suddenly into the camp of the conservatives. David Allison, the land agent of John Gray Blount of Washington, North Carolina, bemoaned the fact that "the damned Pennsylvania insurgents" had brought losses in western land deals.[12] All the men of property saw in the united system of the popular societies a danger that might parallel occurrences in France.[13] Property might be taken for public purposes, confessed Fisher Ames; the democratic societies would do to America what had been done to Geneva, said the patroon, William Van Schaack; political mischief would destroy the security of property, said John Jay; the societies "want to go down the current and stop at the cataract," stated William Vans Murray.[14] For this reason more than any other, namely, that the wealthy classes trembled at the thought of radical social change and its accompanying shift in property relationships, the popular societies were dreaded and viciously attacked. Better, it was, to follow the smug advice of Fisher Ames and "Let wealth lie snug in its iron chest, and let its defence be committed to the wit, learning and talents of a few." [15]

The apprehensiveness of "the few" approached irrational fear, which breeds spleen and invective, when they saw the close association that existed between the democratic societies and a democratic militia. Here, indeed, was the power to enforce popular demands.

[12] Allison to Blount, Sept. 25, 1794, John G. Blount Papers, in the North Carolina Historical Commission Library.

[13] Chas. Nisbet to Alex. Addison, April 18, 1795, Nisbet Collection, Darlington Library, University of Pittsburgh; Wolcott to Wm. L. Smith, Nov. 29, 1798, Smith Papers, Library of Congress; E. Hazard to J. Morse, April 20, 1795, Morse Family Collection, Yale University Library.

[14] The Works of Fisher Ames, ed. by Seth Ames, p. 143; Van Schaack to Sedgewick, Dec. 29, 1794, Sedgewick Papers, Massachusetts Historical Society; Jay to King, May 3, 1794, King Papers, New York Historical Society; Wm. V. Murray to James McHenry, Dec. 16, 1794, McHenry Papers, Vol. III, Library of Congress.

[15] Ames to Gore, Dec. 13, 1802, Ames Papers.

Here was the *enfant terrible*, the incisive instrument for transferring power, that by hook or crook must be smashed. A closer observation of this crucial problem is necessary.

Since the first shots heard around the world, the men of wealth kept a wary eye on the citizen soldiers, distrusted them, and feared them. Washington had no confidence in the militia, called it "a broken reed," and proceeded at times to be unnecessarily harsh with the common soldiers.[16] Hamilton belittled the volunteer militia. He failed to credit it with the important victories at King's Mountain and Cowpens during the war for freedom. He declared it was "the mimicry of soldiership."[17] It was held in circumspection because, democratic body that it was, electing its officers and making its rules,[18] it demanded to know against whom, and for what, it was asked to fight. Sometimes these questions were too pertinent, and the militia hesitated to follow blindly orders from on high, especially when these orders turned farmers against their fellow farmers, as in the Shays's or the Whiskey Rebellion.[19] Again, many soldiers objected to the lack of adequate pay. This was true particularly along the frontier, where, because of low wages, the militiamen were none too friendly toward the central government and its highly paid officials.[20] Finally, the militia riflemen, renowned in Europe as well as America, were a formidable foe to any enemy.[21] The technicway, the long squirrel rifle, gave its user a more careful control over food supply and an advantage over those victims of the cultural lag who stuck by the old musket. The accuracy of the

[16] Knollenberg, *Washington and the Revolution*, pp. 24, n., 216–19.

[17] Hamilton, *Works*, ed. by Lodge, V, 97.

[18] "Minutes of the New York Hibernian Volunteers," MS in the New York Historical Society.

[19] William Sullivan says (*Familiar Letters on Public Characters and Public Events*, p. 5) that the militia could not be relied upon to put down the insurrection in Massachusetts in 1784–85.

[20] Peale, *Charles Willson Peale and His Public Services during the American Revolution. Paper Read before the Society of the Sons of the American Revolution*, pp. 27–28; see Cumberland County town meeting, Aug. 4, 1794, in Affaires Étrangères, Vol. XLI, Part 4; *Pittsburgh Gazette*, Sept. 7, 1793.

[21] The consuls Mangourit and Hauterive both tried to raise rifle corps in America to send to France. Mangourit proposed calling his "The Legion of South Carolina"; see Mangourit to Genet, June 14, 1793, Genet Papers.

frontier riflemen at a great distance would have been baneful to oppressors, and the oppressors knew it.[22]

Moreover, too many militia companies were Francophile in spirit, and at one with the purposes of the popular societies, to give the Federalists comfort. Genet was repeatedly invited to be the honored guest of the various regiments in Philadelphia, and at one of these dinners the assembly lifted a toast to him, but refused to do the same for Washington.[23] As late as 1798, the Republican Blues of Norfolk, Virginia, were challenging the Alien and Sedition Acts, commemorating the Fourth of July, and toasting the names of Jefferson and Madison.[24] In the same state, at Richmond, the militia proclaimed itself as opposed to any curbs on freedom, for, it said, you "cannot cut off the shoot of licentiousness, without seri-

[22] The writer is indebted to Dr. George S. Counts for insight into the use and significance of the rifle. It has proved a fascinating side study, and the facts which relate to the subject before us are offered here.

Germans and Swiss, who probably got the idea of the rifle from Italy, came to Pennsylvania about 1700 and settled near the frontier as gunsmiths. The demands of their locale brought the rifle gun into prominence, and soon they were making better arms than could be imported. (Horace Kephart, "The Rifle in Colonial Times," *Magazine of American History*, XXIV [Sept., 1890],179). During the Revolution, the Pennsylvania riflemen startled the people at Boston and Cambridge with their expert marksmanship, and the English were awe-stricken when colonials with their rifles were able to pick off the redcoats as they stood on the decks of ships in the harbors. (Heller, *The Gunmakers of Old Northampton*, pp. 1–14; James Jarvis, "Reminiscences of Virginia," pp. 31–34, in MS Room, Library of Congress.) So valuable was the rifle on the advancing frontier after the Revolution that it could hardly be purchased for love or money. In Western Pennsylvania it was worth two horses and a good wagon; in Kentucky, two cows and two calves. (Williams, "Education in Greenville County, South Carolina, prior to 1860," p. 9; Breckinridge Papers, Vol. X, No. 1622, in Library of Congress.) John Bernard, who traveled in America in the 1790's, wrote in his *Retrospections of America* (p. 181) of the baffling accuracy of our riflemen in the militia. They could "enlarge the eye of a tin cock on a church steeple," he said, and added that they played the game of "Shooting the Cup" off one another's heads, standing at a distance of one hundred paces! A good general discussion of the importance of the rifle may be found in Burlingame's *The March of the Iron Men*. Several of the Pennsylvania gunsmiths offered their newest inventions to Genet, for they wanted them to be used for and not against the Rights of Man. (Joseph G. Chambers to Genet, May 15, 1793, Genet Papers.) In the light of the effectiveness of the militiaman's rifle, it is little wonder that Hamilton mobilized a ridiculously large army to send against the Whiskey Rebels.

[23] See in the Genet Papers the following dates: Jan. 1, 1793, Jan. 2, Feb. 7, 1794.

[24] *Norfolk Herald*, May 12, 26, July 10, 1798.

ously injuring the plant" of liberty.[25] As a matter of fact, many of the democratic clubs were formed around a militia company that made up the nucleus of the organization. We have already seen this to be true in two of the Western Pennsylvania societies. It was equally true at Charleston, where the Republican Society was formed around the Charleston Battalion of Artillery; and at Paris, Kentucky, where the Democratic Society was composed, in part, of representatives from the militia companies in Bourbon County; and at Rutland, Vermont, where Cutler's Artillery Company met with the society; and again at Portland, Maine, with the local artillery company forming the core of the republican club.[26]

Most of the Federalists remembered too well how the Sons of Liberty had formed armed units, closely associated with their societies, to take lightly these new Liberty Boys and their control over the militia.[27] Where the popular clubs and the militia were not integrally related, there existed a friendly spirit and a common understanding. The two celebrated Independence Day together, and frequently one or more of the officers of the democratic society was captain or colonel of the local militia. True, there were Federalist militia units. Newark, New Jersey, for instance, had the Federal Blues and the Republican Fusiliers, but the latter had for its officers Matthias and Thomas Ward, John Simonson, and others, all of whom were active in the Republican Society of that town.[28] William Dickson, the printer of Lancaster, Pennsylvania, commanded the Republican Blues and presided over a popular society.[29] The Republican Blues of Philadelphia were commanded at one time by Blair McClenachan and at another by William Duane.[30] John Steele, David Stodder, and James A. Buchanan were captains of

[25] *Virginia Argus*, July 9, 1799.

[26] Benj. Legare to Mangourit, Feb. 6, 1793, in "The Correspondence of the Republican Society of Charleston, S.C." in the Boston Public Library; *American Daily Advertiser*, Aug. 11, 1794; *Rutland Herald*, July 13, 1795; "Minute Book" of the First Portland Artillery Company (1791–97), MS in the Maine Historical Society.

[27] Morais, *op. cit.*, p. 272.

[28] *History of the City of Newark*, I, 456; *Newark Gazette*, March 19, 1794.

[29] Worner, "Standard Presented to the Republican Blues," *Lancaster Historical Society Publications*, XXXIV (1930), 256.

[30] *Aurora*, July 7, 1798; July 6, 1799.

Baltimore militia companies, one of which was called the Sansculottes, and often met with the Baltimore Republican Society.[31] Pamphlets on military tactics were written by the democrats Alexander Smyth and William Duane. The latter called his *A Handbook for Riflemen;* in it he states the importance of the rifle. Developed in America, the rifle won the battle of Saratoga and aided France in her revolution, according to Duane.[32] Furthermore, the societies commonly drank toasts to the militia, and the Franklin Society of Pendleton, South Carolina, defended the democratic character of the citizen army. It resolved:

That it is the inherent right of every free man to vote and elect the officers who are to command them in a military character; and he who dares to attempt a contravention of the right, forfeits all protection from this country, is a tyrant and a despot, and an enemy to the people.[33]

In the light of these close relationships between the militia and the patriotic societies, a condition that was tantamount to arming the citizens,[34] one can readily appreciate the restlessness of the "monocrats."

In order to relieve their fears, the conservatives advanced the idea of a standing army. This, they reasoned, would halt the rebelliousness shown when the call went out for any army to march into Western Pennsylvania. The officers, who were "generally for turning out" for the western army, could then force the reluctant

[31] Scharf, *Chronicles,* p. 247; State Papers, April 9, 1794, in the Maryland Historical Society. Other outstanding militia leaders in the democratic clubs were Isaac Clarke, known as "Old Rifle," because of his skill in using the gun (Hemenway, *Gazetteer,* I, 907); Absalom Baird (Frontier War Series, 1792, Wisconsin Historical Society); Henry Rutgers and Jacob De La Montagnie (*New York City Directory,* 1793, p. 205); Thomas Newton, of Norfolk, Va. (Governor's Letterbook, Oct. 9, 1794, in the Virginia State Library); Walter Crockett, of Wytheville, Va. (Broadside, "A Topographical Analysis of the Commonwealth of Virginia" [1790–91] in folder No. 180, Library of Congress.)

[32] Smyth, *Regulations for the Field Exercise, Manoeuvres and Conduct of the Infantry of the United States;* Duane, *A Handbook for Riflemen.*

[33] *Baltimore Daily Intelligencer,* July 7, 1794; *City Gazette,* June 30, 1794.

[34] Only the Portland Republican Society actually urged arming, so far as the records reveal. The English popular societies were suspected of arming, and suppressed; see Birely, *op. cit.,* p. 26.

commoners to join them.[35] Or in the case of "riots," as the Federalists called them, where a crowd gathered to hail a hero or defend a cause, the standing army could attack and disperse the people, instead of defending them as the militia did in Baltimore in 1794.[36] Or again, an army would end the actions of the Charleston republicans in using the militia to disarm British ships, and the actions of a militia company in Washington, North Carolina, which protected pro-French privateering.[37]

These acts and others like them on the part of an armed citizenry irritated the Federalists and gave them premonitions. Even though the democrats defended their militia by insisting that it was the bulwark of their liberties and by championing its effectiveness during the Revolution, the opposition was not mollified. George Cabot, of the Essex Junto, was worried over Genet's associations with military units that could be used to advance French principles in the United States.[38] Another Federalist suggested to Governor Mifflin that the people be deprived of choosing their officers, because, under such methods, the officers always support "the turbulent." [39] Hamilton wrote to Oliver Wolcott, July 28, 1795, to say that because of the Jacobinic complexion of the New York City militia, it could not be relied upon and that it would be some time before a good substitute could be organized.[40] The partisans of France, among the commanders of the militia, at the height of the

[35] "Captain David Ford's Journal," *Proceedings of the New Jersey Historical Society*, VIII (1856), 83.
[36] David Stodder, a popular leader in Baltimore, was arrested and charged with stirring the populace against an Englishman who derisively hoisted a French flag upside down on his ship's mast. A large crowd gathered at the jail and demanded Stodder's release. The Federalist judge, Samuel Chase, was disturbed by the threats from the people and by the fact that the militia would not aid in halting the outbreak. See the report of Samuel Chase to Gov. Thomas Lee, May 6, 1794, Emmet Collection, New York Public Library.
[37] Governor to Assembly of North Carolina, Dec. 4, 1793, Governors Letterbook, 1792–95, Library of the Historical Commission of North Carolina; *American Daily Advertiser*, Jan. 23, 1794; Woodfin, "Citizen Genet and His Mission," p. 268.
[38] Cabot to Parsons, Jan. 8, 1794, in Parsons, *Memoir of Theophilus Parsons*.
[39] S. Bryson to Mifflin, March 4, 1794, Mifflin Papers, Vol. XXVII, p. 21, in the Pennsylvania State Library.
[40] Wolcott MSS, Vol. VII, No. 7, in the Connecticut Historical Society.

anti-French feeling in 1798, disturbed Charles Nisbet.[41] And the Federalist governor, John Jay, so long as he was in office, prevented the formation of an Irish militia unit in New York City. Jay refused to allow the company to convene by withholding commissions from the elected officers of the Hibernian Volunteers. Hence there was no wearing of the green uniform.[42] It was obvious enough that the gentlemen of consequence were out to annihilate the people's militia and to set up in its place a centrally controlled army.

The nightmare of the inhabitants of the southern states was the slave revolt. In the decade from 1790 to 1800, these revolts increased 150 percent over the previous decade.[43] The "Tyrannical Libertymen" or "Republican Pharaohs," as the northerners dubbed the southern slaveholders, wondered if talk of French liberty did not fan the hot sparks of revolt. The New England Federalists certainly thought this true, and had no hesitation, since it served their ends, in reminding the southern democrats as graphically as possible how democracy and insurrections were blood brothers.[44] Realities seemed to bear out the warnings of the Federalists, and fears increased as men began to read the handwriting on the wall.

The Negro up-surge in the French West Indies sent a shudder through the planter families in all the states from Virginia southward. An attempted insurrection in Norfolk, Virginia, in 1793, where the population ratio was about two whites to one black, was attributed to the Santo Domingo uprisings.[45] The most lurid broadsides and pamphlets were scattered about, telling in detail of the horrors perpetrated upon white people in the islands. At once, men began to write and agitate for restraint on the importation of Negroes from territories where they had been exposed to ideas of rebellion.[46]

---

[41] Nisbet to Chas. Wallace, Oct. 25, 1798, Nisbet Papers, New York Public Library.

[42] New York Hibernian Volunteers, "Minutes" from Jan. to March, 1796, in the New York Historical Society. See also A. E. Morse, *op. cit.*, p. 147.

[43] Carroll, *Slave Insurrections in the United States*, pp. 41–45.

[44] *Tyrannical Libertymen. A Discourse upon Negro Slavery in the United States.*

[45] *Norfolk Directory*, 1801, p. 66; Executives Letterbook, Aug. 16, 23, 1793, in the Virginia State Library; Josiah Parker to the Sec. of State, Jan. 8, 1794, Misc. Letters, Department of State; T. A. Boyd, *Light Horse Harry Lee*, p. 206.

[46] Three letters on the danger of harboring the Negroes from the French West Indies, in manuscript, and signed "Rusticus," are of interest. They are in the

Moreover, it was unsafe for the slaves to gather, from ardent democrats in America, that "equality is the natural condition of man." Such teachings were sure to bring the fate of the West Indies to the southern shores.[47] Not only Norfolk, but also Charleston, Wilmington, Richmond, and other towns heard the rumblings of revolt.[48] Jefferson warned of the danger.[49] South Carolinians awakened to the fact that large bodies of Negroes were assembling under the pretense of religious services and were hearing doctrines "highly detrimental to the welfare and policy of the state." [50] Peter Freneau discovered that nearly 200 copies of his republican newspaper were taken daily, from his printing office, by slaves.[51] Insurrection seemed so imminent to Hugh Williamson, of North Carolina, in 1794 that he was startled to find the white people from Maryland southward poorly armed.[52] It was time for curtailment of all talk of liberty and equality. As the astute and conservative Nisbet saw the situation:

It seems that there are black as well as white opinions, and that the love of liberty is a very black one, whenever it is adopted by anything in black.[53]

"Too much of the new-fangled French philosophy" had gotten to the Negroes, according to John Rutledge,[54] and the popular

---

library of the South Carolina Historical Society. A broadside in the 1795 collection of the American Antiquarian Society upholds the exclusion of Negroes from Santo Domingo. Also see *Fayetteville Gazette*, Aug. 7, 1792; Du Bois, *The Suppression of the African Slave Trade*, p. 81.

[47] "Phocion" [William L. Smith] in *City Gazette*, Nov. 26, 1794.

[48] British Archives, F.O.5, Vol. I, No. 20; *Pittsburgh Gazette*, Dec. 12, 1795; *Gazette of the United States*, Sept. 5, 1794; *State Gazette of North Carolina*, July 30, 1795.

[49] To Monroe, July 14, 1794, Monroe Papers, New York Public Library; also Jefferson warned Moultrie, of South Carolina, that French agents were inciting insurrection, Jefferson Papers, Vol. XCVI, Item 16402, Library of Congress.

[50] *South Carolina State Gazette*, May 10, 1795.

[51] Thomas, *op. cit.*, I, 78.

[52] Williamson to J. G. Blount, July 3, 1794, J. G. Blount Papers. Both Saint-Mery (*Voyage aux États-Unis de l'Amérique, 1793–1798*, pp. 330–32) and Bayard (*Voyage dans l'intérieur des États-Unis*, chap. v) describe the inhuman treatment dealt the slaves in America and say that because of the cruelties, the slaves often started fires in hateful protest.

[53] To Addison, Sept. 29, 1791, Nisbet Collection, Darlington Library, University of Pittsburgh.

[54] Du Bois, *op. cit.*, p. 82.

societies had been instrumental in spreading this philosophy. Brissot had founded the Société des Amis des Noirs and Genet was a member. The discovery of this fact did much to discredit the ambassador in the South.[55] It likewise tended to mark the democratic societies as pro-Negro and therefore as a threat to a labor system that was proving more lucrative as the decade advanced.[56] Men like Alexander Smyth, of Wytheville, Virginia, and John Breckinridge, of Lexington, Kentucky, vehement democrats though they once were, turned to vigorous opposition to emancipation. Interestingly enough, both believed the antislavery crusade was an attack upon private property.[57] Furthermore, cartoons were circulated, portraying a meeting of a democratic club with its members pulling down the pillars of government. In the background was a Negro awaiting his turn to create havoc with "good order." [58]

We have presented the principal apprehensions that dogged the life of the conservative groups after the American Revolution. Whether Federalist or republican, the wealthy feared the populace, with its leveling tendencies and its military power, and southern America sat on the lid of slave unrest brought to a boiling point by the heat of a revolutionary era. By 1794 these dangers to the social order stood out sharply. It was the hour for the counter-revolutionists to attack democracy without restraint.

When men's standards of living are seriously threatened, they are apt to pay little heed to ethical or moral precepts. This would seem to be a truism, unless we remember that it applies as much to those on the top rungs of the ladder of fortune as to those nearer the bottom. So much is made of the chaos, disorder, and horror of a revolutionary period, and so little is said of the unbearable cruel-

<hr />

[55] *American Historical Association, Annual Report,* 1897, p. 573; Woodfin, *op. cit.,* pp. 416, 418.

[56] Ashe (*History of North Carolina,* p. 139) indicates that in 1790 America exported no cotton. By 1794 we were exporting 1,500,000 pounds, and by 1795, 5,000,000 pounds. Such increases would soon make Negro slavery highly profitable to cotton planters.

[57] *Speeches Delivered by Alexander Smyth,* pp. 18–26; Martin, *Anti-Slavery Movement in Kentucky prior to 1850,* p. 27.

[58] See "The Anti-Federal Club" in cartoon collection (*c.* 1795) in the Ridgeway Library, Philadelphia.

ties and injustices that men suffer between revolutions. We readily spurn words from the lips of the bedraggled and uncouth who come forward during rapid social change, while we accept with ineffable credulity the utterances of those with wealth, power, and influence. The Federalists had everything to lose and nothing to gain by the social dislocation that swept Europe and America at the close of the eighteenth century. Desperate men forget the ethical niceties, and the desperate Federalists were no exception.

A number of unethical methods of attack were applied to the democrats in general. A few of these are worthy of note. William Maclay was shocked at the high-handed way in which Rufus King, in 1791, altered the minutes of Congress to suit his own purposes.[59] Other Federalists employed the sting of the economic lash effectively, for in 1793 the big merchants of Philadelphia agreed to boycott Clement Biddle, marine insurance business man, because of his pro-French activities.[60] The same technique was used by certain of these merchants upon their employees. Either the employees voted Federalist, or they lost their jobs, according to a writer in the *Aurora*.[61] Frederick Wolcott wrote to his brother, Oliver, May 2, 1796, that with difficulty he had prevented the people of his town from petitioning Congress upon the Jay Treaty. The Wolcotts, like their friend Hamilton, disapproved of the right of petition.[62] The democrats had to take care lest their mail be intercepted; lest rowdies turn their meetings into riots and give opportunity for the pandering press to brand democracy as riotous; and lest, by some connivance, the popular will was subverted at election time.[63] Actual physical violence was used on Benjamin Bache at Philadelphia, on Benjamin Austin in Boston, and upon William Keteltas in New York.[64]

[59] *The Journal of William Maclay*, p. 374.
[60] *The Burd Papers*, ed. by Walker, p. 179.
[61] Issue of Feb. 22, 1798, article signed "Order."
[62] Wolcott MSS Connecticut Historical Society. Hamilton favored criminally prosecuting a body of citizens who petitioned the government; see Randolph to Washington, April 14, 1794, Misc. Letters, Department of State.
[63] Massachusetts Constitutional Society to the Portland Republican Society, undated, in Portland Republican Society Papers, Maine Historical Society; *Aurora*, Feb. 19, 22, 1798; *Albany Register*, Aug. 26, 1799.
[64] *New London Bee*, May 8, 1798.

Unfair and corrupt dealings breed, in those practicing them, an atmosphere of apathy and acceptance, until, finally, discernment itself is dulled. The consciences of the big merchants no longer troubled them. Many were smugglers before the American Revolution and they continued as such into the 1790's. At dinners, it was alleged, they joked about smuggling and humorously accused one another of practicing the subterfuge. The merchants, they admitted, were too close friends of the government officials to have the laws enforced.[65]

What were some of the specific methods used by the counter-revolutionists against the democratic-republican societies? For one thing, the opposition organized counter-societies to offset the influence of the popular organizations. Of course, they already had the Society of Cincinnati and the chambers of commerce, both doing yeoman service for them.[66] But the new societies were brought forward to contravene the acts of the democratic societies so long as they thrived. Elizabeth-town, New Jersey, had one called The Constitutional Association; and Norfolk, Virginia, formed a Society of Constitutional and Governmental Support.[67] The purpose of both of these was to "check the wild and Jacobinical self-created clubs." Daniel Morgan wrote Benjamin Biggs in the summer of 1794, telling him to form a secret chain of informants and clubs among the Whiskey Rebel counties and to prevent people's joining the popular societies. Morgan added that these instructions came from the President of the United States.[68] Soon an anti-democratic club appeared and took for its name, The Association of Pittsburgh.[69]

[65] Extract of a letter from a merchant in Boston to Nicholas Gilman, Feb. 14, 1798, Wolcott MSS, Vol. X, No. 32.
[66] The New England Cincinnati was much more conservative and aristocratic than was this same organization in the South. The northern members had heavy investments in six per-cent stocks. The southerners were not generally so fortunate; some of them were members of democratic societies, and the Cincinnati at Charleston celebrated the Fourth of July, 1793, with Mangourit as a special guest. (Misc. Papers, Society of Cincinnati, June 4, 1793; also "Records of the Connecticut State Society of Cincinnati, 1783–1807," New York Public Library.)
[67] Federal Intelligencer, Jan. 27, 1795; New Jersey Journal, Feb. 4, 1795; Norfolk Herald, March 4, 1795; Wertenbaker, Norfolk: Historic Southern Port, p. 99.
[68] Biggs Papers, undated (c. 1794), Wisconsin Historical Society.
[69] Craig Letterbook, Sept. 26, 1794, Carnegie Library, Pittsburgh, Penn.

The work of these clubs was insignificant, as compared with the gargantuan efforts of the Federalist press to annihilate democracy in every form. John Fenno published the *Gazette of the United States* in Philadelphia. Federalists gave his paper wide circulation and kept it afloat financially. Hamilton raised funds for Fenno in the capital city; King collected contributions for the printer in New York City; and conservatives everywhere subscribed for extra copies, to be sent to corners of the country darkened by democracy.[70] George Bunce, of the *New York Minerva*, had less than 250 subscribers. According to Noah Webster, it took 500 subscribers to keep a paper going. The *Minerva* was saved by gifts from Federalist merchants.[71] Benjamin Russell, editor of the *Columbian Centinel* at Boston, was spokesman for the Essex Junto. Joseph Dennie was backed by the same clique. And William Cobbett, even though in his writings he stooped to the crude and indecent, and even though the Federalists privately recognized that his statements were often inaccurate, still got the support of the conservative classes.[72] We may agree, therefore, with Thomas Amory that the Federalists had wealth and that the press was "controlled by those who supported it." [73] Except for a few notable exceptions, the greater part of the American newspapers seemed to be lock, stock, and barrel in the hands of anti-democrats.[74]

[70] Hamilton to King, Nov. 11, 1793, King Papers, New York Historical Society; Fisher Ames to T. Dwight, Dec. 17, 1793, Ames Papers, Dedham Historical Society.
[71] N. Webster to King, June 28, 1794, King Papers.
[72] Jeremiah Smith to Wm. Plumer, Jan. 7, 1797, Plumer Papers, New Hampshire State Library; also W. P. Hall, *British Radicalism, 1791–1797*, p. 66. Cobbett recognized his purpose in America to be to destroy the principles of the American Revolution; see his writings in the *Anti-Jacobin Review.*
[73] Amory, *Life of James Sullivan*, II, 127.
[74] *Aurora* and the *New York Journal* believed "the far greater part of the American presses have entered into an alliance, offensive and defensive, with the monarchical and despotic combined powers, against the republican states." (See issue of latter, June 29, 1799.) Charles Holt, democratic editor of the *New London Bee*, said in his paper, June 6, 1798, that nine-tenths of the Connecticut papers were Federalist. Other influential Federalist printers were Isaiah Thomas, who had a circulation covering Massachusetts, Connecticut, Rhode Island, New Hampshire and Vermont (see Thomas's *Almanack* [Worcester, Mass., 1795]); Loring Andrews, at Stockbridge, Mass., who was supported by speculators like Sedgewick and land barons like W. Van Schaack, (see Loring Andrews to T. Sedgwick, March 13, 1794,

The attack upon the popular societies by the subsidized press included sins of omission as well as commission. Just as the press often boycotted news of Independence Day celebrations, so did it, as often, completely ignore the democratic societies. Upon turning the pages of the Boston *Mercury* and the *American Apollo* for the year 1794, one can discover no mention of the Massachusetts Constitutional Society, nor of any of the popular societies. Yet the societies were a critical current issue in that year. Those newspapers which did mention the clubs either printed William Willcocks's or David Osgood's tirades against them, or spoke of their members as addicted to "lying, cheating, whoredom, adultery, gaming, peculation, bribery, bankruptcy, fraud, atheism, etc.," or associated the organization with incendiarism, the devil, or the "bloody French Jacobins." [75] Because of newspaper propaganda it was widely believed that "French gold" was undermining American government and that the Democratic societies were "under foreign influence." [76]

One of the most glaring press prevarications about the societies was the announcement that first one and then another had disbanded. Loring Andrews, of Stockbridge, Massachusetts, started this propaganda technique to silence the popular clubs. He first published a statement that the Chittenden County, Vermont, society had only twelve members. This was published by other Federalists, to make the societies seem negligible. Anthony Haswell, the democratic printer of Bennington, Vermont, called Andrews a "liar" and said he could prove the club had eighty-four members. This did not daunt the redoubtable Federalist printer, for he next announced that the Democratic Society of Addison County, Vermont, passed

---

in Sedgewick Papers, Massachusetts Historical Society); and Abraham Hodge, who had a virtual monopoly on the presses of North Carolina and who, if the extant copies of his newspapers tell the whole truth, printed almost nothing about the democratic societies (see Weeks, *The Press of North Carolina in the Eighteenth Century*).

[75] For William Willcocks's polemics, see the *Philadelphia Gazette*, Jan. and Feb., 1795; the *Connecticut Courant* was a bitter enemy of democracy; see Feb. 4, May 27, 1793; Dec. 8, 1794; Nov. 23, 1795.

[76] Nisbet to Addison, Oct. 3, 1795, April 25, 1796, in Nisbet Papers, Darlington Library; Pickering to N. Webster, Feb. 18, 1796, in N. Webster Papers, New York Public Library; *New London Bee*, June 6, 1798; *Courier of New Hampshire*, Oct. 24, 1795.

a motion to burn its papers and adjourn *sine die*.[77] This we know to be false. The statement appeared February 3, 1795, and the *Rutland Herald*, as late as June 1 and August 17 of that year, tells of the regular meetings of the "dead" society. Andrews was relentless, for a year later he announced that the Philadelphia society had voted to dissolve. Spooner's *Vermont Journal*, another conservative paper, joined the sepulchral attack and published a statement, November 18, 1796, that the Chittenden Society, born of France and Genet, was dead, even though Udney Hay delivered a Fourth of July oration before that very-much-alive organization in 1797.[78]

Another device used by the enemy to destroy the popular assemblies was to malign Genet and to make unpopular not only "the Citizen" but likewise any clubs giving him support. Before Genet left France, Governeur Morris, Hamilton, and the British ambassador, Hammond, were plotting to trip him in one way or another. They wished to wreck the Franco-American Alliance, discredit the republican ambassador, and bring about his recall.[79] They succeeded by spreading the story of Genet's threatening an "appeal to the people"—a radical phrase with revolutionary implications in that day.[80] The arch-conservatives Jay and King said they heard of Genet's statement from Hamilton and Knox; the latter conspirators claimed they heard it from Alexander Dallas; and Dallas, who had turned against Genet and was publically uttering angry words against him, denied ever having made such a statement.[81] Nevertheless, the accusation against Genet was broadcast to the far corners of the country. The most derogatory names were everywhere applied to him as the hearsay expanded into the grossest dis-

[77] *Newark Gazette*, Feb. 25, 1795; *Vermont Gazette*, Feb. 6, 1795.
[78] *Western Star*, Jan. 19, 1796; *Burlington Mercury*, July 8, 1797.
[79] Woodfin, "Citizen Genet and His Mission," pp. 82, 121, 147, 165 (Woodfin is excellent on the plot against Genet); Hammond to Grenville, Sept. 17, 1793, British Archives, F.O.5, Vol. I, No. 19.
[80] Henry Adams, *Life of Albert Gallatin*, p. 80.
[81] *State Gazette of North Carolina*, Jan. 4, 1794; also Genet Papers, Aug. 12, 1793; Dallas to Gallatin, Nov. 8, 1793, Gallatin Papers. In Dallas's letter to Gallatin he says that Genet has said "he would appeal to Congress." Jay and King might easily have amplified this as "an appeal to the people over the head of Washington." Anyway, it seems fairly clear that the whole story originated with the "liberal" Dallas, who called the House of Representatives' jurisdiction "inquisitorial."

tortions of fact. New England circles heard the harrowing news that George Washington had been assassinated by the French minister! [82] Although Genet repeatedly asserted his innocence of any attempt to "appeal to the people," the chicane was effective, Genet was disgraced and recalled, and the democratic clubs placed in greater disesteem.[83] As Monroe stated to John Breckinridge, August 23, 1793, "the monarchy party" charged the French ambassador with indiscretions, for it was "labouring to turn the popularity of this respectable citizen against the French Revolution, thereby to separate us from France and pave the way for an unnatural connection with Great Britain." [84]

Further to discountenance the societies and in fact all democratic tendencies of the time, the conservatives made use of the glorified personage of George Washington. Because of his Revolutionary War service, Washington was highly respected. The Federalists, noting his conservatism, sought to enhance adoration of him, so that when he spoke it would carry finality. Ignoring Independence Day, they proposed that two other days should always be remembered—the discovery of America by Columbus and Washington's birthday. Bache was quick to catch this intrigue, and wrote:

Thus the friends of Order, as they call themselves, would exult had they in their power to annihilate the remembrance of the Fourth of

---

[82] Woodfin, *op. cit.*, pp. 456, 457, n., gives a list of the uncomplimentary names Genet was called. For the assassination story, see the *Mirrour* (Concord), Dec. 16, 1793.

[83] Genet's denials of the charge brought against him are numerous. He wrote to Washington, who declined to take part in the controversy (*Connecticut Courant*, Aug. 26, 1793); he next wrote to the Attorney General of the United States, saying that the statement of Jay and King was false (Genet Papers, Nov. 14, 1793). His friend Moultrie, governor of South Carolina, wrote asking whether or not the charge was true. Genet again denied it and added that he was willing to have Congress make an investigation of all his papers (Genet Papers, Oct. 15, 1793). Thirty years after his recall, Genet was still insistent that he had had no intention of appealing to the people (*Western Monitor*, Sept. 23, 1823). In 1800 Genet received a letter from Monroe which stated that the writer always had sympathy and respect for the Frenchman and that he had suffered from the "hands of Injustice" (Genet Papers, July 30, 1800). Andrew Jackson wrote the elderly Genet in 1832 and greeted him as an enlightened and worthy citizen of America (Jan. 2, 1832, in Misc. MSS, J, New York Historical Society).

[84] Emmett Collection, New York Public Library.

July, and losing sight of *Measures*, introduce in its stead the adulation of men.[85]

Some Federalists went to ridiculous lengths to apotheosize the first President. The *Federal Orrery* of Boston compared him with Moses, as a leader of his people. "By night your pillar, and your cloud by day, he fought your battles," said the paper.[86] A toast ran "To Washington—loved as a father, as a god adored." [87] Songs were composed about him and sung to the tune of "America," and poetry grew lavish in his praise as it contrasted "dauntless" and "illustrious" Washington with the mob—"like lice in Egypt swarms." [88]

As early as 1790, William Maclay had noted how the name of Washington was "brought forward as the constant cover to every unconstitutional and irrepublican act." [89] With the appearance of the popular societies, the name came forward again. Washington frowned on them and, as a mystic voice from the Delphic oracle, he pronounced them "self-created," secretive, Genet-inspired, "diabolical" and formidable.[90] The awe-inspiring denunciations, however, failed to intimidate all people. At once, it was noticed that the President did not include the chambers of commerce or the Cincinnati in his category of self-created organizations.[91] The republicans were on guard. Madison saw the attempt to "play up the popularity of the President"; [92] James Lyon heard the talk of the "god-like excellencies of a *man*" and identified it as a soporific; [93] and John Beckley confided to Madison that public confidence was withdrawing itself from the President. Friends were attempting to exalt his name and exaggerate his past services, thought Beckley.[94] Deification, the democrats agreed, was but an attempt painlessly to cut

---

[85] *Aurora*, March 7, 1798.
[86] Callender, *History of the United States for 1796*, p. 37.
[87] *New London Bee*, July 11, 1798.
[88] *American Daily Advertiser*, July 22, 1793; *The Echo, or A Satirical Poem on the Virtuous Ten*, p. 20.
[89] *Op. cit.*, Dec. 14, 1790.   [90] *Writings*, ed. by Ford, XII, 453, 464.
[91] *City Gazette*, Oct. 20, 1795.   [92] *Writings*, ed. by Hunt, VI, 222–23.
[93] *Scourge of Aristocracy*, Nov. 1, 1798.
[94] Sept. 10, 1795, Madison Papers, New York Public Library.

away the liberties that had been gained.[95] Playing up the clubs as a stench in the nostrils of the reigning deity was a subtle method of attack upon democracy, second only in effectiveness to the fears of insurrections.

Because of the aura of sacredness around the name of Washington, his pronunciamento against the societies did affect their progress in some measure. But it also hurt Washington. Leading moderates and all the radicals were critical of the President's words. The "half-way democrats" spoke up for the societies and wrote that Washington had made a serious mistake, which would limit his popularity.[96] For example, Jefferson indicted Genet as an individual radical, but defended the popular society as an organization. In this, Jefferson exhibited his political shrewdness, while Washington tripped and lost much of his popularity. St. George Tucker, a defender of the societies, remarked that Washington really got his light from Hamilton and then reflected it back upon his Secretary of the Treasury.[97] Another influential moderate, Garritt Minor, of Fredricksburg, Virginia, said:

Although I differed in opinion with him [Washington], on many principles both abstract and practical, though I disapproved of many of his acts while an officer of the government, though I am convinced his opinions of our Constitution and government were improper, erroneous and subversive of our liberties, I have never impeached the purity or goodness of his heart.[98]

And Elbridge Gerry, a mild republican, wrote in 1797 that Washington failed in having a broad basis of support for his policies. His support, said Gerry, came from "the union of the funded, bank, commercial, Cincinnati and anti-revolutionary or monarchical

---

[95] *Boston Gazette*, Dec. 16, 1793. William Manning, too, was alert to the trick in the magic of Washington's name; see his *Key of Libberty*, p. 56.

[96] Jefferson to Madison, Dec. 28, 1794, Madison Papers, Vol. XVII, No. 124; Madison to Monroe, Dec. 4, 1794, *Writings*, ed. by Hunt, VI, 222; Joseph Jones (letter to Madison, Dec. 26, 1794, Madison Papers, Vol. XVII, No. 122) says the condemnation of the societies was not well received in his part of Virginia.

[97] [St. George Tucker], *The Probationary Odes*, p. 35.

[98] Minor to Jos. C. Cabell, Jan. 17, 1800, Cabell Collection, University of Virginia Library.

interest," and this was not sufficient to keep him in power! [99]

The radicals openly and publicly turned the most caustic fire of criticism upon the President. Judge Aedanus Burke, critic of the Cincinnati and of Jefferson as a "half-way Republican," said that a lethargy and stupefaction had crept upon the Republic because of "idolatry for a popular citizen." [100] Dr. Nathaniel Ames asserted that "the President is a rebel against General Washington and the United States." [101] Commodore Nicholson, in New York, who distrusted the "pusillanimity" of many republicans, especially those from Virginia, called Washington's conduct in office "notoriously base," but hastened to add that "it is next to treason to apply it to him." [102] Another democratic society president, Colonel Thomas Newton, of Norfolk, Virginia, refused to attend a ball celebrating the President's birthday in 1795.[103] Still another popular leader wrote that Washington was controlled by Hamilton and that there was no difference between the administrations of the first and second President of the United States.[104] And a member of the Republican Society of Newark, New Jersey, rose to toast Washington as "a despot from the South, with Democracy on his lips and tyranny in his heart." [105] The criticisms of Washington's actions by the democrats Benjamin Bache, William Duane, James T. Callender, and Thomas Paine are familiar to historians and need

[99] Gerry to President Adams, April 25, 1797, Gerry Papers, Library of Congress; Weld (*Travels*, p. 88) speaks of encountering a dislike for Washington and of seeing groups of men who refused to celebrate his birthday and to toast him. William Plumer, although pro-Washington, admitted that the hero's influence was declining in 1795; see Plumer's "Autobiography" (1759–1844), p. 60, MS in Library of Congress.

[100] Burke to Genet, Feb. 16, 1794, Genet Papers.

[101] Morison, "Squire Ames and Doctor Ames," *New England Quarterly*, I (1928), 16.

[102] Nicholson to Gallatin, July 2, 1797, Gallatin Papers, New York Historical Society.

[103] Alex. F. Cochrane to Hammond, April 23, 1795, British Archives, F.O.5, Vol. IV, Library of Congress.

[104] Publicola, *Features of Federalism*. John Beckley also believed that Washington was under Hamilton's thumb. He not only, like Genet, used the term "old Washington," but also "old automaton." See Beckley to Monroe, Oct. 17, 1796, Monroe Papers, New York Public Library.

[105] *History of the City of Newark*, p. 449.

not be repeated. However, in Joel Barlow's notebook is a quatrain called "Thomas Paine's direction to the Sculptor who should make the statue of Washington" and it reads:

> Take from the mine the coldest, hardest stone,
> It needs no fashion, it is Washington;
> But if you chisel, let your strokes be rude,
> And on his breast engrave *Ingratitude!* [106]

So, while Washington may have written Ichabod over the doors of some of the popular societies, we may conclude that he likewise placed a fatal sign on the portals of his Federal party.

Washington's verbal assault was taken up by Congress, whence came the next attempt to stigmatize the "self-created" organizations. The conservatives wanted Congress to condemn the clubs and thus end sedition once and for all. The Senate, less amenable to the public will, passed a motion of censure; but the House, after a four-day debate, refused to condemn specifically democratic societies and actually gave them a sort of sanction.[107] Economic interests swayed the voting of the lower house on this issue. John Beckley named to Jefferson, in 1793, those whom he was certain were "paper-men" in Congress. With his help we discover fifteen speculators voting to censure all *sui generis* societies, and only one voting "no." Furthermore, with Beckley's help we discover that Fitz-

---

[106] Barlow Papers, Box IV, Harvard Library. Genet, too, recognized that he was "at war with Washington." (To Bertholet, Dec. 9, 1793, Affaires Étrangères, Vol. XXXIX, Part 7). It would be enlightening to try to discover why Genet was kept in America after his recall (Genet Papers, undated, c. Nov., 1793), and his friend Thomas Paine was held (by imprisonment) in France, even though both wanted to return home. Washington would not intercede to free Paine for return to America. Similarly, David Bradford, not wishing to be hunted by a personal enemy and killed, as the Federalists wished, asked Washington to guarantee him a safe passage to Philadelphia for a fair trial. Elizabeth Bradford, his wife, wrote twice to the President, making this request and begging that a father not be killed. Washington ignored the entreaty. (See Jared Ingersoll to Jasper Yeates, Nov. 2, 1794, Emmett Collection, New York Public Library; Elizabeth Bradford to Washington, Dec. 10, 1794, and Jan. 22, 1795, in "The Pennsylvania Insurrection," Vol. II, Library of Congress.)

[107] Hammond to Grenville, Dec. 1, 1794, British Archives, F.O.5, Vol. IV; Joseph Jones to Madison, Dec. 26, 1794, *Massachusetts Historical Society Proceedings*, Vol. XV, 2d series, p. 146.

simmons, anti-society spokesman for Hamilton in the House, was a "director" in six per-cent projects.[108]

By 1795 the Federalists had the aid of the clergy in assailing the iniquitous clubs. The preachers were presenting arms. They suddenly became discomposed over the irreligion and atheism of the times. Not only the Calvinistic clergymen of New England, with their close tie to Federalism, went into action, but also ministers in the other states as well.[109] The democratic societies were brought into the pulpit and the evil of mixing politics and religion was momentarily forgotten.

The arch-reactionary of all the ministers to attack democracy was the tea-sipping owner of bank stocks, David Osgood, of Medford, Massachusetts.[110] Osgood was so conservative that he would not accept his friend Webster's "new intended spelling," and for a while refused to read even the anti-French publications of Webster.[111] Three different times this pulpit energumen turned his fire upon the popular clubs, using every scare phrase and alarmist technique he could conjure up.[112] The French, the sponsors of the societies, were "execrable monsters" who had abolished the sabbath, and had denied God, immortality, and the resurrection. Furthermore, they had massacred 2,000,000 people, including 250,000 women, 230,000 children, and 24,000 ministers! The mothers' hands were cut off, as they pleaded for their children! These were the wretches

[108] Beckley's list of speculators in Congress is in the Jefferson Papers, Vol. LXXXII, Item 14232, Library of Congress.

[109] James K. Morse, *Jedidiah Morse*, p. 107; Welling, *Connecticut Federalism, or Aristocratic Politics in a Social Democracy*, p. 35; *Minutes of the Methodist Conferences, 1773–1813*; Letterbook of the Rev. Stith Mead, 1793–95, in the Virginia Historical Society, speaks of Mead's attempts to convert "Republican spots" in Georgia and Kentucky; John McMillan (letter to Gallatin, May 2, 1796, Gallatin Papers, Vol. V) tells how Rev. McMillan called upon his congregation to petition in behalf of the Jay Treaty.

[110] "Diary of the Rev. David Osgood, D.D.," from Jan., 1776, to Dec., 1822, in the Medford Public Library, Medford, Mass. See entries for the years 1794 and 1795, *passim*. Peter Chardon Brooks, the Boston financier, was a close friend of Osgood's, according to Freeman Hunt, *Lives of American Merchants*, p. 162.

[111] T. Dawes to N. Webster, Feb. 9, 1795, Webster Papers.

[112] Osgood, *A Discourse Delivered on the Day of Annual Thanksgiving, November 19, 1795*; and the one most hailed by the conservatives, *The Wonderful Works of God Are to Be Remembered*.

who were striving to stir imaginary grievances in our "free and happy land," according to Parson Osgood.[113] His sermons, particularly that of November 20, 1794, received extensive circulation. Die-hards like Van Schaack, Gore, Wm. L. Smith, and Fisher Ames underwrote the cost of having the Thanksgiving sermon put into pamphlet form. Said Van Schaack in a letter to Theodore Sedgewick, on this subject, January 22, 1795:

A burned child dreads the fire, but not me, if another revolutionary government comes—I go for it!

Shortly before this he had written, again to Sedgewick:

I love your plain speaking ministers—they do good, and will become more useful if encouraged by our federal rulers.[114]

Because of publicity given Osgood's sermon, it went through six editions, was widely quoted in all sections of the country, and performed invaluable service for the cause of the counter-revolution.[115]

Jedidiah Morse, the minister from Charleston, Massachusetts, was a friend of Osgood's and exchanged pulpits now and then with him. Morse stirred the next tempest in the teapot when he burst forth with the sensational news that the popular societies were secret adjuncts of the international organization known as the Illuminati.[116] Of course Illuminism was grossly wicked, antireligious, and anarchical; so also were the democratic societies, in the eyes of Morse. Hence two plus two made three; they were from the same egg of sedition, and both must be destroyed. Copies of the domine's sermon were sent to every clergyman in the commonwealth of Massachusetts, and its frightening words were quoted up and down

[113] Osgood, *Some Facts Evincive of the Atheistical, Anarchical and in Other Respects, Immoral Principles of the French Republicans.*

[114] For Van Schaack's statements, see his letters to Sedgewick of Dec. 20, 1794, and Jan. 22, 1795, Sedgewick Papers, Massachusetts Historical Society.

[115] For the extent of circulation and influence of Osgood's sermons, see the following: J. Morse to Wolcott, March 18, 1795, Wolcott MSS, Vol. VIII, No. 10; Ames to Gore, Feb. 24, 1795, Ames Papers; Jeremiah Smith to Wm. Plumer, Jan. 10, 1795, Plumer Papers, New Hampshire State Library; W. De Loss Love, *The Fast and Thanksgiving Days of New England*, p. 367; Woodfin, *op. cit.*, p. 520.

[116] J. K. Morse, *op. cit.*, p. 49; Stauffer, *New England and the Bavarian Illuminati*, p. 271.

the land.[117] Timothy Dwight, the president of Yale, took up the words in psittaceous fashion to say that the purpose of the Illuminati was to infiltrate into a peaceful nation, divide it, and leave it weakened before the enemy.[118] William Willcocks, Hamilton's pawn, relished Morse's morsel and announced that nourishment for the Jacobin clubs of France and America was supplied by Illuminism.[119] Charles Nisbet and William Cobbett did their bit.[120] Few of the people who were aroused and misled by this barrage of propaganda ever knew that Jedidiah Morse was totally unable to substantiate his claims.[121] The charges were a deterrent to democracy, however, no matter how false and unfair their basis.

Although other ministers, such as Hezekiah Packard, David Tappan, Thomas Barnard, and John Lowell, joined Osgood and Morse in a chorus of invective against the Enlightenment in general and the popular societies in particular, an isolated pulpit voice, here and there, was lifted to counteract the wave of reaction. Notable among the courageous divines was Ebenezer Bradford, of Rowley, Massachusetts, who welcomed the democratic societies as protectors of liberty. For his forthrightness he soon was given the name "Rowley Vandal" by the Federalists, and it was whispered that he was a brother to David Bradford, the insurrectionist.[122] Samuel Stillman, of the Baptist Church of Boston, and Samuel Miller, New York Presbyterian, whom we have already mentioned, were also excep-

---

[117] *Ibid.*, p. 276. Elihu Palmer, in his *The Political Happiness of Nations*, defends the Illuminati of Europe and says that they uphold democracy and freedom from superstition.

[118] *New London Bee*, June 19, 1799. Here Charles Holt, the editor, criticizes Dwight's statements and defends the Illuminati. He says the society actually started in America in 1768.

[119] *Springer's Weekly Oracle*, Aug. 6, 1798.

[120] *Porcupine's Gazette*, Feb. 26, 1799; Nisbet to Addison, June 9, 1797, Nisbet Papers, Darlington Library.

[121] J. K. Morse, *op. cit.*, p. 58. Jedidiah Morse also uncovered a society in Europe called "The Propaganda," whose object was to free the entire human race from tyrants. (Newspaper clippings, 1798, in the Morse Family Collection, Yale Library.) In the Pickering Papers, Massachusetts Historical Society, is an item which Pickering labeled "Illuminati," but it was only a French Masonic Society which was organized at Portsmouth, Va., about 1795. (Letters from Correspondents, Vol. XLII, pp. 37–41.)

[122] J. K. Morse, *op. cit.*, p. 132.

tions to the rule that the clergy served the Federalists faithfully.[123] By 1799 religious revivals were sweeping over the New England states and it was said "some of our most noted Deists have bowed the knee to King Jesus." [124] The clergymen rattled the witchcraft gourd of otherworldliness and repeated the Mumbo Jumbo about sinful, depraved man. The Children of Reason were turning to follow.

Finally, we must weigh the success of the counter-revolutionists in their endeavors to make all popular societies infamous and to quell them for evermore. Some authorities have been too ready to believe that Washington, speaking *ex cathedra*, put a quietus on the clubs, and that in 1795 they petered out and were heard of no more.[125] This is hardly true, as the first chapter of this study indicates. Let us see just what did happen.

A series of actions by the national government had a quieting effect upon certain exacerbated leaders in the patriotic societies. Hamilton, to the surprise of many, categorically demanded compensation at once for American ships captured by the English in the West Indies.[126] Wealthy traders with these islands breathed more easily. Pinckney's Treaty of 1795 gained the right of the use of the Mississippi River and poured oil on the troubled waters in the West. The nefarious Jay Treaty was accepted by many westerners because it gained the evacuation of the western forts. Many more trans-Alleghenians welcomed the relief from the fear of Indian depredations occasioned by Wayne's decisive victory over the red men.[127] New promises for wealth loomed up,[128] and land speculators marched on to new lucrative ventures.

[123] Stillman, *A Sermon Delivered on November 20, 1794*. John Jay in a letter to King, Nov. 14, 1797, (King Papers, Vol. XLI), admits the clergy has aided and promoted Federalism.

[124] *A Brief Account of the Late Revivals of Religion*. Cf. Koch, *Republican Religion*, p. 292.

[125] Stauffer, *op. cit.*, p. 109; Miller, *The Democratic Clubs of the Federalist Period*, pp. 114–15.

[126] Hammond to Simcoe, Aug. 10, 1794, British Archives, F.O.5, Vol. IV.

[127] McFarland, *Twentieth Century History of the City of Washington and Washington County, Pennsylvania*, p. 114.

[128] Whitaker, *The Spanish-American Frontier*, p. 222; David to Isaac Shelby,

Developments in France also had an effect upon the American societies. Most American democrats were cordial to the French Girondin party, led by Brissot, and looked with approval upon its mild reforms. Thomas Paine was a member of this party. When the French Revolution turned into more radical channels and elevated Robespierre to power, it tended to dampen the spirit in the democratic societies. They were, as has already been pointed out, organized in America to preserve the fruits of a revolution and not to take extreme measures. Accompanying the stories in American newspapers of the sudden changes in French governmental administrations was a steady flow of writings associating the French leaders with arson, rapine, and murder. The radical turns in France, together with the exaggerations about them in America, must be considered as an influence in the demise of the popular societies.

These factors, together with the fears that the societies might get out of hand and run to extremes, alienated many of the most influential leaders and divided the membership. The landed gentlemen, David Redick and Hugh H. Brackenridge, of Western Pennsylvania, petitioned the House of Representatives to support the Jay Treaty. In fact, William Findley was stunned at the way so many western leaders turned hypocrite, called the treaty the "damned treaty" before their constituents, and voted for it in Congress.[129] Alexander Smyth, of Wytheville, Virginia, wrote in 1796 to indicate his changed thought regarding the need for war:

But the state of things is changed. Liberty is secure; and aggression has decreased on the part of Britain, and thus at present, neither my *interest* nor my *feelings* leads me, or I presume any other member of the society who published that address [of July 4, 1794], to be solicitious for such an event.[130]

June 2, 1795, Draper Collection, Wisconsin Historical Society, says that the navigation of the Mississippi has greatly changed the West for the better.

[129] Petitions for the support of the Jay Treaty bearing "democratic" westerners' names are in the Gallatin Papers, March 21, April 7, 1796, Vol. V; and in Findley to Addison, May 6, 1796, Nisbet Papers, Darlington Library.

[130] Smyth, *The Third and Last Letter from Alexander Smyth to Francis Preston*, p. 34.

Alexander J. Dallas and John Swanwick, prosperous Philadelphians, did a *volte-face* because of the western insurrection and would have nothing more to do with popular democracy.[131] Their actions and the split in the Philadelphia Democratic Society, which has been already noted, marked a difference between the East and the West which the Federalists worked for and welcomed.[132] Moreover, Dallas, the "half-way," started the story that Genet intended appealing to the people.[133] Hence Federalist sops to opportunistic democrats and the acts of chameleonic liberals divided the democratic societies, caused the death of many, and lessened the influence of others.[134]

Even though the particular societies discussed in these pages disappeared, for the most part, in 1795 and 1796, this was not their

[131] *A Translation of Citizen Fauchet's Intercepted Letter, No. 10; The Quid Mirror* speaks of Dallas as one who "betrayed and deserted" the Democratic Society. John Beckley wrote Madison, Sept. 10, 1795 (Madison Papers, New York Public Library) that the democrats of Philadelphia could no longer confide in Dallas and Swanwick.

[132] J. Swanwick in the *Gazette of the United States*, Sept. 17, 1794, takes up his pen to argue against the radical westerners. Wm. V. Murray wrote to James McHenry, Dec. 16, 1794 (McHenry Papers, Vol. III, Library of Congress) to say that the western insurrection would bring a crisis which would divide the "eminent, sound men" from the "puzzling, disorganizing politicians" of the frontier.

[133] Jay to King, Dec. 12, 1793, King Papers. Jefferson also said he heard this statement from Dallas.

[134] Monroe's criticisms of the French Jacobins were published with great glee by the Federalists and did much to injure the patriotic societies; see *City Gazette*, March 23, 1795; Jeremiah Smith to Plumer, Jan. 10, 1795, Plumer Papers, New Hampshire State Library; Woodfin, *op. cit.*, p. 528. There is considerable evidence to prove that some men joined the democratic societies in order to keep them in control and to prevent radicalism. These men were Federalist at heart, and not democrats. William Eustis, wealthy Bostonian, was probably one. He attended meetings on Madison's resolutions and the Jay Treaty in order to stop any extreme actions. Fisher Ames confided in Eustis, and George Cabot of the Essex Junto said Eustis went into the democratic movement "to prevent greater mischief." (See *The Life and Correspondence of Rufus King*, ed. by Charles King, I, 547; II, 19; *The Works of Fisher Ames*, ed. by Seth Ames, p. 136; *The Works of Alexander Hamilton*, ed. by Lodge, p. 82.) John McDonald stated that he joined the Society of United Freemen because he thought a club would set the people to deliberating instead of acting. (Brackenridge, *Incidents of the Insurrection in the Western Parts of Pennsylvania*, III, 25.) And David Redick said of the Washington, Pennsylvania, society, "Indeed, one of the principal views of the institution was to prevent the people from undue influence at elections." (*Independent Chronicle*, Feb. 2, 1795.) J. Paul Selsam (*The Pennsylvania Constitution*, p. 77) points out how this same trick of boring from within was used by conservatives against the Associators in 1775.

final fate. The democratic impulse which the societies represented blended into new social forms and political arrangements. Some of the societies continued in existence into 1796 and the years following. Members of the Portland, Maine, society were toasting "May the wing of Liberty never lose a feather" as late as December 30, 1796.[135] The Massachusetts Constitutional Society was meeting in 1796, though this fact was never published in a newspaper.[136] The Baltimore club held its Fourth of July celebration in 1797, and the New Yorkers carried on into 1799.

The threatened war with France and the Alien and Sedition Laws aroused new societies in Virginia and Connecticut in 1798. The Constitutional Society of Norfolk, Virginia, was presided over by Arthur Lee. Said an older critic of the young Lee,

I heard not long since that Arthur had carried his Democratic principles so far as to make the common mechanicks and apprentices of Norfolk his intimate friends, and that he would sometimes attempt to declaim in this society. How very dangerous it is for young men [blank] on the wide theatre of the world without having acquired any fixed principles. He resembles a ship in a tempestuous ocean without a rudder.[137]

---

[135] *Independent Chronicle*, Jan. 30, 1797.

[136] Papers of the Portland Republican Society. The reactionary attack upon the popular societies drove a number of "liberal" newspapers into the conservative ranks. They ceased to publish democratic news. For example, Thomas and Samuel Green's *Connecticut Journal* was in 1792–93 carrying news of Paine and the French Revolution. But in 1794–95 it ignored even the Fourth of July and had assumed a strong Federalistic tone. Benjamin Titcomb, printer in Portland, Maine, at first presented republican items. In 1795 he refused not only such writings, but also the announcements of meetings of the popular society. Later he became a Baptist preacher. (Griffin, *History of the Press in Maine*, p. 34.) Elijah Russell, editor of *The Mirrour*, Concord, N.H. is another case in point. At first pro-republican, he later turned and printed attacks on the popular clubs. By April, 1795, he had changed the name of his paper to the *Federal Mirror*. Just one more illustration of the press seeking the fleshpots of Israel: John Wood of the *Newark Gazette* received letters from subscribers threatening that if he did not cease printing material on politics and societies, they would cancel their subscriptions and bring another printer into the community (*Newark Gazette*, March 4, 1795). After this threat there was no more information on the local Republican Society in this paper. Instead William Willcocks, enemy of the society "got the ink." (*Newark Gazette*, Jan. 21, Feb. 11, 1795.)

[137] I. A. Coles to St. George Tucker, July 20, 1799, *William and Mary College Quarterly*, IV (1st series), 108; *Norfolk Herald*, Oct. 2, 1798. This paper ridiculed and belittled the society.

This Virginia enthusiast had a rudder that his dogmatic contemporaries did not perceive. His Constitutional Society called attention to the fact that the Federalists were stirring up a war with France, in order to draw men's minds from internal affairs and to rob them of their liberties. The society expressed this thought in a letter to Edward Livingston, of New York. Livingston answered and complimented the society on its attempts "to discuss and disseminate political truth." [138] At the same time this body "of common mechanicks and apprentices" were raising money to print and circulate a pamphlet against the Alien and Sedition Acts.[139] Societies in Stamford and Norwalk, Connecticut, arose to resist war with France, and in Philadelphia the True Republican Society was organized by the leaders of the erstwhile Democratic Society. The True Republicans drank a toast to "The people of France,—if any of their servants have been corrupt, may they be more successful than we have been in their chastisement." [140] The word "republican" carried less stigma than "democrat," so by and large these later societies used the less odious name.

If popular societies retreated under the assault of the enemy, the "town meetings" held the fort and were directed by the same generals. Lexington, Kentucky, to mention one, dropped the name Democratic Society in August, 1794, but continued to hold meetings of the citizens of the town under the old leaders. The club members here and in other places may have met secretly.[141] At least, John

---

[138] *Albany Register,* May 3, 1799. [139] *Norfolk Herald,* March 16, 1799.

[140] *Aurora,* May 3, 1798, May 6, 1799; May 7, 1800. This Republican Society was organized in May, 1797, but it became most active when it took up Jefferson's cause a year or so later.

[141] There are a number of evidences of the popular clubs continuing their work, but covering their tracks. The Massachusetts Constitutional Society we have mentioned. Noah Webster expressed to Wolcott, Sept. 17, 1800 (Webster Papers, New York Public Library) his astonishment at the secret, disciplined exertions of the democrats, which were gaining them victory. Sulte, "Les Projets de 1793 à 1810," *Proceedings and Transactions of the Royal Society of Canada,* V (1911), 59 is authority for the statement that secret assemblies thrived in Vermont throughout the 1790's and that the democrats were involved. One of the most interesting instances is revealed through the pages of Deborah Logan's writings (MS Logan Papers, Historical Society of Pennsylvania.) Jefferson, McKean, and others knew that Dr. George Logan planned to go to France, unauthorized by the government, and settle the difficulties the Federalists had prompted. In fact, Jefferson gave

Adams received resolutions and a broadside in 1798 from popular meetings in Kentucky, objecting to war and to the Sedition Act. "Take care, John Adams," said the anonymous note enclosed with the resolutions, "an evil day is approaching. Traitors will be punished." [142] The *New York Journal*, April 21, 1798, stated that "The spirit of *Yeomanry Meetings* pervades almost every part of the Union." The article mentions the town meetings held in Massachusetts, New Jersey, Maryland, and Virginia, where the citizens expresesd their opposition to war with France and to the hateful "gag act." The *Salem Gazette* on August 4, 1795, announced that the town meetings were the same as democratic societies and mobs; that all were organized by the same men, with the same radical ends in mind. In 1799 the House of Representatives received a petition signed by more than a thousand citizens, a great number for that day, stating their opposition to the procedures adopted by the Federalists toward France.[143] Though suppression was strong, the popular will was ever-present and organized. The town meeting was the mode of popular expression. The popular society leaders worked more safely if hidden among their fellow citizens.[144]

Just as Madison and Jefferson defended the democratic societies and studied their progress, so also did these wise statesmen watch the results of the hundreds of town meetings in the closing years of the century.[145] That "cool, casuistic, Frenchified fellow," as Hamil-

---

Logan a letter of introduction. All of this had to be secret, for the conservatives were so bent upon crushing the democratic element, according to Mrs. Logan, that the republicans were even forced to go armed in order to protect themselves from physical violence. Dr. Logan's friendly approach was successful. It scattered the war hysteria rolled up by the Federalists and reflected on the sincerity of those who dealt with Mr. X, Y, and Z. (See also Gallatin Papers, Vol. XV, "Notes made by Gallatin" [1799].)

[142] Pickering MSS, Aug. 15, 1798, Vol. XIII.

[143] *Aurora*, Feb. 12, 1799; Ambler (*Sectionalism in Virginia from 1776 to 1881*, pp. 67–68) speaks of the great number of mass meetings protesting the Federalist program in 1798.

[144] Wm. Miller ("First Fruits of Republican Organization," *Pennsylvania Magazine of History and Biography*, LXIII [1939], 120) supports the statement that popular society leaders were backing the town meetings.

[145] Madison to Jefferson, May 2, 1798, *Works of Madison*, ed. by Hunt, II, 143. Deborah Logan wrote that when Jefferson returned from France he wore ruffles and an "elegant topaz ring," but that he soon changed to more republican garb.

ton called Jefferson, saw in the organization behind the patriotic clubs and the town meetings a new political alignment of strength and promise. As citizens first in the societies and then in the town meetings and celebrations lifted the pewter mug or tilted the dinner glass to Thomas Jefferson, the numbering of the days of the Federalists began.

The democratic societies laid the groundwork for the Republican party.[146] They believed in local governmental institutions—small units that could register the opinions of the common man and awaken his interest in his government. They brought out voters who had previously never taken part in government.[147] They clarified the issues and prompted concern in the outcome. As Frederick Jackson Turner has rightly concluded, the societies produced a party crystallization.[148] Men divided and took one side or the other. If they chose the cause of the democrats, they believed in the ability of the average man to enter into all decisions that affected his wellbeing. And if they could see, with Jefferson, that this wider democracy was inevitable, that its power would overwhelm the aristocratic forces, they could struggle *ad astra per aspera*. Each election year, from 1794 on, the democratic republican power gained momentum.[149]

The Federalist worries mounted from the time the first popular society appeared until they were forced to accept the victory of 1800. They struck at the democratic-republican clubs, and in 1795 Noah Webster warned Oliver Wolcott that laws were needed to curtail not only the societies but also the "irregular town meet-

She also said that Jefferson told her how angry Washington was when he saw Freneau's paper and that Jefferson "knew but too well who had caused it to appear." Cf. Marsh, "Freneau and Jefferson," *American Literature*, VIII (1936), 189, where Marsh concludes that there was no collusion between Jefferson and Freneau on issuing the *National Gazette*.

[146] John Taylor, in his *A Definition of Parties, or The Political Effects of the Paper System Considered*, recognizes two parties in Congress in 1794; Gibbs, *op. cit.*, p. 77; Wm. Miller, *op. cit.*, p. 119.

[147] Jameson, "Did the Fathers Vote?" *New England Magazine*, Jan., 1890, pp. 484–90; Luetscher, *Early Political Machinery*, p. 60.

[148] *American Historical Review*, III, 650.

[149] Leutscher (*op. cit.*, chap. iii) has traced the victories of the republicans; also Woodfin, *op. cit.*, p. 487; and Wm. Miller, *op. cit.*, p. 218.

ings." [150] For the "Jacobins," the opposition all agreed, certainly had unity and industry. The master mind of the Federalists, Alexander Hamilton, marveled at the way in which the "mobocrats" were organized, for he thought "the devil was in the Republicans for system." [151] But the republicans had a long heritage of effective organization, running back into colonial days. This has been traced. Once brought forward, it would harass the "few" and, if opposed, sweep them aside. "The few" defied the resurgence of democracy, and "the many" in 1801 sang to the victory of their leader— "The Reign of Terror Is No More." [152]

Democracy is a method, not a fixed system of government. It is a constant, ongoing process of changing and reconstructing old forms and adapting to the new conditions of social life. Just as the Federalists failed to throttle the method of democracy, so the Jeffersonians fell short of instituting the rule of the people.[153] After 1800, men were still divided and active with the more democratic of them criticizing the less democratic—many of whom were at one time members of the popular societies. New Jersey called forth democratic associations in 1802 and their members remembered well the victory of the Republican Society of Newark in the previous decade.[154] Dr. James Tilton and his colleagues, of Newcastle, Dela-

---

[150] Wolcott MSS, Vol. X, No. 31. Connecticut Historical Society.

[151] James Nicholson to Gallatin, April 20, 1798, Gallatin Papers.

[152] One of the songs in Jefferson's Scrapbook (1801) in the University of Virginia Library.

[153] The reader will recall it was pointed out in an earlier chapter of this study that Joel Barlow was uncertain of the "thoroughgoingness" of Jefferson's democracy. There is other evidence to show that popular societies would be needed after the revolution of 1800. For example, numbers of anti-Federalists had profited by the funding system. In 1801 these were wondering if Jefferson would attempt to change that system. Most of them agreed that he would not do so. (Phil. Livingston to Jacob Read, Feb. 23, 1801, *Columbia University Quarterly, XXIII* [1931], 200). Again J. Yeates of Lancaster, Penn., wrote to E. Burd, Jan. 5, 1801: "The changes in the public officers of the Government effected no alteration in my mind, as to confidence in its measures. I feel no difficulty in persuading myself, that Mr. Jefferson as President will pursue the path trod by his predecessors. No doubt there will be an alteration of some of the superior officers but the general measures of the union will wear their former complexion from necessity if not from choice." This letter is in the Burd, Strohm, Yeates, Shippen Letters, in the State Library, Harrisburg, Pennsylvania.

[154] Sloan, *An Oration before the Democratic Association of Glouster County, New Jersey;* Fee, *The Transition from Aristocracy to Democracy in New Jersey,* pp. 132, 133.

ware, were still using popular assemblies in 1805.[155] That same year, old democrats such as Thomas Leiper, William Duane, and Dr. Michael Leib started a new Democratic Society in Philadelphia. Its constitution began with words taken directly from its forbear; "With a view, therefore, to cultivate a just knowledge of rational liberty," and so on. The Declaration of Independence was its ideal.[156] Two years later, in 1807, Harrisburg, Pennsylvania, established the Democratic Society of Friends of the People. Hear the clash of opposing ideas in its constitution:

At this eventful period, when men are combined, who have heretofore professed opposite political doctrines, and have acted to produce opposite political ends; when a suggestion to convene the people in their sovereign character, is deprecated as an evil, is denounced as an innovation, and proscribed as a revolution; when the form of our government is said to have arrived at a perfection incapable of further improvement, its imperfections blazoned as republican symmetry, and it is insinuated that the people are incompetent to manage their own affairs or to be trusted with their own welfare; and when their rights and happiness are to be made subservient to the views of ambition or interest; it becomes the solemn and bounden duty of the people to unite their efforts, to preserve themselves against insidious attacks, concealed conspiracy, or open treachery.[157]

In 1810 popular societies were behind the candidacy of "the radical" Simon Snyder for the governorship of Pennsylvania.[158] Andrew Jackson proudly accepted the name "Democratic" for his party, an outgrowth of and a criticism of Jeffersonian democracy.

The conservatives were not idle. In 1802 the clever Hamilton set on foot the Christian Constitutional Society, to defend Christianity and the Constitution.[159] Some years later the Washington Benevolent Societies arose to celebrate the birthday of the "illus-

[155] See Broadside dated 1805, in Collection No. 13 (Delaware), Library of Congress.

[156] *Constitution of the Democratic Society of Friends of the People.*

[157] *The Democratic Society of Friends of the People, Oracle of Dauphin*, July 9, 1808.

[158] *Two Addresses of the Democratic Society of Philadelphia to Their Democratic Brethern.*

[159] Beard, *Economic Origins*, p. 213, n.

trious Washington" and to oppose "Anarchy, Despotism and Democracy." [160]

The work of the democratic societies in the 1790's was only a
beginning. The birth of freedom did not guarantee its longevity.
Constant vigilance was the watchword of the popular societies and
their friends in similar organizations. Tammany, with its political
complexion derived from the Democratic Society, as late as 1832
was celebrating Thomas Paine's birthday and defending not only
his *Rights of Man*, but also his *Age of Reason!* [161] The Cooper and
Mechanic Societies, and later the Cordwainers, stood with the
people in the struggle to maintain and perpetuate democracy. Both
William Duane and Caesar A. Rodney were found in 1806 defending the Cordwainers' right to unite, to pass resolutions, and to
defend their civil liberties.[162] So the story goes on beyond the limits
of this study, to other times and other places, where the sons of
the lowly and the humble worked together to free the spirit of man.

[160] The Harvard Library has a badge and an armband of the Washington
Benevolent Society of Franklin County, Mass.; Jay, *Correspondence*, ed. by Johnston, p. 326.

[161] Morrison, *An Oration Delivered in Tammany Hall in Commemoration of
the Birthday of Thomas Paine*.

[162] Commons, *et al.*, *A Documentary History of American Industrial Society*,
III, 67, 162–206.

Chapter Nine

THE ACHIEVEMENTS AND INFLUENCE OF THE SOCIETIES

He that would make his own liberty secure must guard even his enemy from oppression.

THOMAS PAINE

THE attempt has been made in these pages to portray a stage in the growth of American democracy. The fact that most of the popular societies in America called themselves "Democratic" does not mean that they were fully democratic in practice. Some individual members were as selfishly motivated as were certain spokesmen for the opposition. An attempt has been made to show the ax they were grinding. Sometimes they were moved by rivalry, or by disappointment over not being politically recognized by the party in power, or more often by hope of economic aggrandizement—all in the name of democracy. The societies themselves did not represent the propertyless, the slaves, and the indentured servants. There is no record of Negroes, even those who held property and were educated, being admitted to membership in these "democratic" clubs. Nevertheless, beneath these inconsistencies—a characteristic of all social movements—was a forceful, humane philosophy of life. In actions no less than in words the democratic societies reveal a social force driving toward man's right to self-determination and the fulfillment of his creative possibilities.

The principal achievements of the popular societies in our early national history may be roughly divided into two categories: (1) the political, and (2) the social.

By accepting democracy and a secular, democratic education as inseparable partners, the societies made a basic contribution to political science. They indicated that, by fostering discussion on public problems, foggy and muddled thinking and acting could be avoided and the real issues could be discovered and made clear to all. Moreover, they saw that in a democracy one must always be ready to hear and weigh the arguments of the opposition. They were aware of the function of conflicting opinion as a process which must never be dispensed with. For, as the Patriotic Society of Newcastle, Delaware, wrote, "The collision of opposite opinions produces the spark which lights the torch of truth." It is politically significant that the societies recognized this principle and that from it they derived not only a new party but also the recognition of the validity of the two-party system in the United States.

The social contribution of democracy and education, functioning together in post-Revolutionary times, may be summarized in the following manner. In the first place, citizens, acting collectively and concerned over their social problems, were able to warn against and check antidemocratic tendencies. Secondly, it was "the many" and not "the few" who acted to preserve and uphold republican ideals. In the third place, the free play of intelligence was relied upon, for the democracy of these included freedom of speech, press, and assembly at critical times. Lastly, the societies pointed to the fact that untrammeled public education, for young and old alike, was basically essential to the continuance of democracy: Information must be "communicated" and diffused freely and from every source possible. That the popular societies championed these ideals is of importance to the social historian who wishes to discover more fully America's democratic heritage.

BIBLIOGRAPHY

Where source is known, credit is given.
—BENJAMIN FRANKLIN

I. PRIMARY SOURCES

This list includes only manuscripts and works in which material was actually found and used in the dissertation. It encompasses in a rough way the period between 1785 and 1800.

Manuscripts

Adams, Samuel. Papers. New York Public Library.

Affaires Étrangères. Correspondance Politique, États Unis, Vols. 30 to 43 inclusive and Supplements, Vols. 5, 28, and 30. Photostats in the Library of Congress.

Ames, Nathaniel, and Fisher Ames. Papers. Dedham Historical Society, Dedham, Massachusetts.

Allen, Ira. Papers. Fleming Museum, University of Vermont.

Bache, Benjamin F. Papers. In the possession of Mr. Franklin Bache of Philadelphia.

Baird, Absalom. Papers. Wisconsin Historical Society.

Barbour Collection. University of Virginia.

Barlow, Joel. Papers. Harvard University.

Barrows, Rev. David. Journal. Wisconsin Historical Society.

Biggs, Benjamin. Papers. Draper Collection, Wisconsin Historical Society.

Blount, John Gray. Papers. North Carolina Historical Commission Library.

Brackenridge, Hugh H. Papers. Darlington Library, University of Pittsburgh.

Breckenridge, John. Papers. Library of Congress.

British State Papers. Canada, Colonial Correspondence, Vols. 41, 47, and 49. Transcripts in the Library of Congress.
Burd, Strohm, Yeates, Shippen. Letters. State Library of Pennsylvania.

Cabell, Joseph C. Papers. University of Virginia.
Carnes, Thomas P. Papers. Duke University.
Carter, Benjamin. Sea Journal. Essex Institute.
Carter, Robert. Papers. Virginia Historical Society.
Clark, George Rogers. Manuscripts. Draper Collection, University of Wisconsin.
Collins, Stephen. Papers. Library of Congress.
Cornwall, Vermont. First Congregational Church Minutes. In the possession of Mr. Edward H. Matthews, church clerk.
Craig, Isaac. Letterbook. Carnegie Library, Pittsburgh, Pennsylvania.

Democratic Society of Pennsylvania. Minutes. Historical Society of Pennsylvania.
Dennie, Joseph. Papers. Harvard University.
Du Ponceau, Peter S. Papers. Historical Society of Pennsylvania.
Durrett Collection. University of Chicago.

Emmett Collection. New York Public Library.

Fitch, Jabez. Diary. Society of Mayflower Descendants, Boston, Massachusetts.
French Legation Letters. Department of State. National Archives.
Friends of Liberty and Equality. Minutes of the society. Historical Society of Pennsylvania.
Frontier War Series (1792). Wisconsin Historical Society.

Gallatin, Albert. Papers. New York Historical Society.
Gates, Horatio. Papers. New York Public Library.
Genet, Edmund Charles. Papers. Library of Congress.
Gerry, Elbridge. Papers. Library of Congress.
Governor's Letterbook (North Carolina). North Carolina Historical Commission.
Governor's Letterbook (Virginia). Virginia State Library.
Great Britain. Archives, Public Records Office (United States), Foreign Office 1, 4, 5, and 115. Transcripts in Library of Congress.
Great Britain, Notes from. Department of State. National Archives.

Hamilton, Alexander. Papers. Library of Congress.

Hartshorne, William. "Diary of a Journey from New York to Detroit, 1793." Photostat in New York Public Library. Original is jointly owned by New York Yearly Meetings of Friends.

Hauterive, Alexandre Comte D'. Diary (1793). New York Historical Society.

Hay, Udney. Letters. New York State Library.

Heth, Will. Papers. University of Virginia.

Innes, Harry. Papers. Library of Congress.

Jarvis, James. "Reminiscences of Virginia" (1853). Library of Congress.

Jefferson, Thomas. Papers. Library of Congress. Massachusetts Historical Society.

King, Rufus. Papers. New York Historical Society.

Lamb, John. Papers. New York Historical Society.

Lee, Richard Bland. Papers. Library of Congress.

Logan, Dr. George. Miscellaneous Papers. Historical Society of Pennsylvania.

Logan, Deborah Norris. "Biographical Sketches of the Life and Character of Dr. George Logan." Historical Society of Pennsylvania.

Lyon, Matthew. Collection. (Mostly written after Lyon's death.) Vermont Historical Society.

McGavock, James. Papers. William and Mary College Library.

McHenry, James. Papers. Library of Congress.

Madison, James. Papers. Library of Congress.

Manning, William. Papers. Harvard University.

Marine Insurance Papers (1789–1802). New England Historical Genealogical Society.

Massachusetts. Journal of the House of Representatives. State Library of Massachusetts.

Mead, Rev. Stith. Letterbook (1793–95). Virginia Historical Society.

Mifflin, Thomas. Papers and Documents. State Library of Pennsylvania.

Minor-Watson Papers. Library of Congress.

Miscellaneous Letters. Department of State. National Archives.

Miscellaneous Manuscripts (alphabetically arranged). New York Historical Society.

Monroe, James. Papers. New York Public Library.
Morse, Jedidiah. Family Papers. Yale University.

New York Hibernian Volunteers. Minutes (1796). New York Historical Society.
Nisbet, Charles. Letters. Darlington Library, University of Pittsburgh.
—— Papers. New York Public Library.
Nicholson, Joseph. Papers. Library of Congress.

Osgood, Rev. David. Diary (1776–1822). Medford, Massachusetts, Public Library.

Pennsylvania Insurrection. Papers. Library of Congress.
Pickering, Timothy. Papers. Massachusetts Historical Society.
Pinckney, Thomas, and Charles C. Pinckney. Papers. Library of Congress.
Pinckneyville District. Papers. Union County Courthouse, Union, South Carolina.
Plumer, William. Letters. New Hampshire State Library.
—— Autobiography. Library of Congress.
Portland Artillery Company (First). Minute Book (1791–97). Maine Historical Society.
Portland Republican Society Papers. Maine Historical Society.

Rawle, William. Papers, Vol. I, "Insurrection in Western Pennsylvania." Historical Society of Pennsylvania.
Republican Society, New York. Minutes (1788). New York Historical Society.
Rodney, Caesar A., and Thomas Rodney. Papers. Delaware Historical Society.
"Rusticus." Letters on Slavery (c. 1794). South Carolina Historical Society.

Sargeant, Winthrop. Papers. Massachusetts Historical Society.
Sayward, Judge Jonathan. Diary. American Antiquarian Society.
Schoolbred, John. Letterbook. Charleston (South Carolina) Library Society.
Sedgewick, Theodore. Papers. Massachusetts Historical Society.
Senate of South Carolina. Journal. South Carolina Historical Commission.

Shelby, Isaac. Papers. (Only a few.) Historical Society of Kentucky.
Shepard, Samuel. Diary. Massachusetts Historical Society.
Shippen, William. Papers. Library of Congress.
Smith, William L. Papers. Library of Congress.
Sons of Liberty. Correspondence. New York Historical Society.
Society of Cincinnati. Records of Connecticut, 1783–1807. New York
    Public Library.
—— Miscellaneous Papers. New York Public Library.
Society of Mechanics and Tradesmen. Minutes. Mechanics and Trades-
    men Society Library, New York City.
State Governors, Letters from. Department of State. National Archives.
Sumter, Thomas. Manuscripts. Wisconsin Historical Society.

Tammany Society, New York City. Minutes. New York Public Library.
Thornton, William. Papers. Library of Congress.
Todd, John Clark. Papers. Filson Club Library, Louisville, Kentucky.
Transylvania Seminary. Records of the Proceedings of the Board of
    Trustees. Transylvania University.

Washington Academy. Minutes and Proceedings of the Board of Trus-
    tees. Washington and Jefferson College.
Washington Benevolent Society. Collection. (A few items only.) Har-
    vard University.
Washington, George. Papers. Library of Congress.
Webster, Noah. Papers. New York Public Library.
Whig Club. Papers Relating to the Whig Club (1777). In Maryland
    Miscellaneous (1771–1838), Library of Congress.
Whig Society. "Free and Independent Whig Society of Observation."
    Constitution and Minutes, 1778–1780. Boston Public Library.
Will and Deed Books. (Used in several courthouses, principally in the
    South.)

Yeates, Jasper. Papers. Historical Society of Pennsylvania.

Books

American State Papers. Miscellaneous, Vol. I. Documents Legislative
    and Executive of the Congress of the United States. Washington, 1834.
American State Papers. Foreign Relations, Vol. I. Washington, 1832.

Ames, Seth, ed. The Works of Fisher Ames. Boston, 1854.

Annals of Congress. Third Congress. Washington, 1794.

Annals of the General Society of Mechanics and Tradesmen of the City
of New York from 1785 to 1820, ed. by Thomas Earle and Charles
T. Congdon. New York, 1882.

Asbury, Francis. Journal of the Reverend Francis Asbury. 3 vols. New
York, 1821.

Ashe, Thomas. Travels in America, Performed in the Year 1806. London, 1809.

Austin, Benjamin. Constitutional Republicanism in opposition to Fallacious Federalism. Boston, 1803.

A View of the Relative State of Great Britain and France at the Commencement of the Year 1796. London, 1796.

Baird, Absalom. Copies of Authentic Letters and Papers Throwing Some
Light on the History of Dr. Absalom Baird. Pittsburgh, 1909.

Bayard, Ferdinand M. Voyage dans l'interieur des Etats-Unis. Paris,
1797.

Bentley, William. Diary. Salem, Mass., 1907.

Bernard, John. Retrospections of America. New York, 1887.

Biddle, Charles. Autobiography, 1745–1821. Philadelphia, 1883.

Blanchard, J. P. "The Journal of My Forty-fifth Ascension, Being the
First Performed in America," The Magazine of History, extra numbers, XVI (1918), 271.

Bonnet, J. E. Etats-Unis de L'Amerique a la fin du XVIIIe siecle. Paris,
1802.

—— Political Miscellany. New York, 1793.

Brackenridge, Hugh H. Incidents of the Insurrection in the Western
Parts of Pennsylvania in the Year 1794. 3 vols. in one. Philadelphia,
1795.

—— The Standard of Liberty, Philadelphia, 1802.

—— Gazette Publications. Pittsburgh, 1806.

Brackenridge, H. M. Recollections of Persons and Places in the West.
Philadelphia, 1868.

Brissot de Warville, J. P. New Travels in the United States of America.
London, 1794.

Callender, James T. American Annual Register for 1796. Philadelphia,
1797.

—— The History of the United States for 1796. Philadelphia, 1797.

—— Sedgewick and Company, or a Key to a Six Percent Cabinet. Philadelphia, 1798.

—— The Political Register, or Proceedings in the Session of Congress. Philadelphia, 1795.

—— A Short History of the Nature and Consequence of Excise Laws. Philadelphia, 1795.

Canadian Archives. Report. Ottawa, 1891.

Carey, Matthew. A Plumb Pudding for the Humane, Chaste, Valiant, Enlightened Porcupine. Philadelphia, 1799.

Charleston [South Carolina] City Directory for 1793, 1794 and 1795.

Clark and Genet Correspondence. American Historical Association, *Annual Report* for 1896, pp. 930–1107.

Cobbett, William [Playfair]. The History of Jacobinism: Its Crimes, Cruelties and Perfidies. 2 vols. Philadelphia, 1796.

Colbert, Le Comte de. Voyage dans l'interieur des Etats-Unis et au Canada. Baltimore, 1935.

Committee of Secrecy Reports. First and Second Reports with an Appendix. London, 1794.

Commons, John R. *et al*, A Documentary History of American Industrial Society. Cleveland, 1910.

Cooper, Thomas. Some Information Respecting America. London, 1795.

Coram, Robert. Political Inquiries, to Which Is Added a Plan for the General Establishment of Schools throughout the United States. Wilmington, Del., 1791.

Crèvecœur, J. Hector St. John. Letters from an American Farmer. Philadelphia, 1793.

Drayton, John. Letters Written during a Tour through the Northern and Eastern States of America. Charleston, S.C., 1794.

Duane, William. A Handbook for Riflemen. Philadelphia, 1812.

Erskine, Thomas. A View of the Causes and Consequences of the Present War with France. Philadelphia, 1797.

Feast of Merriment by Well-fed Domine Double Chin, Esq. Burlington, N.J., 1795.

Ford, David. "Captain David Ford's Journal," *Proceedings of the New Jersey Historical Society*, VIII (1856), 77–86.

Findley, William. History of the Insurrection in the Four Western Counties of Pennsylvania. Philadelphia, 1796.

Fraser, Charles. Reminiscences of Charleston. Charleston, S.C., 1854.

Fraser, Donald. A Collection of Select Biography. New York, 1798.

—— The Columbian Monitor. New York, 1794.

—— The Mental Flower Garden. Danbury, Conn., 1800.

Gallatin, Albert. The Speech of Albert Gallatin. Philadelphia, 1795.

Georgia-Florida Frontier. "Papers relating to the Georgia-Florida Frontier, 1784–1800," *Georgia Historical Quarterly*, Vol. XXIV (1940), Nos. 1, 2, and 3.

Gibbs, George. Memoirs of the Administrations of Washington and Adams. New York, 1846.

Graham, John A. A Descriptive Sketch of the Present State of Vermont. London, 1797.

Hamilton, Alexander. The Works of Alexander Hamilton, Edited by Henry C. Lodge. 9 vols. New York, 1886.

Hamilton, J. G., ed. "A Society for Preservation of Liberty," *American Historical Review*, XXXII (1884), 550–52.

Hardie, James. The Philadelphia Directory and Register. Philadelphia, 1793.

Hedges, Phineas. Strictures on the Elementa Medicinal of Doctor Brown. Goshen, N.Y., 1795.

Henry, William Wirt. Patrick Henry, Life, Correspondence, and Speeches. New York, 1891.

Hobson, Bulmer, ed. The Letters of Wolfe Tone. Dublin, n.d.

Jay, John. The Correspondence and Public Papers of John Jay, edited by Henry P. Johnston. 4 vols. New York, 1893.

Jefferson, Thomas. The Writings of Thomas Jefferson, edited by Paul L. Ford. 10 vols. New York, 1895.

Johnson, Thomas. Kentucky Miscellany. Lexington, 1821.

Kelsey, Rayner W., ed. A Record of the Journey of Theophile Cazenove through New Jersey and Pennsylvania. "Haverford College Studies," No. 13, 1922.

King, Rufus. The Life and Correspondence of Rufus King, edited by Charles King. 6 vols. New York, 1894.

Knox, Alexander. Essays on the Political Circumstances of Ireland. . . . With an Appendix Containing Thoughts on the Will of the People. . . . London, 1799.

La Rochefoucauld-Liancourt, F. A. F., Duke de. Travels through the United States of North America. 4 vols. London, 1799.

Locke, John. Two Treatises on Civil Government. New York, 1884.

Lodge, Henry. The Life and Letters of George Cabot. Boston, 1877.

Maclay, William. The Journal of William Maclay. New York, 1927.

M'Knight, John. God the Author of Promotion. New York, 1794.

McRee, Griffith J. The Life and Correspondence of James Iredell. New York, 1858.

Madison, James. The Writings of James Madison, edited by Gaillard Hunt, 9 vols. New York, 1906.

Mangourit, M. A. B. Mémoire de Mangourit. Paris, 1795.

—— "The Mangourit Correspondence in Respect to Genet's Projected Attack upon the Floridas, 1793–1794," edited by F. J. Turner, *American Historical Association, Annual Report*, 1897, pp. 569–679.

Manning, William. The Key of Libberty. Billerica, Mass., 1922.

Marshall, Humphrey. History of Kentucky. Frankfort, 1824.

Mechanics and Tradesmen of the City of New York. Annals of the General Society of Mechanics and Tradesmen of the City of New York, edited by Thomas Earle and Charles T. Congdon. New York, 1882.

Michaux, André. "Journal de André Michaux," *Proceedings of the American Philosophical Society*, XXVI (1889), 99.

Miller, Samuel. A Brief Retrospect of the Eighteenth Century. New York, 1803.

Minutes of the Methodist Conferences, 1773–1813. New York, 1813.

Monroe, James. Writings of James Monroe, edited by S. M. Hamilton. 7 vols. New York, 1900.

Moore, Maurice A. Reminiscences of York [County, South Carolina]. N.p., n.d.

Mitchell, Clarence B., ed. Mitchell-Boulton Correspondence, 1787–1792. Princeton, N.J., 1931.

Mount Zion Society. Minutes and Other Records of the . . . Winnsborough, South Carolina. Columbia, S.C., 1934.

222 BIBLIOGRAPHY

New York City. Directories, 1790 to 1800 inclusive.
Norfolk, Virginia. Directory (1801).

Otis, Harrison Gray. The Life and Letters of Harrison Gray Otis, edited by Samuel E. Morison. 2 vols. Boston, 1913.

Palmer, Elihu. The Political Happiness of Nations. New York, 1800.
Parsons, Theophilus. Memoir. Boston, 1859.
Philadelphia. City Directories, 1793 to 1799 inclusive.
Prince, Hezekiah. "Diary of Hezekiah Prince," *New England Magazine*, IX (1835), 733–750.

Revolution Society in London. Correspondence of the Revolution Society . . . with the National Assembly and with Various Societies of the Friends of Liberty in France and England. London, 1792.
Rousseau, Jean J. The Social Contract. New York, 1923.
Rowan, Archibald H. Autobiography. Dublin, 1840.

Saint-Mery, Moreau de. Voyage aux États-Unis de l'Amerique, 1793–1798, edited by Stewart L. Mims. New Haven, 1913.
Scott, Job. Journal of the Life, Travels and Gospel Labours of That Faithful Servant and Minister of Christ. Wilmington, 1797.
Smyth, Alexander. Speeches Delivered by Alexander Smyth in the House of Delegates and at the Bar. Richmond, 1811.
——— Regulations for the Field Exercise, Manoeuvers and Conduct of the Infantry of the United States. Philadelphia, 1812.
Sparks, Jared. Life of Gouverneur Morris. 3 vols. Boston, 1832.
Sullivan, William. Familiar Letters on Public Characters and Public Events. Boston, 1834.

Taylor, John. An Inquiry into the Principles and Tendencies of Certain Public Measures. Philadelphia, 1794.
——— A Definition of Parties, or The Political Effects of the Paper System Considered. Philadelphia, 1794.
Thomas, E. S. Reminiscences of the Last Sixty-Five Years Commencing with the Battle of Lexington. 2 vols. Hartford, 1840.
Thomson, R., ed. A Tribute to the Swinish Multitude, Being a Choice Collection of Patriotic Songs. London and New York, 1795.
Tone, William T. W., ed. Memoirs of Theobald Wolfe Tone. London, 1827.

[Tucker, St. George.] The Probationary Odes of Jonathan Pindar. Philadelphia, 1796.

United Irishmen. Proceedings of the Society of United Irishmen. Philadelphia, 1795.

Vermont. Records of the Governor and Council of the State of Vermont. 8 vols. Montpelier, 1876.
Vermont Register for 1795. N.p., 1795.

Walker, Lewis B., ed. The Burd Papers (Phil., 1899).
Wansey, Henry. An Excursion to the United States of North America in the Summer of 1794. Salisbury, 1798.
Waring, William. South Carolina and Georgia Almanac for 1793. Charleston, 1793.
Warren, Charles, ed. Jacobin and Junto, or Early American Politics as Viewed in the Diary of Dr. Nathaniel Ames, 1758–1822. Cambridge, 1931.
Washington, George. The Writings of George Washington edited by Worthington C. Ford. 14 vols. New York, 1889.
Webb, Samuel Blachley. Correspondence and Journals of Samuel B. Webb. New York, 1894.
Weld, Isaac. Travels through the United States of North America and the Provinces of Upper and Lower Canada during 1795, 1796 and 1797. London, 1800.
Winterbotham, William. An Historical, Geographical, Commercial and Philosophical View of the United States of America. 4 vols. New York, 1796.
Wood, John. A Full Exposition of the Clintonian Faction and the Society of the Columbian Illuminati. Newark, 1802.

Pamphlets

Address of a Convention of Delegates from Twenty Towns and Five Plantations, etc. Portland, 1795.
Address to the People of South Carolina by the General Committee of the Representative Reform Association. Charleston, S.C., 1794.
Address of a Convention of Delegates on the Separation from Massachusetts. Portland, 1795.

A Brief Account of the Late Revivals of Religion. Boston, 1799.

Anfrer, Anthony. Cannibal's Progress. Portsmouth, N.H., 1798.

An Emetic for Aristocrats. Boston, 1795.

A Definition of Parties, or the Political Effects of the Paper System Considered. [John Taylor?] Philadelphia, 1794.

A Twig of Birch for a Butting Calf, by a Brother of the Birch. New York, 1795.

A View of the New England Illuminati. Philadelphia, 1799.

Austin, Benjamin. Constitutional Republicanism in Opposition to Fallacious Federalism. Boston, 1803.

Barlow, Joel. A Letter to the National Convention of France. New York, 1795.

Barnard, Thomas. A Sermon, Delivered on the Day of the National Thanksgiving, February 19, 1795. Salem, 1795.

Bentalou, Paul. Pulaski Vindicated from an Unsupported Charge. Baltimore, 1824.

—— A Reply to Judge Johnson's Remarks. Baltimore, 1826.

Bird, Henry M. A View of the Relative Situation of Great Britain and the United States of North America. London, 1794.

Bishop, Abraham. An Oration on the Extent and Power of Political Delusion. Newark, 1800.

Boyd, William. Woman. Boston, 1796.

Bradford, Ebenezer. The Nature of Humiliation, Fasting, and Prayer Explained. Boston, 1795.

Bradley, William C. The Rights of Youth. Westminster, England, 1794.

Buchanan, Archibald. An Oration Composed and Delivered at the Request of the Republican Society of Baltimore on the Fourth of July, 1794. Baltimore, 1795.

Cautionary Hints to Congress Respecting the Sale of the Western Lands. [Thomas Paine?] Philadelphia, 1794.

[Chauvet, David.] The Conduct of the Government of France towards the Republic of Geneva. Trenton, 1798.

Clinton, George, Jr. An Oration Delivered on the Fourth of July, 1798. New York, 1798.

Cobbett, William. A Little Plain English Addressed to the People of the United States. Philadelphia, 1795.

Constitutional Society of Sheffield. The Spirit of John Locke on Civil

Government Revived by the Constitutional Society of Sheffield. Sheffield, n.d.

Correspondence between Citizen Genet, Minister of the French Republic, to the United States of North America and the Officers of the Federal Government. Philadelphia, 1793.

Democratic Society of New York. Circular of the Democratic Society of New York. New York, 1794.

—— Constitution. New York, 1794.

Democratic Society of Philadelphia. Two Addresses to Their Democratic Brethren. Philadelphia, 1811.

Democratic Society of Friends of the People. Constitution. Philadelphia, 1805.

Democratic Society of Friends of the People. Constitution. Harrisburgh, 1807.

Democratic Society. Principles, Articles and Regulations Agreed upon by the Members of the Democratic Society of Philadelphia, May 30, 1793. Philadelphia, 1793.

Demos in Council. Boston, 1799.

Duane, William (Jasper Dwight, pseud.). A Letter to George Washington, President of the United States. Philadelphia, 1796.

Echo, The, or A Satirical Poem on the Virtuous Ten. Hartford, 1795.

Farmer, A [George Logan ?]. Five Letters Addressed to the Yeomanry of the United States. Philadelphia, 1792.

Fauchet, Joseph. A Translation of Citizen Fauchet's Intercepted Letter, Number 10, October 31, 1794. Philadelphia, n.d.

Features of Federalism, by Publicola [pseud.]. Wilmington, 1803.

(Franklin, pseud.). Letters of Franklin on the Conduct of the Executive and the Treaty. Philadelphia, 1795.

Freneau, Philip (Robert Slender, pseud.). Letter on Various Interesting and Important Subjects. Philadelphia, 1799.

Gallatin, Albert. The Speech of Albert Gallatin. Philadelphia, 1795.

Goddard, William. The Prowess of the Whig Club. Baltimore, 1777.

Harper, Robert Goodloe (Appius, pseud.?). An Address to the People of South Carolina by the General Committee of the Representative Reform Association. Charleston, 1794.

226 BIBLIOGRAPHY

Haswell, Anthony. An Oration Delivered at Bennington, Vermont, August 16, 1799. Bennington, 1799.

Hedges, Phineas. An Oration Delivered before the Republican Society of Ulster County. Goshen, N.Y., 1795.

Johnson, John I. Reflections on Political Society, New York, 1797.

Lee, Richard. Account of the Proceedings of a Meeting of the London Corresponding Society. London, 1795.

Leib, Michael. Dr. Leib's Patriotic Speech. New London, 1796.

Lezay-Marnezia. Lettres ecrites des rives de L'Ohio. Paris, 1801.

Logan, George. Fourteen Agricultural Experiments to Ascertain the Best Rotation of Crops. Philadelphia, 1797.

—— Five Letters Addressed to the Yeomanry of the United States. Philadelphia, 1792.

—— A Letter to the Citizens of Pennsylvania on the Necessity of Promoting Agriculture, Manufacturing and the Useful Arts. Philadelphia, 1800.

London Corresponding Society. Address of the London Corresponding Society. London, 1792.

—— The London Corresponding Society's Addresses and Regulations. London, 1794.

—— To the Parliament and People of Great Britain. London, 1795.

Massachusetts Constitutional Society. Constitution. Boston, 1794.

McMurray, William. A Sermon Occasioned by the Death of Colonel Henry Rutgers. New York, 1830.

Miller, Samuel. A Sermon, Delivered in the New Presbyterian Church, New York, July 4, 1795. New York, 1795.

Morrison, John. An Oration Delivered in Tammany Hall in Commemoration of the Birthday of Thomas Paine. New York, 1832.

Morse, Jedidiah. A Sermon Delivered at Charleston in the Commonwealth of Massachusetts, February 19, 1795. Boston, 1795.

Moultrie, Alexander. An Appeal to the People on the Conduct of a Certain Public Body in South Carolina Respecting Colonel Drayton and Colonel Moultrie. Charleston, 1794.

New England Mississippi Land Company. Memorial of the Agents of the Mississippi Land Company. Washington, 1804.

Ogden, John C. A View of the Calvinistic Clubs in the United States. Litchfield, Conn., 1799.

Osgood, David. The Wonderful Works of God Are to Be Remembered. Boston, 1794.

—— A Discourse Delivered on the Day of Annual Thanksgiving, November 19, 1795. Boston, 1795.

—— Some Facts Evincive of the Atheistical, Anarchical and in Other Respects Immoral Principles of the French Republicans. Boston, 1798.

Packard, Hezekiah. Federal Republicanism Displayed in Two Discourses. Boston, 1799.

Paine, Thomas. Letter to George Washington on Affairs Public and Private. Philadelphia, 1796.

—— Dissertation on First Principles of Government. Philadelphia, 1795.

—— The Rights of Man. Philadelphia, 1792.

Paine, Thomas, and Other Supporters of the Rights of Man. Tom Paine's Jests; Being an Entirely New and Select Collection of Patriotic Bon Mots, Repartees, Anecdotes, Epigrams, Observations, etc. on Political Subjects. Philadelphia, 1796.

Palmer, Elihu. The Principles of Nature, or a Development of the Moral Causes of Happiness and Misery among the Human Species. New York, 1797.

—— An Enquiry Relative to the Moral and Political Improvement of the Human Species. New York, 1797.

Patriotic Society of Newcastle, Delaware. Circular. 1795.

Pinckney, Charles. On the Right of Expatriation. Philadelphia, 1799.

Price, Richard. Observations on the Importance of the American Revolution and the Means of Making It a Benefit to the World. Trenton, 1785.

Puglia, S. F. A Short Extract (Concerning the Rights of Man and Titles) from the Work Entitled Man Undeceived. Philadelphia, 1793.

Puglia, James P. The Federal Politician. Philadelphia, 1795.

Quid Mirror, The. New York, 1806.

Rights of Asses, The. A Poem. Burlington, N.J., 1793.

Rush, Benjamin. A Plan for the Establishment of Public Schools and the Diffusion of Knowledge in Pennsylvania; to Which Are Added, Thoughts upon the Mode of Education Proper in a Republic, Addressed to the Legislature and Citizens of the State. Philadelphia, 1786.

Rushton, Edward. Expostulatory Letter to George Washington of Mt. Vernon on His Continuing to Be a Holder of Slaves. Lexington, Ky., 1797.

Sanders, Daniel C. A Discourse on Occasion of the Death of William Coit, Esq. Burlington, Vt., 1802.

Sheffey, Daniel. Speech of the Honorable Daniel Sheffey. Alexandria, Va., 1814.

Sloan, James. An Oration before the Democratic Association of Glouster County, New Jersey. Trenton, 1802.

Smith, Melancton (A Plebeian, pseud.). An Address to the People of the State of New York. New York, 1788.

[Smith, William Pitt.] Observations on Conventions. New York, 1793.

Smyth, Alexander. A Letter from Alexander Smyth to Francis Preston, Wythe Courthouse, March 10, 1795. Richmond, 1795.

—— The Third and Last Letter from Alexander Smyth to Francis Preston. N.p., 1796.

Society for Promoting Christian Knowledge and Piety. Constitution. New York, 1794.

Stillman, Samuel. A Sermon Delivered on November 20, 1794. Boston, 1795.

Sullivan, James. Thoughts upon the Political Situation of the United States of America. Worcester, Mass., 1788.

—— Observations upon the Government of the United States of America. Boston, 1791.

—— The Altar of Baal Thrown Down. Boston, 1795.

Swanwick, John. Poems on Several Occasions. Philadelphia, 1797.

—— A Roaster; or A Check to the Progress of Political Blasphemy. Philadelphia, 1796.

Tappan, David. Christian Thankfulness Explained and Enforced. Boston, 1795.

Taylor, John. Disunion Sentiment in Congress in 1794. Washington, 1905.

Tilton, Dr. James. The Biographical History of Dionysius. Philadelphia, 1788.

Tyrannical Libertymen. A Discourse upon Negro Slavery in the United States. Hanover, N.H., 1795.

Tytler, James. The Rising of the Sun in the West. Salem, Mass., 1795.

United Company. To the Honourable General Assembly of Connecticut, to Be Holden at Hartford in May, 1776. The Memorial and Petition of a Numerous Body of the Inhabitants of Said Colony [Connecticut], Known by the Name of the United Company. N.p., 1776.
United Irishmen of Dublin. Proceedings of the Society of the United Irishmen of Dublin. Philadelphia, 1795.

(Veritas, pseud.). Six Letters on the Intrigues, Apostacy and Ambition of Dr. Michael Leib. By the Society of Independent Democrats. Philadelphia, 1807.

Warner, George James. Means for the Preservation of Public Liberty. New York, 1797.
Whig Club. The Declaration and Form of Association Adopted by the General Committee appointed by the Whig Club. London, 1796.
—— [William Goddard]. The Prowess of the Whig Club. Baltimore, 1777.
Wortman, Tunis. An Oration on the Influence of Social Institution upon Human Morals and Happiness. New York, 1796.
—— A Treatise Concerning Political Enquiry and the Freedom of the Press. New York, 1800.
—— An address to the Republican Citizens of New York. New York, 1801.
—— [Timoleon]. A Solemn Address to Christians and Patriots. New York, 1800.

Newspapers

Albany Register.
American Daily Advertiser (Philadelphia).
American Gazette (Norfolk, Va.).
Aurora and General Advertiser (Philadelphia).

Baltimore Daily Advertiser.
Baltimore Daily Intelligencer.
Baltimore Daily Repository.
Baltimore Telegraphe.
Boston Gazette.
Burlington Mercury (Vermont).

Carlisle Gazette (Pennsylvania).
Catskill Packet (New York).
City Gazette (Charleston, S.C.).
Columbian Centinel (Boston).
Columbian Mercury (New York).
Columbian Mirror and Alexandria Gazette (Virginia).
Connecticut Courant.
Connecticut Gazette.
Connecticut Journal.
Courier of New Hampshire.

Delaware and Eastern Shore Advertiser.
Delaware Gazette.
Diary (New York).

Eastern Herald (Maine).

Farmers Library (Vermont).
Fayetteville Gazette (North Carolina).
Federal Gazette (Philadelphia).
Federal Intelligencer (Baltimore).

Gazette of Maine.
Gazette of the United States.
Goshen Repository (N.Y.).
Guardian (New Jersey).

Independent Chronicle (Boston).

Kentucky Gazette.

Lancaster Intelligencer (Pennsylvania).
Lancaster Journal (Pennsylvania).

Maryland Gazette and Frederick-Town Weekly Advertiser.
Massachusetts Spy.
Mercury (Boston).
Mirrour (Concord, N.H.).

National Gazette (Philadelphia).
Newark Gazette.

New Hampshire Gazette.
New Jersey Journal.
New London Bee.
New York Daily Gazette.
New York Journal.
Norfolk Herald.
North Carolina Gazette.
North Carolina Journal.
Norwich Packet (Connecticut).

Oracle of Dauphin (Harrisburg, Penn.)

Pennsylvania Gazette.
Pennsylvania Packet.
Philadelphia Gazette.
Pittsburgh Gazette.
Porcupine's Gazette (Philadelphia).
Providence Gazette (Rhode Island).

Republican Journal (Dumfries, Va.).
Rising Sun (Kingston, N.Y.).
Rutland Herald.

Scourge of Aristocracy (Richmond, Va.).
South Carolina State Gazette.
Springer's Weekly Oracle (New London, Conn.).
State Gazette of North Carolina.

Vermont Gazette.
Vermont Journal.
Virginia Argus.
Virginia Chronicle.
Virginia Gazette and General Advertiser.
Virginia Herald (Fredericksburg).

Western Monitor (Lexington, Ky).
Western Star (Stockbridge, Mass.).

Broadsides

These include the especially fine collections in the Library of Congress
and The New York Historical Society; and the good collections in the

Harvard Library, the American Antiquarian Society and the New York Public Library.

Cartoons

The Historical Society of Pennsylvania has a collection of cartoons for this period separate from its good broadside files. The Ridgeway Library of Philadelphia also has some rare and interesting cartoons.

II. SECONDARY SOURCES

Adams, A. N. A History of the Town of Fairhaven, Vermont. Fairhaven, 1870.

Adams, Henry. Life of Albert Gallatin. Philadelphia, 1879.

Adams, William F., ed. Commodore Joshua Barney. Springfield, Mass., 1912.

Alger, John G. Englishmen in the French Revolution. London, 1889.

Ambler, Charles H. Sectionalism in Virginia from 1776 to 1861. Chicago, 1910.

Amory, Thomas C. Life of James Sullivan. 2 vols. Boston, 1859.

Ashe, Samuel A. History of North Carolina. Raleigh, 1925.

Austin, Mary S. Philip Freneau, the Poet of the Revolution. New York, 1901.

Beard, Charles A. Economic Origins of Jeffersonian Democracy. New York, 1915.

Bemis, Samuel F. "Jay's Treaty and the Northwest Boundary Gap," *American Historical Review*, XXVII (1922), 465–84.

—— Pinckney's Treaty. Baltimore, 1926.

Benson, Mary S. Women in Eighteenth Century America. New York, 1935.

Birley, Robert. The English Jacobins from 1789 to 1802. London, 1924.

Boucher, John N. A Century and a Half of Pittsburgh and Her People. New York, 1908.

Bowers, Claude G. Jefferson and Hamilton. New York, 1933.

Boyd, Julian P. "The Sheriff in Colonial North Carolina," *North Carolina Historical Review*, V (1928), 151–80.

Boyd, Thomas A. Light-Horse Harry Lee. New York, 1931.

Brailsford, H. N. Shelley, Godwin, and Their Circle. New York, 1913.

Brigham, Clarence S. "Bibliography of American Newspapers, 1690–1820," *Proceedings of the American Antiquarian Society*, XXIII to XXXVII (1914–27, in each issue).

Brinton, Clarence C. The Jacobins: an Essay in the New History. New York, 1930.

—— "Political Ideas in the Jacobin Clubs," *Political Science Quarterly*, XLIII (1928), 249–62.

—— "The Membership of the Jacobin Clubs," *American Historical Review*, XXXIV (1929), 740–56.

Brown, John M. Political Beginnings of Kentucky. Louisville, 1889.

Brown, Phillip A. The French Revolution in English History. New York, 1924.

Buck, Solon J. The Planting of Civilization in Western Pennsylvania. Pittsburgh, 1939.

Burlingame, Roger. The March of the Iron Men. New York, 1940.

Burt, Alfred L. The Old Province of Quebec. Minneapolis, 1933.

Butler, Mann. A History of the Commonwealth of Kentucky. Louisville, 1834.

Carroll, Joseph C. Slave Insurrections in the United States. Boston, 1938.

Channing, Edward. History of the United States. 6 vols. New York, 1929.

Charleston, City of. Yearbook. 1887.

Cheyney, Edward P. History of the University of Pennsylvania. Philadelphia, 1940.

Childs, Frances S. French Refugee Life in the United States, 1790–1800. Baltimore, 1940.

Clark, Dora M. British Opinion and the American Revolution. New Haven, 1930.

Clark, Harry H., ed. The Poems of Freneau. New York, 1929.

—— "Thomas Paine's Relation to Voltaire and Rousseau," *Revue Anglo-Americaine*, IX (April and June, 1932), 305, 393.

—— "Toward a Reinterpretation of Thomas Paine," *American Literature*, V (1933), 133–45.

Clark, Thomas D. A History of Kentucky. New York, 1937.

Clearwater, Alphonso T., ed. The History of Ulster County. Kingston, 1907.

Conover, Charolette R. Concerning the Forefathers. New York, 1902.

234 BIBLIOGRAPHY

Conrad, Henry C. History of the State of Delaware. 3 vols. Wilmington, 1908.
Conway, Moncure D. The Life of Thomas Paine. New York, 1892.
—— Writings of Thomas Paine. 3 vols. New York, 1895.
—— "Thomas Paine et la revolution dans les deux mondes," *La Revue hebdomadaire*, VI (May, 1900), 221–46, 322–56, 453–82.
Corbin, John. The Unknown Washington. New York, 1930.
Coulter, E. M. "The Efforts of the Democratic Societies of the West to Open the Navigation of the Mississippi," *Mississippi Valley Historical Review*, XI (1924), 376–86.
Coyle, Wilber F. The Mayors of Baltimore. Baltimore, 1919.
Crane, Ellery B. "Shays' Rebellion," *Proceedings of the Worcester Society of Antiquity*, V (1881), 61–111.
Creigh, Alfred. History of Washington County, Pennsylvania. Philadelphia, 1882.
Curti, Merle E. "The Great Mr. Locke, America's Philosopher, 1783–1861," Huntington Library Bulletin, No. 11 (1937).

Dallas, George M. The Life and Writings of Alexander J. Dallas. Philadelphia, 1871.
Davenport, C. H. "The History of Vermont Politics," *The Vermonter*, VII (1909), 378–94.
Davidson, Phillip G. "Sons of Liberty and Stamp Men," *North Carolina Historical Review*, IX (1932), 38–56.
Delaware. Biographical and Genealogical History of the State of Delaware. Chambersburg, Pa., 1899.
X Dictionary of American Biography. 20 vols. New York, 1929.
Dictionary of American History. 5 vols. New York, 1940.
Dodd, William E. The Life of Nathaniel Macon, Raleigh, 1903.
Dorfman, J. "The Economic Philosophy of Thomas Paine," *Political Science Quarterly*, LIII (1938), 372–88.
DuBois, W. E. B. The Suppression of the African Slave Trade. New York, 1896.
Dunbar, Louise B. A Study of "Monarchical" Tendencies in the United States from 1776 to 1801. Urbana, Ill., 1923.
Dyer, Walter A. "Embattled Farmers," *New England Quarterly*, IV (1931), 460–81.

Easterby, J. H. A History of the College of Charleston. Charleston, 1935.

Ellis, Franklin. The History of Columbia County, New York. Philadelphia, 1878.

Farmer, James E. Essays on French History. New York, 1897.

Faust, Albert B. The German Element in the United States. 2 vols. Boston, 1909.

Faÿ, Bernard. The Revolutionary Spirit in France and America. New York, 1927.

—— The Two Franklins. Boston, 1933.

—— "Early Party Machinery in the United States," *Pennsylvania Magazine of History and Biography*, LX (1936), 375–90.

Fee, Walter R. The Transition from Aristocracy to Democracy in New Jersey, 1789–1829. Somerville, N.J., 1933.

—— "The Effect of Hamilton's Financial Policy upon Public Opinion in New Jersey," *Proceedings of the New Jersey Historical Society*, L (1932), 32–44.

Ferguson, Russell J. Early Western Pennsylvania Politics. Pittsburgh, 1938.

—— "Albert Gallatin," *Western Pennsylvania Historical Magazine*, XVI (1933), 183–95.

Fitzpatrick, Edward A. The Educational Views and Influence of De Witt Clinton, New York, 1911.

Foote, William H. Sketches of North Carolina. New York, 1846.

Forman, S. E. "The Political Activities of Philip Freneau," *Johns Hopkins Studies in Historical and Political Science*, Series XX, No. 9 and 10 (1902), 9–103.

Fox, Dixon R. The Decline of Aristocracy in the Politics of New York. New York, 1919.

Franken, Paul L. "New England Whig; or a Study of the Boston Constitutional Society." Honors Thesis, Harvard University, 1940.

French, Janie, and Zella Armstrong. Notable Southern Families. Bristol, Tenn., 1928.

Genet, George C., Washington, Jefferson and "Citizen" Genet, 1793. New York, 1899.

Gilpatrick, Delbert H. Jeffersonian Democracy in North Carolina, 1789–1816. New York, 1931.

—— "The English Background of John Miller," *Furman* Bulletin, XX (1938), 14.

Gooch, G. P. "Europe and the French Revolution," *The Cambridge Modern History.* New York, 1904, 754–90, VIII.

Gottschalk, Louis R. "Communism during the French Revolution, 1789–1793," *Political Science Quarterly,* XL (1925), 438–50.

Gray, Lewis C. History of Agriculture in the Southern United States to 1860. Washington, 1933.

Griffin, Joseph. History of the Press in Maine. Brunswick, Me., 1872.

Griswold, Rufus W. The Republican Court. New York, 1867.

Grossman, Mordecai. The Philosophy of Helvetius. New York, 1926.

Hall, Courtney R. A Scientist in the Early Republic; Samuel L. Mitchill, 1764–1831. New York, 1934.

Hall, Walter P. British Radicalism, 1791–1797. New York, 1912.

Hansen, Allen O. Liberalism and American Education in the Eighteenth Century. New York, 1926.

Harper's Encyclopedia of United States History. 10 vols. New York, 1902. Vol. III.

Harpster, John W. "Eighteenth Century Inns and Taverns of Western Pennsylvania," *Western Pennsylvania Historical Magazine,* XIX (1936), 5–16.

Hartman, Kathryn M. "Presbyterianism as a Social Institution on the Western Pennsylvania Frontier, 1790–1810." Seminar paper, University of Pittsburgh, 1933.

Hazen, Charles D. Contemporary American Opinion of the French Revolution. Baltimore, 1897.

Headley, Russell, ed. The History of Orange County. Middletown, N.Y., 1908.

Heller, William J. The Gunmakers of Old Northampton. Philadelphia, 1908.

Hemenway, Abby M. The Vermont Historical Gazetteer. 5 vols. Rutland, 1923.

Henderson, Archibald. "Isaac Shelby and the Genet Mission," *Mississippi Valley Historical Review,* VI (1920), 451.

—— "Richard Henderson: The Authorship of the Cumberland Compact and the Founding of Nashville," *Tennessee Historical Magazine,* II (1916), No. 3, 155–74.

—— "A Pre-Revolutionary Revolt in the Old Southwest," *Mississippi Valley Historical Review,* XVII (1930), No. 2, 191–212.

Henry, W. H. Patrick Henry; Life, Correspondence and Speeches. 3 vols. New York, 1891.

Hildreth, Richard. History of the United States of America. 6 vols. New York, 1851.

Hosmer, James K. The Life of Thomas Hutchinson. Boston, 1896.

Hunt, Freeman. The Lives of American Merchants. 2 vols. New York, 1856.

Jacob, Rosamond. The Rise of the United Irishmen, 1791–1794. London, 1937.

James, Thomas. Three Years among the Indians and Mexicans. St. Louis, 1916.

Jameson, J. F. "Did the Fathers Vote?" *New England Magazine*, January, 1890, pp. 484–90.

Jensen, Merrill M. The Articles of Confederation. Madison, Wis., 1940.

Jones, Howard M. America and French Culture. Chapel Hill, 1927.

Kephart, Horace. "The Rifle in Colonial Times," *Magazine of American History*, XXIV (1890), 179–91.

Kerr, Charles. History of Kentucky. Chicago, 1922.

Kilpatrick, W. H. "Democracy and Respect for Personality," *Progressive Education*, XVI (Feb., 1939), 83–90.

Kilroe, Edwin P. Saint Tammany and the Origin of the Society of Tammany or Columbian Order in the City of New York. New York, 1913.

King, William L. The Newspaper Press of Charleston, South Carolina. Charleston, 1872.

Knauss, James O. Social Conditions among the Pennsylvania Germans in the Eighteenth Century, as Revealed in German Newspapers Published in America. "Pennsylvania German Society Publications." Lancaster, 1922.

Knight, Harry S. "Early Judges of Northumberland County," *The Northumberland County Historical Society Proceedings*, I (1926), 38–48.

Knollenberg, Bernhard. Washington and the Revolution. New York, 1940.

Koch, G. Adolf. Republican Religion. New York, 1933.

Lamprecht, Sterling P. The Moral and Political Philosophy of John Locke. New York, 1918.

Lancaster County [Pennsylvania] Historical Society: Historical Papers and Addresses. Lancaster, 1904.

Leake, Isaac Q. Memoir of the Life and Times of General John Lamb. Albany, 1850.

Lerner, Max. "John Marshall and the Campaign of History," *Columbia Law Review*, XXXIX (1939), 407–20.

Link, Eugene P. "The Democratic Societies of the Carolinas," *North Carolina Historical Review*, XVIII (1941), 259–77.

Locke, Mary S. Anti-Slavery in America from the Introduction of African Slaves to the Prohibition of the Slave Trade, 1619–1808. Boston, 1901.

Lockitt, C. H. The Relations of French and English Society, 1763–1793. London, 1920.

Loring, James S. The Hundred Boston Orators. Boston, 1852.

Lossing, Benson J. The Pictorial Field-Book of the War of 1812. New York, 1869.

Love, W. De Loss. The Fast and Thanksgiving Days of New England. Boston, 1895.

Ludlum, David. Social Ferment in Vermont. New York, 1939.

Luetscher, George D. Early Political Machinery in the United States. Philadelphia, 1903.

Lutz, Alma. Emma Willard, Daughter of Democracy. New York, 1929.

Lyon, Elijah. Louisiana in French Diplomacy, 1759–1804. Norman, Okla., 1934.

McCrackan, William D. "The Real Origin of the Swiss Republic," *American Historical Association, Report*, 1898, 355–363.

McFarland, Joseph F. Twentieth Century History of the City of Washington and Washington County, Pennsylvania. Chicago, 1910.

McLaughlin, A. C. "The Western Posts and the British Debts," *American Historical Association, Report*, 1894, 413–44.

McMaster, John B. A History of the People of the United States. 8 vols., New York, 1921. Vol. II.

McMurtrie, Douglas C. John Bradford: Pioneer Printer of Kentucky. Springfield, Ill., 1931.

Marsh, Philip M. "Freneau and Jefferson: The Poet-Editor Speaks for Himself about the National Gazette Episode," *American Literature*, VIII (1936), 180–193.

⸺ "Philip Freneau and His Circle," *Pennsylvania Magazine of History and Biography*, LXIII (1939), 37–59.

Martin, Asa E. Anti-Slavery Movement in Kentucky prior to 1850. Louisville, 1918.

Matthews, Lyman. The History of the Town of Cornwall, Vermont. Middlebury, 1862.

Mead, George H. Movements of Thought in the Nineteenth Century. Chicago, 1936.

Meigs, Wm. M. The Life of Charles Jared Ingersoll. Philadelphia, 1897.

Miller, William. "The Democratic Clubs of the Federalist Period, 1793–1795." Master's thesis, New York University, 1937.

⸺ "First Fruits of Republican Organization," *Pennsylvania Magazine of History and Biography*, LXIII (1939), 118–43.

⸺ "The Democratic Societies and the Whiskey Insurrection," *Pennsylvania Magazine of History and Biography*, LXII (1938), 324–49.

⸺ "The Effects of the American Revolution on Indentured Servitude," *Pennsylvania History*, VII (1940), 131–41.

Minnigerode, Meade. Jefferson, Friend of France, 1793. New York, 1928.

Mitchell, Clarence B. The Mitchell Record. Privately printed, Princeton, 1926.

⸺ The Mitchell-Boulton Correspondence, Princeton, 1931.

Moore, Maurice A. The Life of General Edward Lacey. Spartanburg, S.C., 1859.

Morais, Herbert M. Deism in Eighteenth Century America. New York, 1934.

Morison, Samuel E. The Maritime History of Massachusetts, 1783 to 1860. New York, 1921.

⸺ "Squire Ames and Doctor Ames," *New England Quarterly*, I (1928), 5–31.

Morris, Richard B., ed. The Era of the American Revolution. New York, 1939.

Morse, Anson E. The Federalist Party in Massachusetts to the Year 1800. Princeton, 1909.

Morse, James K. Jedidiah Morse. New York, 1939.

Mudge, Eugene T. The Social Philosophy of John Taylor of Caroline. New York, 1939.

Muhlenberg, Henry A. The Life of Major-General Peter Muhlenberg. Philadelphia, 1849.

Mullett, Charles E. "Classical Influence on the American Revolution," *Classical Journal,* XXXV (1939), 92–104.

Newark. The History of the City of Newark. New York, 1913.

Parrington, Vernon L. Main Currents in American Thought. 3 vols. New York, 1927–30.

Pattee, Fred L., ed. The Poems of Philip Freneau. Princeton, N.J., 1902.

Peale, Albert Charles. Charles Willson Peale and His Public Services during the American Revolution. Paper Read before the Society of the Sons of the American Revolution. Washington, 1896.

Perrin, William H. The Pioneer Press of Kentucky. "Filson Club Publication," No. 3, Louisville, 1888.

Peter, Robert. History of Fayette County, Kentucky. Chicago, 1882.

Pomerantz, Sidney I. New York, An American City. New York, 1938.

Poole, William F. Anti-Slavery Opinions before the Year 1800. Cincinnati, 1873.

Preble, George H. Origin and History of the American Flag. Philadelphia, 1917.

Purcell, Richard J. Connecticut in Transition, 1775–1818. Washington, 1918.

Ravenel, Mrs. St. Julien. Charleston, the Place and the People. New York, 1925.

Richards, George W. German Pioneers in Pennsylvania. Philadelphia, 1905.

Riley, I. Woodbridge. American Philosophy. New York, 1907.

Robinson, William A. Jeffersonian Democracy in New England. New Haven, 1916.

Ruschenberger, W. S. W. An Account of the Institution and Progress of the College of Physicians of Philadelphia. Philadelphia, 1887.

Scharf, J. Thomas. History of Delaware. 2 vols. Philadelphia, 1888.

—— The Chronicles of Baltimore. Baltimore, 1874.

Scharf, J. Thomas, and Thompson Westcott. History of Philadelphia. 3 vols. Philadelphia, 1884.

Scherger, George L. The Evolution of Modern Liberty. New York, 1904.

Schlesinger, Arthur M. The Colonial Merchants and the American Revolution, 1763–1776. New York, 1918.

Schouler, James. History of the United States of America. 7 vols. New York, 1904.

Sellers, Charles C. The Artist of the Revolution: The Early Life of Charles Willson Peale. Hebron, Conn., 1939.

Sellers, Leila. Charleston Business on the Eve of the American Revolution. Chapel Hill, 1934.

Selsam, J. Paul. The Pennsylvania Constitution. Philadelphia, 1936.

Sherrill, Charles H. French Memories of Eighteenth Century America. New York, 1915.

Simons, A. M. Social Forces in American History. New York, 1925.

Simms, Jeptha R. The Frontiersmen of New York. 2 vols. Albany, 1883.

Smith, H. Perry. Addison County, Vermont. Syracuse, N.Y., 1886.

Snowden, Yates, ed. History of South Carolina. 5 vols. New York, 1920.

Sonne, Niels H. Liberal Kentucky. New York, 1939.

Speed, Thomas. The Political Club, Danville, Kentucky, 1786–1790. Louisville, 1894.

Stauffer, Vernon. New England and the Bavarian Illuminati. New York, 1918.

Stevens, Wayne E. "The Northwest Fur Trade, 1763–1800," *University of Illinois Studies in the Social Sciences*, XIV (1928), 407–610.

Sulté, Benjamin. "Les Projects de 1793 à 1810," *Proceedings and Transactions of the Royal Society of Canada*, V (1911), 19–67.

Swift, Samuel. History of the Town of Middlebury. Middlebury, Vt., 1859.

Thompson, Zadock. History of Vermont. Burlington, 1842.

Tuckerman, Frederick. William Cooper. Amherst, Mass., 1885.

Turner, Frederick J. The Significance of Sections in American History. New York, 1932.

—— "The Policy of France toward the Mississippi Valley in the Period of Washington and Adams," *The American Historical Review*, X (1905), 249–79.

Van Duzer, Charles H. Contributions of the Ideologues to French Revolutionary Thought. Baltimore, 1935.

Veech, James. The Monongahela of Old. Pittsburgh, 1910.

Washburn, Israel. "The Northeastern Boundary," *Collections of the Maine Historical Society*, VIII (1897), 41–50.

Washington and Jefferson College. Biographical and Historical Catalogue of Washington and Jefferson College. Cincinnati, 1889.

Weeks, Stephen B. The Press of North Carolina in the Eighteenth Century. Brooklyn, 1891.

Welling, James C. Connecticut Federalism, or Aristocratic Politics in a Social Democracy. New York, 1890.

Werner, Raymond C. "War Scare and Politics, 1794," New York Historical Association, Quarterly Journal, XI (1930), 324–34.

Wertenbaker, Thomas J. Norfolk: Historic Southern Port. Durham, N.C., 1931.

Wescott, Thompson. The Life of John Fitch. Philadelphia, 1878.

Wharton, Anne H., Salon Colonial and Republican. Philadelphia, 1900.

Whitaker, Arthur P. The Spanish-American Frontier. New York, 1927.

Whitman, John A. The Iron Industry of Wythe County. Wytheville, Va., 1935.

Williams, Antoinette M. "Education in Greenville County, South Carolina, prior to 1860." Master's thesis, University of South Carolina, 1934.

Wilson, Erasmus, ed. Standard History of Pittsburgh, Pennsylvania. Chicago, 1898.

Winsor, Justin, ed. Narrative and Critical History of America. 8 vols. New York, 1889.

Wolfe, John H. Jeffersonian Democracy in South Carolina. Chapel Hill, 1940.

Woodbury, Margaret. Public Opinion in Philadelphia, 1789–1801. Durham, 1919.

Woodfin, Maude H. "Citizen Genet and His Mission." Doctor's thesis, University of Chicago, 1928.

Worner, William F. "Standard Presented to the Republican Blues," Lancaster Historical Society Publications, XXXIV (1930), 256–59.

Wright, Ernest H. The Meaning of Rousseau. London, 1929.

Yoshpe, Harry B. The Disposition of Loyalist Estates in the Southern District of the State of New York. New York, 1939.

INDEX